PRAISE FOR
*An Ordinary Age*

"*An Ordinary Age* is an antidote for young people everywhere who are sick and tired of being sick and tired that the lives they wake up to every day don't match the ones they see on Instagram. It is a book for those who deserve to know that their lives and their efforts aren't just good enough; they are well and truly *good*."

—Meg Jay, PhD, author of
*The Defining Decade* and *Supernormal*

"Rainesford Stauffer is a brave writer who takes us to places that we haven't been yet and gives us companionship when we're there. I'd love to hand out thousands of copies of this book. You will find comfort and empowerment in every chapter. *An Ordinary Age* is a gentle but urgent call to embrace the fullness of life, and that's a reminder we can use at any stage of life."

—Mari Andrew, author of *Am I There Yet?*

"Rainesford Stauffer asks all the important questions in *An Ordinary Age*, which is in many ways a coming-of-age manifesto about how it feels and what it means to grow into adulthood in the digital age when we're all told we should be living our quote-unquote *best lives*."

—Kate Fagan, author of *What Made Maddy Run: The Secret Struggles and Tragic Death of an All-American Teen*

"The quest for perfection and excellence has left us exhausted, pissed off, and bewildered. If you want to turn away, at whatever point in your life, from the endless cycle of burnout, this beautifully written, endlessly empathetic book is for you."

—Anne Helen Petersen, author of *Can't Even: How Millennials Became the Burnout Generation*

"Reading this book made me feel a lot less alone—it captures what it is to be young in America with so much empathy and intelligence. Stauffer centers the voices and experiences of young adults while also investigating the systemic forces that define this life stage with clarity."

—Masuma Ahuja, author of *Girlhood: Teens around the World in Their Own Voices*

# AN ORDINARY AGE

# AN ORDINARY AGE

## Finding Your Way in a World That
Expects Exceptional

## RAINESFORD STAUFFER

HARPER PERENNIAL

NEW YORK • LONDON • TORONTO • SYDNEY • NEW DELHI • AUCKLAND

HARPER ● PERENNIAL

HarperCollins books may be purchased for educational, business, or sales promotional use. For information, please email the Special Markets Department at SPsales@harpercollins.com.

FIRST EDITION

*Designed by Jamie Lynn Kerner*

Library of Congress Cataloging-in-Publication Data has been applied for.

ISBN 978-0-06-299898-9

21 22 23 24 25   LSC   10 9 8 7 6 5 4 3 2

*To all of us, in all our ordinariness.*

*For my mom, the first to teach me the power of ordinary things, and my sister, who is everything extraordinary; my best friends.*

# CONTENTS

# CONTENTS

# AN ORDINARY AGE

# ON BEING ORDINARY

You always think the moments that will change your life the most are the ones we've been trained to recognize: At graduation we move our tassel, we get a job we don't mind, we label our boxes and move to new cities, we take our Polaroid camera with us when we stay out late with our best friends in a new place, meeting new people. We know it when we're in it: These are the times of our lives, so they say.

It's implied everywhere—and sometimes said explicitly, by well-meaning parents and mentors, popular culture that illustrates coming of age as self-exploration and adventure tidily wrapped up by the finale scene, and maybe even a fixation on youth and "being young." *These are the best years of your life. These are the times you can't get back. This is the chance you have to make your life extraordinary.* It echoed in my brain like a 2000s pop hit I didn't remember memorizing during my own checkered collection of "milestones" in young adulthood: Dropping out of college. Returning to my hometown like life was rewinding. Searching for ways to make myself *more*—braver, and bolder; more fearless, less cautious; more likable—whatever that means. What should have been singsong aspiration sounded more like a threat: When anything can happen, the pressure is on to make sure *everything* does.

If you're a young adult today (or even just know a young adult today), it's a challenge not to feel as though finding yourself has been turned into a competitive sport. Now, it seems, striving to be extraordinary, being exceptional, and being special are the same as being capable, being fulfilled, and being happy. We have so-called dream jobs and side hustles just to try to pay the bills, college rankings that tell us where our formative years fall on the scale of public opinion, and which education is supposedly worth all the debt. Omnipresent illustrations of best lives, bodies, and selves constantly play out on Instagram, and the churn of perfectionism has radically amped up expectations that turn "perfect" into a theoretically meetable standard. There are new timelines for entering young adulthood, and what it means to be a fulfilled young person is being rethought in real time. But the myth of a best self, and a best life, following certain patterns and meeting certain benchmarks, remains.

Within that, there are the real-life pressures: lack of a helpful, substantial social safety net, systemic racism and discrimination, and a world literally on fire. Figuring out how to avoid getting sick so you don't rack up medical debt. Doing math on a napkin to assess how you'll ever be able to take care of your parents on your current salary. Pondering whether all the messy pieces of your life will eventually feel steady and cohesive. There's lifestyle expectations that are just not a practical part of life for a lot of young adults, sprawling from saving a certain amount of money by a certain age, pressure to "make memories" before the moment has even passed, knowing what you're good at and going after it, the right kind of social life so you never feel lonely, and above all: proceeding with total confidence that whatever you're doing is the best thing you *could* be doing. There are milestones we're supposed to be hitting—moving out and apartments that are furnished, "real" jobs, and being "prepared" enough to map out a five-year plan for our dreams, despite a world that makes thinking that far in advance all but impossible. At the same time, young adults are supposed to be having the wild-and-free adventures that supposedly define this life period. There's a lot going on.

This time of life also marks a point when you're conscious of growth occurring. It can be seen, with young adulthood being hyped as the part meant for moves for jobs or school, new circles of friends, all the big "firsts" of becoming an adult, from being able to pick your own groceries to landing a job that puts the college degree you went into debt for to use. It can be felt, too, when we start asking the big questions: *What matters to me? Who am I supposed to be in the world? Is everyone else as overwhelmed as I am?* Everything is just beginning, young adults are told. You can be anything. And sometimes, it feels so much effort and time are spent living up to the people we could be, it's almost as if the people we *are* become an afterthought.

Every time I ventured off the prescribed path that supposedly marks how you find yourself and build your life as a young adult, I felt scatteredness and shame: When I left college after my freshman year to work even more hours than I did as a student, only to eventually return to school as an online student and full-time employee. When I moved home, a reality for lots of people for all kinds of reasons and one of the first that gets flagged as a young person having not "made it." When I moved for jobs that never fully eliminated the need for a second job as a safety net. When I watched my hometown friends marry the loves of their lives and buy houses with fireplaces. All of this necessitates privilege that isn't a reality for all young people. And none of it is the enduring trauma or hardship of my own life. Instead, it felt like a pattern: Life was messier than how I'd anticipated this time of life being, and the more people I spoke to, the more that feeling was echoed back to me. There's a lot of lofty praise around being young and having it "together," and the emphasis on having a particular kind of extraordinary adulthood felt as though it was telling in a couple ways: First, it treated young adults as a monolith, as if everyone was racing from the same starting line. Second, it also seemed to indicate that this was the time in which *everything* had to happen in order for your life to feel fulfilling, as if young people were in a buzzer-beater game of finding themselves and figuring out what matters to them, rather than those discoveries being lifelong. This pressure to know what your "best life" entails, and how to create it in young adulthood, felt worthy of a closer look to see where it stems from, how it shapes young people, and what systems and power structures enable it.

As I moved through my early twenties into my mid-to-late-twenties, I found myself yearning for simple things that rarely made the list of dream jobs, big moves, and adventures that have been marketed as cornerstones of young adulthood. I thought about the steadiness of a partner and community when I was supposed to feel confident and proud to go it alone. A sense of self that wasn't tethered to what I achieved or who I pleased. Framed photos of people I love in a home and a dresser in my bedroom, signs of staying instead of looking toward the horizon of the next new place. Over and over, I realized that no amount of cautious perfectionism was going to stop *truly* bad stuff from happening to me, or to my loved ones, and that there wasn't some threshold of achievement that would tidy up my messy parts, doubts, and uncertainties. It had never occurred to me that some of that, the false starts and self-doubt and everything coming with a side of chaos, was normal. And since these markers of what it means to be an extraordinary young adult were never a reality for all, anyway, I wondered why the averageness of coming of age wasn't talked about as much as achieving your wildest dreams.

Not all young adults have the opportunity to think about this at all. Within these pages, young people describe worrying about their parents' lack of retirement savings, experiencing housing insecurity, the stress of chronic illnesses, and the pressure of working while in school. Thousands of others are breadwinners for their families, dealing with medical debt, experiencing abuse, and grappling with economic hardship. The enduring conception of emerging adulthood—a time for wild and free exploration, identity experimentation, and creating your "best self"—isn't separate from factors including socioeconomic status, race, gender, geographic region, and class. While there might be characteristics or milestones traditionally aligned with young adulthood, it's far from a one-size-fits-all time of life. Though society's fixation on youth can be seen in beauty standards, "30 Under 30" lists, and ageism rampant in the workforce, it feels like a version is illustrated in the pressure to have your life fully figured out, sense of self fully established, and achievement locked down by the time you make it to your mid-twenties. It's not realistic. And, in a way, it's sad: When all the pressure is on to have the time of your life during *one* time of life, it could make the bad things feel worse, and the good feel fleeting. The scramble for "achievement" early in life feels like yearning for any sense of security rather than craving supernatural specialness, and there's a case to be made for a more nuanced conversation around young adulthood—one less about our best selves, and more about what it means to create who we are.

Everyone has different versions of ordinary, too. Some pinpointed a basic level of respect too many people still do not receive, like having their name pronounced correctly or being referred to by the right pronouns. Others articulated it as finding somewhere that feels like a place you can stay, or the ability to buy groceries without worrying your card will get declined. In conversations I've had with young adults from all different locations and backgrounds, "a sense of home," "community," "having time to do my laundry," "work that feels fulfilling," "not living for social media," "getting to slow down," and "having my best be enough" all popped up. Lingering about all of this was the pervasive sense that so many of us are looking for a permission slip to opt out of hustling to live our best lives, and instead embrace our ordinary ones.

For years, I lived my life in afters. After I moved away from my hometown, my real life would begin. After I finally finished my hodgepodge college degree, I'd find the right job. After I made myself into a perfect person—no insecurities or hang-ups—I'd be worthy of love. After I proved I could do it—whatever it was—I'd be fulfilled. It's not hard to see how slippery this could get, the sensation that once you've found the perfect home, secured the perfect job, locked down the perfect and unshakable sense of security, and found the perfect circle of friends, "real life" will begin. Life will start once we become the extraordinary people we're destined to be, and then we can relax a bit and enjoy it.

But what if we're missing it? I wondered. What if—by waiting until we have it all figured out to care for ourselves or notice our needs, or what we actually want as opposed to what we're supposed to—we're late to the party? What if some of the most enlightening and important and meaningful parts of young adulthood are actually the ordinary ones?

Mid-conversation with young adults describing this pressure "to be special," "to be the best," "to make sure I'm making the most of life," "to live up to what my parents/my mentors/my friends believe I can do," "to do the right things," I realized it felt as though we were all asking different versions of the same questions: *How can I ensure I have worth in the world, how can I guarantee I have meaning?* How we ask that—and who is asking it—deserves attention. Young people have complex identities, lives, and experiences, and when we talk about growing up, what's important to note is that isn't going to feel, let alone look, the same for everyone. If you're constantly trying to change or better yourself, it leaves little room to actually get to know yourself at all—to recognize that goodness and worthiness don't find you after you've fixed yourself first. "At this time, I was supposed to have more things figured out than I do right now," Lexi, twenty-one, said. She graduated with a job lined up that was canceled as a result of COVID-19. Her mom is an immigrant, and her dad grew up poor, and she described education as something viewed, especially in immigrant communities, as "your ticket to the world," a means of life being good from there on out that she's been working toward her whole life. "I think a lot of things I worry about are so interconnected," she said. "In terms of social issues, you really can't extract any single one without touching anything else." Young adults get this on a profound level. Her fear of being unable to get a job and pay off student loans is inherently connected to the fact that the job market is dismal, and she pointed out that her generation has grown up with a particularly heavy backdrop: Her college years were bookended by the election of Donald Trump and the COVID-19 crisis; she was a young teenager when the Sandy Hook Elementary School shooting happened, and described the general sentiment as "something's going to boil over eventually." Then, she added, there's the social pressure—"to move out of your parents' home and have a beautiful apartment, and live in a glamorous city with your friends, and go to expensive dinners every night." If that sounds like fantasy, not reality, it's one reason to look twice at the stories we tell young adults about timelines, what adulthood feels like, and what they ought to be doing. And the stereotype of young people craving being special? "I think that's also part of us, like, clinging on to those last remaining strands of the American Dream," Lexi said. "That if we can just be special or be different, that dream will be ours in some way, but we need to stand out in the crowd to make that happen."

Laney, a twenty-two-year-old first-generation college graduate who was working full-time out of her childhood bedroom when we spoke, likened the urge to always keep moving forward, to pursue novelty or adventure, to getting knocked over by a wave—the momentum feels good; it doesn't matter where it's taking her, the fact that she's moving is enough. It felt like an apt metaphor for trying to make it in the world right now. "And for a lot of people, including me, that movement has been a marker of *I'm doing something, therefore I'm doing something right,*" she said, noting that, for a lot of young adults, there is increased autonomy over what you find meaningful and how you spend your time for the first point in your life. It echoed conversations of every extraordinary thing young adults explained they pursued just because they believed it was the thing they *should* be doing. For one of the first times, Laney said, it feels like, "Oh, how do I actually spend my time? Yes, I'm doing something, but am I doing something that I believe in?" Rarely is time for that consideration built into the framework of young adulthood, and it gets overshadowed by the pervading sense that we should've had that figured out already, regardless of circumstances.

"When I would hear my peers talking about how when they reached their twenties they'd start having children and moving into their own houses and collecting all these other milestones that to them signified adulthood, it was hard for me to see that for myself," Brie, twenty-four, told me. She recalled hearing that, being from the South Side of Chicago, she wasn't necessarily expected to "make it out," and realized in her early teens that's because the city's systemic problems became her community's problems, which, in turn, fell to individual people. "Imagine trying to live your very best life in a place that is telling you that your life does not have value," Brie said. Because of the pain, suffering, and generational trauma Black people, and in particular Black women and Black trans women, have had to endure, Brie said, of course that pressure carries on. "It's, well, how are we supposed to live our very best life when you're constantly trying to take our lives away?" Young adulthood doesn't exist in a vacuum: Systemic problems do impact how, or whether, young people meet the so-called milestones of young adulthood. Brie cites her driver's license, or lack thereof, as one example: She knows how to drive, but doesn't have a license or car, and gets pressured by people who say she's not an adult until she accomplishes those so-called adult markers. "That marker is really only buried in, like, 'you should be able to afford a car,'" she said, and added that the moments where she truly feels most "adult" are subtler. "Even just the idea that I could trust my instincts," she explained. "That's the coolest—that sometimes I can just figure something out on my own." It never appears on the "external markers of successful young adulthood" list, and yet, being able to renegotiate what matters to you, solve problems, and learn to trust yourself are ordinary things with remarkable power for young people.


The concept of the "best life" serves as a social script: Do these things, in this order, and you'll end up happy, or fulfilled, or, at the very least, on par with the same kind of lives your peers are leading. This is not realistic. We're never without the next best thing we should be doing, on the path to growing into our next best selves. It's worth looking closer at what a "best life" means, and remembering that it's going to look different for everyone. One of the high points of young adulthood is getting to define yourself and your life on your terms.

While these moments of reflection, of "finding yourself," aren't necessarily unique to any particular generation of young adults, the parameters in which one does so have shifted greatly. Decades ago, there was a pattern of fairly universal milestones, allowing you to hopscotch from step to step with a clear-cut trajectory. Some research[1] points to the process of becoming an adult as one associated with the "acquisition of social roles and responsibilities," or "traditional social markers of adulthood" including finishing school, finding a job, leaving home, getting married, and having children (obviously, not everyone followed this social script). With increased independence and opportunity came more variance in the patterns our lives follow—like periods of living out of your parents' house and also not living with a significant other, or choosing not to get married at all, or it often taking longer to find a job post-college, if you went to college. And, as research on becoming an adult and markers of adulthood points out,[2] young people have dramatically different opportunities or experiences depending on their family, socioeconomic factors, or background. Now, the goal posts have moved and shifted some of those priorities: Other research[3] shows the highest-ranked milestones of adulthood for individuals aged eighteen to thirty-four are finishing school or education achievement, and economic security, indicating that priorities have shifted: According to this research, published in 2017,[4] over half of Americans say getting married and having kids aren't important to becoming an adult, with about a third saying they're somewhat important, and only a quarter of Americans think moving out of your parents' home is a very important part of adulthood. Meanwhile, it says that finishing school and economic security rank high. All this doesn't even account for cultural shifts, like social media enabling both a constant prying eye and opportunity for connection, the ability to curate yourself, and, of course most insidious, the ability to track everyone else's milestones and successes. Meanwhile, the workforce remains in chaos as we bounce from economic crisis to economic crisis, vast inequities in higher education persist, and it feels like being perfect is the only option if we want any shot at things turning out okay. And is "okay" really considered good enough, anyway?

In her bestselling book *The Defining Decade*, psychologist Dr. Meg Jay wrote that "to a great extent, our lives are decided by far-reaching twentysomething moments we may not realize are happening at all." In the preface, Jay explains something I wrote on a notecard when I was twenty-two, living in an apartment with a gallery wall, working my first "real" job while finishing my degree, and have carried with me since: *It is easy to imagine that life's significant experiences begin with big moments and exciting encounters, but this is not how it happens.* It offered solace when I was sitting on the floor of my apartment eating frozen pizza into the hours of morning where dawn turns blue, writing papers, sending emails, and wondering if loneliness meant being alone forever. When I mentioned that line to Dr. Jay when I met her in the crowded lobby of a downtown New York hotel that featured the sort of fireplace you'd pin on Pinterest, to talk to her about loneliness for a chapter of this book, it was still how my brain was operating. While I overthought whatever better version of me I should be working toward, it was the little things that were shaping me as I lived through them.

"Research shows and life experience shows that it is these little, unexpected moments that often end up being transformative," explained Jay. "It's because they're unexpected." We didn't plan them; there is no script there, she said. It certainly doesn't mean we don't have agency to change our circumstances or lives, but it's "that person we meet by chance or it's that flyer that we see and think, 'Oh, I didn't know they had a program.'" It got me thinking about the idea of transformation—maybe transformation, as Jay described it, is less about a full-life makeover. It's about slowing down enough to notice the things that truly change our lives, and impact who we are, when we aren't looking. "I think it's being able to see the potential in the ordinary," Jay said.

My own list of what's "transformed" my life the most seems downright mundane—the opposite of flashy plot twists and anecdotes to fill up my nostalgic toasts, or the champagne-popping announcements we're trained to recognize as pivotal moments. It's not that those moments don't matter; of course they do, especially when they hold personal meaning. It's that they aren't the *only* moments that count—and when we orient our lives around climbing the next step on the ladder to get us closer to a "big" moment, we look up, and realize that our identities, and our understanding of what we want out of life, have gotten lost in the shuffle of striving. I thought of the tiny moments that had changed my direction: When I left college, which felt like the world's worst mistake, but allowed me to work full-time all the way through school and gave me space to, over time, shift from a freshman struggling with severe depression, who couldn't even imagine her life several months in advance, to a fulfilled young adult who had goals beyond just making it through. The Twitter message I sent based on nothing more than spur-of-the-moment gut instinct that led to love. The times I wound up at home unexpectedly, because I got sick and needed help, because the organization I worked for went bankrupt and I couldn't pay rent, and as a result was around for moments with my family I'll cherish forever. It's stuff that never popped up in my GPA, or on my résumé, or, a lot of times, on my Instagram feed. It didn't necessarily make me smarter or cooler or better. But it made *me*. And turns out, in young adulthood, that's exactly the point.

This is not a book about millennials. At least, not entirely.

Half the time, it feels like when we talk about "millennials" and "Gen Z"—and the many stereotypes of these two generations, including references to avocado toast and lattes—we're referring to "emerging adults." Emerging adulthood is a life stage; "millennial" and "Gen Z" are names for specific ranges of birth years. And that matters: The generational wars of "who has it worse" seem to mask the fact that the way our society is structured doesn't seem to be working for *most* people, regardless of age, and that it's gone a long time without fundamentally changing to address this. But I was interested in a specific pressure I saw in young adults: How do you build a life, and find yourself, when there's been such a specific outline, timeline, and illustration of what it means to do "your best" handed to you like an instruction manual?

Jeffrey Jensen Arnett, PhD, coined the term "emerging adulthood" for this developmental period,[5] roughly ages eighteen to twenty-nine,[6] in the early nineties, when he was actually researching Generation X. Back then, he told me, people were saying similar things about that generation as they do about millennials now: "'They sure are taking a long time to grow up and they sure are depending on their parents for longer than people did in the past. And they seem kind of selfish and self-absorbed and self-indulgent,'" he explained, pointing out that he found very little evidence for that line of thought. Instead, he noticed that this "later entry" to adulthood included later entry into things like stable work, marriage, and parenthood, things that weren't distinctive to Generation X. "You could see that the changes that were happening in the economy and education and society all were going to continue," Arnett said. And they have. People were waiting longer to marry and have kids, a trend that's continued for young adults today. And the modern economy pushed for more and more higher education to, theoretically, gain financial and job security. And young people were moving back in with their parents then, too: "That's treated by many people as a character defect," Arnett told me. Young people have "grown up in an individualistic society, and by the time they get to their twenties, they believe what the people around them believe, which is that, okay, now you should be independent. You should be self-sufficient. You should be able to fend for yourself."

Though there might be more freedom in building your own path as a young adult, that doesn't mean every option—every freedom, every exploratory venture—is available to everyone. And it doesn't mean that those adult transitions or markers are totally irrelevant to everyone when it comes to how we think about our lives.

In reality, this period of our lives is when we're doing a lot of identity development work. Dr. Dalal Katsiaficas, assistant professor in the Department of Educational Psychology at the University of Illinois at Chicago, explained that we're renegotiating "many of our social identities during this time because we're coming into the ability to navigate the world in very different ways, but also to make contributions to the world." What's happening, she told me, is that we are asking the questions about who we are in a larger society, or world, and who we want to be. Katsiaficas explained that emerging adulthood is when the accumulation of dispossession comes to fruition—meaning that the effects of systemic issues of racism, oppression, marginalization, and disadvantage are so pronounced specifically during this life period. She described "structural dispossession" as dispossessing young adults from basic human needs, "healthcare, financial stability through student loans, from imagining themselves in the future tense, through police violence and white supremacy," which can be seen through a lens of capitalism and racism. "I think that for many emerging adults, they've really internalized these messages [that] somehow they're not measuring up because they can't achieve these elusive markers of adulthood," she continued. "When really, they're part of a system that sets that up and then blames them for it." Major traps of that, she said, are getting locked into this hyper-individualism and feeling alienated from imagining a new, collective future and our own power to change these systems. It feels like a fundamental flaw with *us*: We're not growing up fast enough, or doing enough, or achieving enough. In actuality, we're separate from the things we need.

The characteristics of emerging adulthood, according to the American Psychological Association,[7] include identity exploration, instability, self-focus, a feeling of in-between, and an age of possibilities. In other words: All this wondering what we're supposed to be doing, and who we want to become, is more normal than gets talked about. So many of the compounding pressures of finding yourself and building a life aren't unique to any single generation. It is part of growing up that has been amplified by shifting demands of what it means to be worthy and to be making the most of your life. Some of the things that get dismissed as unimportant during young adulthood—stability, routine, self-worth, community—are actually what fulfill us, not just the extraordinary, "big" stuff.

The circumstances in which young people today are growing up aren't the same as they were even a decade ago. The figures of outstanding student loan debt—over $1 trillion—are so unbelievable that there's now a Twitter account tracking every time that number increases. Late-stage capitalism and an economy that's racist and sexist, according to experts, have altered how we work; "jobs for everyone" is the talking point, while needing three of them to survive is overlooked. The world is aflame because of climate change, and any semblance of a social safety net—that never existed for everyone, anyway—has flaked out from under us. The world we grow into has changed. The standards of what it means to do that successfully have not budged.

In 2020, not only did the COVID-19 pandemic decimate the health of so many people's loved ones, but the job losses were grueling, with workers who were barely making a minimum wage suddenly our essential heroes, even if the people calling them essential didn't care enough to offer them healthcare. Waves of racial justice protests demanded justice for Black lives lost to ongoing police brutality, and were a confrontation of hundreds of years of structural racism, white supremacy, and inequity built into America's systems and structure. School and work closures meant, suddenly, parents had no childcare and gender pay and caretaking disparities were exacerbated, college students were forced out of dorms, even if they had nowhere else to live, going to work was a risk, and traveling was a no-go.

It became obvious, if it wasn't already, that so much of our hyper-focus on being exceptional, individualistic, and extraordinary was built on a foundation of lies that all this would save us; that it would all be enough someday. Extraordinary as a standard of living is inherently inequitable, a standard given to all but attainable for only a few. It's easy to focus on being exceptional, for example, when you aren't worried about paying rent or finding a job. When you have healthcare. When you have a support system. When you aren't staring down racism, bigotry, and prejudice—all of which mean additional standards of extraordinariness just to get by; when you have to do quadruple the work to go half as far and have even less margin for error. There's the insinuation that one kind of life means you've made the most of living: one of adventure that's enough to become the stories you tell when you're older, one of no mistakes or missteps, one where you can hustle your way into anything. But this also occurs within a society that, not coincidentally, relies on us to feed a system in which "never enough" is embedded. Too often, getting to say you're enough, as is, feels like something that has to be earned first.

In other words, this isn't just about Instagram and FOMO and a generation that was told they were special too many times. In fact, the obsession with extraordinary often seems like the inverse of participation-trophy woes. It's as though the perpetual broadcasting of a "best self" means so many young people are working to live up to standards that turned "good" into "average," and "ordinary" into a synonym for boring, lackluster, and perhaps most darkly, failure.

Over and over, young adults vocalized the same rebuttals I'd heard myself. You're wasting years meant for exploring on routine? If you're laying roots now, be it significant others or a sofa you love that you'd never be able to move down the stairs at your current apartment, you will have wasted your time to be choosy. You don't know what to do next? You should've been more prepared. You're burnt out already? Well, the only answer is to work harder, and do more, to get to the job status level where one day, you won't be. You're lonely? Put yourself out there. It's never been easier to meet people, but you should be able to do this alone, anyway. This trope—of being exceptional, self-reliant, and never unsure—instructs us to play by rules we didn't set, encourages criteria that don't feel compatible with everyday existences, and puts us in a constant state of fixing ourselves in hopes life will turn out the way we want.

There is, of course, abundant privilege that accompanies the aspiration of having an extraordinary life—one in which you have time to focus on dreams instead of basic survival. Young people today continue to face systemic oppression, racism, discrimination, and marginalization, and are impacted by everything from economic stratification to gentrification. The social contract, the idea that if you went to school and worked hard and paid your dues, everything will work out just fine, doesn't exist anymore (for many, it never did). I question the idea that appreciating ordinariness is as simple as moving back to your small town, as though it is a hub of family recipes and values that is purer and more wholesome, as if that doesn't disenfranchise people, too. Or that it's as simple as learning to embrace your flaws and celebrate the small things—those are worthy pursuits, of course. But unpacking this feels like it demands acknowledging that young adults are coming of age in a society that's quick to tell them what they ought to be, with little attention paid to the fact that, often, what's significant is small, and what shapes us is the everyday, not always the grand adventure or accomplishment. That's why the everyday circumstances in which we build our lives and selves matter so much. This isn't a manifesto of "Slash everything from your life and retreat to the woods; embrace the ordinary and it'll be fine!" One kind of life does not work best for everyone, and perhaps the greatest gift we can give ourselves is realizing that, and noticing that sometimes, doing what we can, with what matters, where we are, is enough.

So many of the themes explored in these pages are exacerbated by glaring inequities. That can't go unacknowledged: Telling people to embrace their ordinary in the midst of social structures that are, at best, crumbling, or, at worst, working against them, feels twee. While a cultural interrogation can't put into place the structural changes that transforming a society requires, I hope this book can be a balm for the moments young adults feel lonely while finding their way, a comfort when they think they've failed at living up to everything young adulthood "should" be, and gets us talking about how many of our ordinary moments and feelings are actually formative. Being contented, present, and learning as we go should move us closer to the kind of lives and world we actually want to wake up to. It's part of doing what we can to reconsider the milestones we meet and the extraordinary expectations we chase, and decide for ourselves what it means to live a meaningful life.

That also means amplifying the voices of young people who all have unique perspectives, opinions, and experiences in the world. The essays in this book put personal experience in conversation with experts, anecdotes, data, and stories from other people to explore where the pressure to accumulate and broadcast extraordinary experiences comes from, to better understand how we can unravel it. It won't capture every lived experience. The stories of young people in these pages are just a small sampling of how it feels to be making your way in the world right now. There's a myth that if you haven't had every great adventure, every formative life experience, and every major accomplishment during young adulthood, you're behind, or you're broken. And the more young people I spoke to, the more it seemed like living your "best life" was ripe for a reckoning—and revamping parts of that conversation to focus on young adults trying to build their lives in ways that feel truest, most practical, and most fulfilling to them.

These essays examine themes, like work culture and dating and our sense of home, that seem like big inflection points for how we think about and decide on the kind of lives we want to lead. I wrote and researched while working my day job and scrambling to search, with a magnifying glass of desperation, for where the bonus hours in the day were hidden—for actually scheduling the colonoscopy I was supposed to have a year ago, responding to texts, and *as* I attempt to figure things out. Mostly, it was written while talking to people who were experiencing versions of the exact same thing. Dozens upon dozens of people, ranging in age roughly from eighteen to thirty, shared their thoughts, feelings, and pressures for these pages, taking time to think aloud about their own extraordinary expectations, and what they wish people knew about the grind of building life as a young person today.

When we're growing up—which we still are!—seeking contentment, being seen, and a life that feels true to who we are aren't afterthoughts. These things also often aren't found (at least for everyone) in being perfect, powerhouse milestones, certain degrees or job titles, and meeting expectations you didn't set. What we might find is that the big questions—*What matters to me? How do I tune out the noise of what doesn't? Who am I going to be in the world?*—have ordinary answers. Maybe it's embracing the pursuit of those answers that leads us to growth, and shows us who we can grow into. We all grow up, and out. We're not wrong for wondering if there's a different way to navigate through it. This is, after all, an ordinary age.

# 2

## "FOR THE EXPERIENCE"

*On work identities, dream jobs, and doing it "for the experience"*

EVERYONE WHO HAS EVER BEEN PRAISED AS A "HARD WORKER" knows the feeling: the zing of acknowledgment that you've done a good job, followed by the sharp stab of panic—*How do I keep this going?* We know, logically, that we are more than any job title or pay stub—but we exist in a world that's quick to tell us otherwise. Working one job turns into working two or three, because warnings about having a safety net feel as tangible as bills that demand to be paid each month, consistent in their arrival and persistent in their tick-tock urgency. Due to work monopolizing so much of our lives—for the worse, in most cases—it feels like there are few things that intersect more with the various parts of our identities, including what we can afford, our social circles, our ability to identify as a person who does X, where we live, than our jobs.

We grow up hearing we should think about our dream jobs and finding a way to do what we love, right alongside reminders to "do something practical" and "major in something you can make money in." Toddlers get asked what they want to be when they grow up, and we don't stop asking—the question just morphs into "So what do you do?" Never mind that perhaps not everyone dreams of working—no, not everyone has a "dream job"—or can work. Work, theoretically, pays us money to invest in ourselves, from the food we nourish our bodies with, to the places we live, to the hobbies and the luxuries we can afford. And because most of us have to do it, to some degree, it becomes easy to divorce the privilege, opportunities, and access from who gets to do what.

"Good" jobs have never been accessible to everyone, and society still applies judgment about the work people *do* have—as though it is a commentary on their character and their ambition. While "major in something realistic" is a common talking point, with "do what you love and you'll never work a day in your life" serving its aspirational opposite, the realities of jobs and work pop up less: For a lot of young people, working is not a fun hobby to chat about in college interviews or a cool means of presenting identity by Instagramming your business cards. It's a necessity for plain old survival, supporting loved ones, or taking care of yourself. A college degree, even with perfect grades and rock-star internships, doesn't guarantee you anything but debt if you don't have a scholarship or financial support to pay your tuition. And after graduation, overworking doesn't promise promotions, success, or even the stability that lets you live on your own—it just guarantees you're working hours you likely aren't being paid for. These adult versions of straight-A report cards—being called "ambitious," "driven," "a hard worker"—have come to feel like sorry concessions of capitalism, the only thing we get in a culture that underpays people often, treats employees as disposable, and relies on pats on the back instead of equitable wages, healthcare, or job security.

We can't hard-work our way out of it, and yet we have to anyway. There's always someone waiting in line for our job, we're told.

Jobs give us another arena in which we can achieve the extraordinary, from money to acclaim to dreams come true. But thanks to work's monopoly on us, "extraordinary" varies so spectacularly it's impossible to keep up with what it means. It shouldn't be extraordinary, a feat of the impossible, to be able to comfortably pay your bills, and yet, for a lot of young people, that alone feels like an accomplishment beyond comprehension. For others, "extraordinary" looks like job titles that capture an outward signal about your personality, having coworkers who will become friends, or a "cool" work environment, complete with Ping-Pong tables and company-sponsored happy hours. Just as we assess degrees from a select few colleges as holding some weird nobility, there's a stigma around certain kinds of jobs deemed lesser, which is where the "jobs at McDonald's are for teenagers" quips come from. And even for teenagers, summer jobs that were supposed to mean independence and a sense of identity beyond being a student are disappearing, part of the economic upheaval young people have never really experienced a world without. Yet: Jobs are considered part of the foray into adulthood, and how we build our lives within it.

In college, Georgie, twenty-two, said she felt like everyone she knew had a "thing" they were called to do, and she envied the confidence they had in the direction their life was going. The "calling" part hit me in the gut: If you're not getting ahead in what you're "meant" to do, you're already behind. It's like all our meaning can be neatly packaged, ironically not separate from our productivity. We anticipate everyone getting on a single track, and hitting the benchmarks of success within that track, like settling on a course of study or a job. If they don't, we assume they're directionless, instead of just finding their direction. "I was told over and over, 'You've got time to figure it out,' until eventually people stop saying that," she added. Then Georgie moved following graduation: She had decided on a city further south after being guaranteed one job, but the organization changed its mind on where they wanted to place her. So she opted to keep the job she had in her college town and work remotely in her new city—that security allowed her to move. Shortly after, the business pivoted to focus on a service Georgie wasn't needed full-time for, and it left her without full-time work and applying to jobs around the clock. "There was definitely a sense of shame when I realized how dependent my self-sufficiency was on something that could disappear in an instant," she said.

After interviewing six times over the course of seven weeks for a position she had been assured would ultimately be offered to her, she was rejected for not having a large enough network in the area. Georgie got a job at a grocery store, another waiting tables, and quickly realized more of her identity was entwined in her work than she was aware. "I was taken aback by my own insecurity," she said. "I quickly was tracing dots and asking myself questions like, 'If you personally feel insecure telling people you work at a grocery store, does that mean all this time you've been judging people who have jobs that don't require degrees?'" In school, she had been surrounded by "high-achieving, full-ride-earning, perfect-GPA kids," and while she felt she had never fully bought into that culture, she felt she suffered from being deeply implanted in it. "Achievement and identity were often one and the same," she said. Being unemployed for six weeks was more taxing on her sense of self than she could have foreseen. In addition to being financially stressful, it made her question her purpose. Now, when people ask "What do you do?" she wants to say, "Well, there are far more important things about me than what I do, but I work at a grocery store and a restaurant."

She adds, "And then I feel my insecurity wanting to say, 'Just for this year, though; I've applied to go to law school.' We talk to every person we meet like it's the truest, most important thing about them," she said of our jobs. "And maybe, in a culture that sacrifices so much of our time and health at the altar of Work, we simply must believe it to be that important, or else realize we've made grave mistakes due to misaligned priorities."

What's more disturbing is that, in this country, our employment status is directly linked to our access to health insurance, our income is connected to our rent, and our résumés are so often tied to our social perception, so to say we hang in the balance of work, distressingly, isn't an understatement. There was this other facet of extraordinary, though, a means through which unpaid internships, a class and equity divide that pops up in the depths of job-hunting for young adults, remains justifiable: It's *for the experience*. The work is worth doing for the experience of having done that work. Working "for the experience" will hardly pay your rent or allow you to get groceries, but those extraordinary experiences are supposed to be a different form of currency: that we're on a track toward proving ourselves. We made plans and stuck with them. We had dreams and goals for our lives—as if every dream must be tied to the value of productivity.

"Young adults are hearing the message that they should have internship experience from a variety of sources—online, more broadly, but also from career counselors and faculty," Dr. Carrie L. Shandra, associate professor of sociology at the State University of New York at Stony Brook, said. "It wouldn't be surprising to me that the downstream consequence of that messaging is the feeling that one's work history or identity is lacking in the absence of internship experience." While Shandra notes she can't distinguish paid from unpaid internships in the data, the results of the College Senior Survey, a college exit survey administered by UCLA, shows that only 29 percent of seniors reported participating in an internship in 1994. By 2017, that number was 65 percent. "But these numbers tell us that internship participation is ubiquitous among college graduates, and that rates of participation are significantly higher today than they were two decades ago," she said. Because so many are unpaid, or, in some cases, cost tuition money (meaning, you pay your university to work an internship, which counts as college credit), a young person working an unpaid internship has to have some other financial support, whether it is their parents, scholarships, or working a part-time paid job and doing their internship on the side. While Shandra noted that internships themselves aren't inherently inequitable (the policies and practices that create the system of unpaid internships in the United States is, she said), internships can be thought of along a spectrum: "Some are more useful for providing access to social networks, skills training, mentorship, and a potential foot in the door for full-time employment than others. This means that, in addition to the barriers of getting any internship, there are also inequities in getting a good internship," she added. And work, paid or unpaid, doesn't stay at work. It seeps out into how we live our lives or think about ourselves, particularly when it comes to hitting so-called milestones of young adulthood, like moving out and getting jobs. These inequalities have ripple effects, Shandra said. "Young adults are living with parents at unprecedented rates right now. Without access to full-time employment with benefits, they may not have health insurance. And it'll be difficult to become financially independent or build the kind of savings required to buy a home and build wealth."

"Having a job has meant that I'm the friend that never goes out on the weekends. Not getting enough sleep. Not having enough time in my schedule to work a school job or an unpaid job, I can't afford to," Cherisse, twenty-one, said. She worked in high school and got a substantial scholarship for college that paid for her meal plan and tuition but didn't provide any type of living stipend. She works at a Whole Foods, and has never been able to afford to take an unpaid internship or volunteer opportunities. She described some class-mates acting like they don't recognize her when she's at work, and being on the receiving end of disrespect. Working in "the wealthiest and whitest part of the city I was born in [is] a big point of resent-ment already." There are so many Black and Latino young people working to make a living while in school, she pointed out. "How could it be such a taboo concept to pay them a living wage in an internship where their labor and knowledge is being used like ev-ery other employee they interact with?" Working for free is another extraordinary expectation demanded to climb a certain ladder of work. Cherisse's ultimate goal is to be a documentary filmmaker, and she's majoring in journalism—this has also meant investing in her own equipment, which costs money, as does buying clothes for interviews, which she mentioned. With work to survive and work she's working toward, she said sometimes "I think that, because it consumes so much of my time . . . what would I do if I didn't have to work?"

It's a worthwhile question. Who are we when we're not work-ing? Is there any way to support ourselves *and* not feel like work makes up the heft of us? Ambition won't save us, and security and stability have been positioned as luxuries you'll hopefully gain access to after you've proved yourself instead of being considered basic things needed to live. It's as though the line of thought goes: If you do enough now, you'll be comfortable later. If you achieve enough, you'll be safe. It's like jobs are never just jobs.

"Every message I received from my master's program, every entrepreneurial podcast on queue, every Instagram influencer I followed, and every contemporary self-help I listened to on Audible seemingly thinks millennials should build their own career," Kristine, twenty-four, told me. She took one month off between undergrad and starting a master's program for functional nutrition and medicine, which she found through her own healing process, using it to reverse some of what she described as the self-inflicted damage done by chronic stress. Her physical healing came from changing her diet, and the kitchen became a peaceful refuge from the hustle of being in "incessant overdrive doing everything I could to always be the best in my class, jobs, and internships." On the surface, it sounds like the dream job scenario: a passion *but* a practical field; it involved intense training but she *also* had the entrepreneurial streak that rendered her a self-starter, the lofty buzzword that a million job applications ask for and few seem to define. But the day she graduated with her master's, people began asking how the practice was going, curious about her roster of patients less than a week after graduation, which left her feeling like a failure for not meeting those expectations. She kept hearing messaging around millennials building their own businesses: If she didn't, "I'd be a millennial sellout." An extension of "never settle" and "ever upward" motivational talk, pursuing a "better" job is a hallmark of today's working world, where the idea is that we will always be moving up in whatever we do, and if we don't, we're doing it wrong. After taking a hard look at how to stay in the medical field without spending another decade in school, she began a nursing program, with Zoom classes and fourteen-hour shifts two to three times a week.

I think about it at least once a week: how unnerving it is that so much of my identity is tethered to something I could be fired from, and how, the deeper into adulthood I get, the more I side-eye how much of my own self-perception is intertwined with work. I've never known young adulthood without a job of some kind. Which makes me wonder if I've ever known myself as an adult beyond the context of labor, striving, and the all-elusive "earning it," and this doesn't seem, by any means, unique to me. "Hustle culture" pep talks pepper a work culture that suggests young adults should work for free to gain experience and that there's only a certain kind of work that matters. And despite the best intentions around work not consuming our lives, it also feels borderline impossible to escape the sensation that it says something about who we are, even if it shouldn't. Like, do I *really* need to check my email before going to bed? What kind of person—who is not literally saving lives or shaping them—assigns this much energy, conversation, and worry to what is essentially labor? At the start of my working life, as a teenager, I rode high on ambition, and considered the ability to outwork everything and everyone the cornerstone of my personality *and* my safety net. Surely it would all be okay if I just kept hustling, right?

Now I'm just tired, and I worry about work in reverse: Am I *one of those people* so fixated on this one thing, work, I've lost track of everything else? How do I define myself beyond what I do, and the security I chase? What's so wrong with finding your meaning, and even your dreams, outside the scope of what you achieve and earn? I knew I was privileged because I had jobs and was lucky enough to generally like most of them. But it was staggering how much work-place abuse and toxicity didn't register as anything beyond something I had to tolerate in order to secure a paycheck until years after the fact, or how I put off significant medical appointments because of lack of insurance. It feels like a lot of what we tell young adults about work are opposites: This is the time to experiment, chase your dreams, and prove yourself, but on the other hand, you need to be practical, prepared to do anything, and certainly shouldn't expect anything from work—this includes, sometimes, expecting payment for it. If you haven't pursued your passion as a career, are you really making the most of your time on earth? But on the flip side, don't you know there's more to life than work and you should be grateful to have a job at all?

During COVID, the divide between work and sense of self seemed to blur: For some, workplace desks and office plants were replaced by laptops at kitchen tables and employees reheating the same cup of coffee for the duration of the workday—the length of which increased during the pandemic, according to research.[1] While the study said it was unclear whether the increase in the span of the workday was a drawback or benefit—having control over your schedule or working nontraditional hours could be a plus—it stated, "The change in work schedule may be a consequence of a blurred distinction between work and personal life, in which it becomes easy to overwork due to the lack of clear delineation between the office and home."[2] No kidding. For others, the blurred distinction between work life and personal life came in the form of losing their job, being unable to work remotely and thus furloughed, or risking their lives as an "essential worker," sometimes for minimum wage or reliance on tips. Hiring freezes coinciding with job-hunting fresh out of college derailed the plans of some young adults—they did, after all, graduate into the worst job market in a generation.[3] None of the old standby advice—*Apply for everything! Be flexible; be willing to move; be willing to take a job outside your field! Ask a mentor to get coffee!*—felt relevant. The domino effect was gutting: Lack of work meant lack of money (thanks to lack of federal relief) to pay rent or buy food; lack of jobs to apply to meant lack of opportunity to do the thing that's unrealistically celebrated most in America—changing your circumstances by hustle and merit alone. It also thoroughly thwarted the idea of jobs being an obvious marker of stability, security, and success in young adulthood.

"My career has been my identity for so long, and so, I lost all that due to COVID," said Harper, twenty-seven. After leaving a toxic workplace—so toxic that she was diagnosed with workplace PTSD—Harper had landed a dream job, working with an advertising agency that specializes in Broadway, a step toward a life goal of starting a scholarship fund to support musical theater by people who are marginalized. While she said the PTSD was a struggle she brought into her dream job, her colleagues were supportive, and she was so excited about the work she was doing; it was everything she could ever want. She took a massive pay cut, but she said that, at a certain point, "I am selling my soul very literally. And I don't want to be that person anymore." Then COVID hit, and imploded, among other things, the theater industry. Along with the job, she lost "her sense of home," living in New York where she'd spent the majority of her adult life. She's now living with her parents, and mentioned trying to explain the loss of her dream job to her family: When they told her at least she got the opportunity to do something she cared about, when some people go their entire lives without that, she understood. But when her parents were her age, they had two kids. Her younger sister is recently engaged. They all had "bigger" things going on in their lives, she said. "And I really did not have anything." Even her hobbies, over the past years of day-to-day work grind, had fallen away. "And for me, it was like, I'm finally becoming this person that I had in my head, who has the life that I want, you know?" she said, noting that when she tried to explain this to her mother, she said that psychologists have researched and now understand that when we think about our future selves, our brains don't put together that it's still us—it's like a different person we're aspiring to be. "And so, I was really mourning her death." It wasn't just the loss of a job, but showed all the things losing a job can steal: a sense of home; a sense of who you are.

As Jhumpa Bhattacharya, vice president of programs and strategy of the Insight Center for Community Economic Development, pointed out, the unrest in 2020, in which massive layoffs as a result of COVID-19 coincided with racial justice protests around the world, underscored what so many young people know from personal experience: Our economy was designed to benefit the few and strip resources away from the many. Profit has become the "almighty god," she told me, so now, we're not actually caring for the people we're supposed to care for. That includes a tearing away of public goods, things that are meant for the public, including education— education, utilities, and healthcare should all be free, Bhattacharya said. "Because we had such a movement to move away from investment and public goods and we've privatized all of that—most of it— and then you have an influx of corporate power, this generation is really going to feel the impacts of that in a way that no other generation has had to," she added. "It's not y'all's fault at all. It's how we set up the structure and rampant, runaway capitalism."

Bhattacharya described drivers that have kept the millennial generation from accumulating wealth—increasing student debt, "continued pay inequality and occupational segregation on racial and gender lines," and shifting social customs and family formation, like getting married and having kids much later than previous generations. Other young people, especially children of immigrants, Bhattacharya pointed out, are the breadwinners for entire extended families. And people of color in America fall to the bottom of almost every single economic indicator, Bhattacharya explained. "When we think about, 'How do you address racial wealth inequality?,' we're still using kind of traditional measures of wealth, building or buying a home, starting a business, getting a degree, but what we see, time and time again for Black folks, particularly for Black women—those standard wealth levers don't work because we live in a patriarchal, racist society and economy," Bhattacharya said, noting that women hold two-thirds of the nation's student loan debt[4] (and Black women finish undergrad with more debt than other women[5]). For young people in low-income communities, or rural areas that are depopulating, work and pursuing extracurricular freelance work, interning in different fields until you find one you like, or even finding multiple jobs needed to make ends meet can be even more challenging—it's impossible to chase an opportunity if the opportunity doesn't exist to you to begin with.

Plus, there's the wealth aspect of all this to consider ("What wealth?" you might be asking). Wealth, everything you own, your savings, and your social capital, minus everything you owe, like student loans, is, in a capitalist society, Bhattacharya said, what gives us access to power, dignity, and choice. It's impossible to not address who has access to those freedoms and who doesn't. And it's built into our systems of work: Young people of color also face hiring discrimination, and research shows that Black workers experience higher unemployment and work in jobs with lower wages and fewer benefits than those held by white workers.[6] It's not a matter of being a hard worker; it's a matter of systemic racism and barriers that include hiring discrimination, pay inequality, and microaggressions in the workplace. And those barriers are present from the jump: Research from the Urban Institute[7] showed that Black, Latinx, and Asian youth aren't only employed at lower rates than their white peers, they're also paid less. Other research shows those who kick off their working lives in a depressed labor market that oftentimes accompanies a recession could get trapped in a "downward-shifted economic trajectory."[8] And it's not like the playing field has ever been even to begin with.

Bhattacharya pointed to what it feels like a lot of this "hustle culture" thrives on: "toxic individualism," which she explained as "this idea that if you're poor, you made bad choices, and you don't know what you're doing, versus looking at structural inequality issues." There should be no one going hungry, without a home, or having to work two to three jobs to meet the standard of the cost of living in a given area, she said. This has a physical and emotional health impact, too: Bhattacharya spoke about wildfires that impacted the West Coast in 2020, and who could afford an air purifier; it made me think about how even should-be ordinary things, like having money for an emergency, become feats worthy of acclaim or failures worthy of commentary on your character, as if it's divorced from circumstances.

It's all so interconnected: The pivot between work being everything, a necessity for living, and something we're advised not to put our whole worth into—as if these things can coexist. Cobbling together multiple jobs at a time. And the rejection: We see job announcement posts, but never the behind-the-scenes of making it to the final interview round and never hearing a decision, applying to a thousand jobs only to be rejected by one thousand and one. And so we think that we're the *only ones* having this particular experience with work. You can send follow-up email after follow-up email regarding a position you applied for, and never hear from your interviewer again, despite the pleasant conversation you thought you had. You can be told that an offer has been made to someone else, only to see the job description reposted with a lower salary two days later. Young adults described similar horrors: getting an email with an offer, followed by an another email apologizing, saying the offer had been sent to the wrong candidate and they'd meant to send a rejection instead; seeing ideas they offered up on a test or their work samples used by the company that didn't hire them; feeling ashamed for admitting they're disappointed they didn't get something, feeling guilty that they didn't do enough to lock the job down. It's a constant process of reinvention, swallowing your pride, and pretending rejection doesn't rattle you. There's a lot of starting over.

Work doesn't seem to be working for many of us. Melissa and Johnathan Nightingale are the founders of Raw Signal Group, which offers management and leadership training for growing organizations. One of the experiences we aren't getting at work anymore is the promise and potential of longevity. You've seen the headlines: Today's young people are job-hoppers; they have no loyalty; they don't stick around long enough to gain the knowledge they need, because they're constantly looking for something better. On the other side of the coin, employers are no longer investing time or resources into their employees. "One of the key ways that work has changed is that we don't have an expectation of longevity or loyalty," explained Melissa. Thus, employers aren't expected to have to train their employees. According to Melissa, most employers automatically assume new hires won't stick around for long and, instead of making the long-term decision to invest in training someone, they opt to hire someone with a skill set that requires minimal prepping and that they can put to work immediately. It used to be, you could learn from parents or older coworkers what was expected in the workplace. You could learn the rules, but now, the rules don't work anymore, Johnathan added, so this isn't a thing you can learn generationally. But that's another layer: Being loyal to an employer could be an incredibly risky career decision, and a terrible personal one. "What does the word 'loyalty' mean in a context where employers are telling employees they are not allowed to discuss their compensation, right?" Johnathan said. "They write it into job contracts. You're not allowed to discuss your compensation." If you're a woman in the workforce, or a marginalized individual in the workforce, Melissa added, you know you're "actively being screwed" on things like compensation all the time. So, looking to move on and up wouldn't come completely out of left field. "I think part of the reason why people shift roles is upward economic mobility," she said. People know putting your head down, working hard, and hoping your boss notices is no longer a strategy for success.

"So many folks, particularly in the early parts of their career, find that their advancement and their salary gains come much faster when they shift employers," she said. And when we finally come of age and enter the workforce, it may be that the careers we've planned for our entire life aren't what we thought they'd be. "It also happens that folks fall out of alignment with the work that they're doing," said Melissa. "It's somebody else's dream job. It's something that other people get excited about. It looks cool on a résumé." People get excited about your LinkedIn updates about it, she said, but the reality is waking up every day feeling like you're doing the wrong work. It reminded me of something Jhumpa Bhattacharya told me in regard to the current moment in society, which unearthed an opportunity for some of us to challenge everything we've been told to believe, which is that "work equals personhood." Attaching deservedness to jobs pops up in a dozen forms, from shaming people for not "working hard enough" to avoid the need for social services or help of any kind, to spinning everything that isn't grandiose as lackluster. As work dominates more of our waking hours, it also monopolizes more of our identities, meaning career transitions, job losses, or financial strains often double as identity crises.

And honestly, it feels backward to define ourselves by what we do anymore, as if job titles are status symbols and dream jobs don't incite their own version of turmoil: What if everyone else knows their dream job, their calling, their purpose, and you don't? What if you end up unable to get a job in your chosen field, or get your dream job and realize it's not at all what you want? When these notions get encouraged in young adults, it feels like undercutting more realistic expectations around what work is, and how it feels. Maybe if so many of us weren't only focused on defining ourselves by dream jobs, it would give us freedom to reimagine our meaning, purpose, and what matters to us in other facets of our lives. What if we started those conversations earlier, unwinding hyped-up versions of "making it" that comes with "accomplishing your dreams," leaving little room for the fact that dreams or goals might change based on circumstances, realities like finances, or simple shifts in personal preference that happen as we grow up? After all, even passions can feel fatiguing and frustrating.

The "dream job" trope connects directly to the "for the experience" work: Are you *really* going to question whether you should be paid or not, or paid more, if you're just grateful to be in the room? Work from Dr. Erin A. Cech,[9] who does research around what she calls the "passion principle," or self-expression being a guiding force in career decisions, stated that "passion principle thus appears to help neutralize these career aspirants' critiques of the capitalist labor structure—critiques that might, under different circumstances, foster collective demands for shorter work hours, more leisure time, or better work-life balance." "Pursuing your passion" or living out your dreams through work has never been a reality for everyone—and it's worth questioning why work is the place that's supposed to house so much of our self-esteem, meaning, and identity. "The cultural valuation of individualism and self-expression has grown dramatically since the 1950s and along with it the expectation that individuals should have as many opportunities as possible to make autonomous choices about the direction and character of their own lives," Cech's research states.

The combo of individualism and capitalism makes it so we're working more hours, so of course we figure those hours will go by easier and faster if we love the work we're doing—but it can also keep us from critiquing the structure in which this is unfolding. It seems to put the burden of "creating work-life balance" back on individuals, rather than a workforce that takes, takes, takes. Our current system of work tightly ties job titles, income, and dream jobs to ambition, value, and self-worth—but the system is failing us. It's worth reconsideration that if we are what we do, there's value in having dreams and doing things beyond work, and the pressure to have a dream job serve as your sole identifier can feel like a lot. Have you ever known yourself beyond it; do we have enough means of defining who we are outside it? It really is okay for a job to be just a job—just a means of living a fulfilled life in other ways.

Not to mention, "you are what you do" seems like a slimy stance to take when so many factors go into the job you end up in, especially when we know that our most average selves always stand alongside our most exceptional accomplishments. To make it more complicated, you also can't just assume the work we do has nothing to do with how we feel, which might be why you hear young adults craving work that's "fulfilling," "meaningful," or "important." When a job came up at a small company that does some work with clients Harper ethically disagrees with, she was stuck: She needed the job; she needed the money. She has what she described as several chronic mental health struggles, and if she's no longer able to afford her medication, it would make it harder for her to find work, which would make it harder to get treated, a vicious cycle.

"There are plenty of people who, once again, don't have their dream jobs," she added. "What makes me think that I'm so fucking special that I should be entitled to a job that I feel ethically pristine about?" It isn't just a prestige thing. The work we do does affect how we feel about ourselves and our place in the world. Just like we might overestimate how spectacular achievements might change who we are, we underestimate the fact that, for many, a steady paycheck or the chance to escape a toxic work environment does have real ramifications on mental health, stability, and overall well-being.

So, yeah. Work is personal.

And because it's so personal and so deeply linked to how we see ourselves and experience the world, what happens at work matters, too. We spend more time at work, statistically, than we do with our families, Melissa and Johnathan of Raw Signal Group said. It would be hard to spend more time somewhere than you do with your family, Melissa said, and not have it impact your identity, including how you feel about yourself and the people around you. Work also stands in for family in many ways now, as a support system and network in cities where many young people have come, leaving family and familiarity behind in pursuit of building a future. It's natural that people grouped together, especially with some common mission, would end up bonding. "They're standing in for your family because you're not near your family," Melissa said. When we're defining what matters to us and safety, security, and stability all make the list, it makes sense that you'd be drawn to the work environment that counts you as "family," even if that's a farce. "To be fired from that community that you've built, especially early, when you don't have a distinct identity of like, 'I'm a genuinely good copywriter. I'm a genuinely good engineer. I know that about myself internally,' is challenging," Johnathan said. "So much of your validation comes from the fact that this work family thinks that you're valuable, and so to be expelled from that, it's brutal." So, this family is still keenly aware of how valuable you are as a worker, and your very membership is tied to your achievement.

In other ways, our jobs and our work being tied to personal identity pops up in social settings. It becomes a means of relating to a group of people, standing out, or defining yourself, which is why, in introductions at parties and on first dates and small talk, "What do you do?" is a common question—popular belief is that the answer tells us a lot. "What you do" also ties into how you live, and this is where privilege begets privileged choices: If you can stay on your parents' health insurance, if you have a family home to go back to if you're struggling with rent, if you have an employer who supports you taking a sabbatical or puts funding toward continued education, if you can afford to work for free for the experience without panicking over bills, your social capital pays off in ways that aren't considered when we assume all young people should be hitting the same career milestones at the same time. Really, society doesn't just want emerging adults to have work. We want them to have work that is considered worthy and proof they've "made something of themselves." "Making it" gets discussed like it's a fill-in-the-blank for young people: Hustle, work hard, pay your dues, you'll make it! But the problem is that we have fundamentally different definitions as individuals when considering what "making it" means.

Jay, a twenty-five-year-old working as a brand designer at a digital and creative agency, was the second person in her family to attend college. She wanted a steady job, a consistent paycheck, and to learn financial literacy, something she said isn't taught to low-income people. "Making more money than your parents is an awful feeling," Jay explained. With the power that comes from doing something truly extraordinary, like being the first in your family to finish college or secure work, comes pressures that aren't addressed when we talk about what kinds of jobs young adults should pursue or pressures they may be under. "Seeing your parents age without a retirement plan in place because they can't afford it is awful," she said. When she was a college senior, Jay got a jump on the extraordinary career she aspired to, taking an unpaid apprenticeship with a successful artist in order to gain experience and have someone who could vouch for her professionally, a benefit to jobs she'd pursue later on. After two months of trekking to and from the studio, she couldn't afford to get there. "That's when I realized that working for free is expensive," she said. The common talking point is that it all pays off later—the unpaid internship leads to a full-time job, the college degree in a practical major leads to a career that pays the loans off, the right job leads to the markers of "real" adult life, like buying a house or owning a car. But many young adults today have witnessed the financial impact of multiple recessions play out for their parents and older friends, if they weren't impacted by it themselves. You're not going to budget your way out of a financial recession, and increasingly, young people know you can't always hard-work your way to fulfillment and security.

Despite now having a career in her field, Jay said she felt she was "struggling to keep up" the act. She wants to switch careers, but the transition terrifies her, because of the threat of entering the gig economy and "seeming less 'impressive' within my friend group." Jay has a dog and a cat and wants to take care of them, in addition to giving her mother "a little pocket change when she needs it," something she's not sure would be possible if she started over in a different career sector. And it always seems like the advice is that there is something more we could've done: Major in something different. Skip college altogether (a nugget of advice that usually seems to come from people with college degrees). Work harder. Spend less—that ten-dollar candle you bought or the lunch you splurged on was the ticket to financial insecurity. If you have two jobs instead of three jobs, well, that explains why you can't pay off student loans. People crowdfund for medical bills, as if they can control unexpected illnesses or severe accidents, and there are wedding-planning websites that offer registry options for couples who want guests to contribute to a cash fund for refinancing student loans. It's not as simple as "Just quit and find something else!" You feel lucky for having work at all, even though our work culture is not set up for us to have full lives outside of it. It is only set up for us to be workers. You see this in the lack of paid family leave (despite today's twenty- and thirtysomethings being reprimanded for being "selfish" and not having kids), sick days being a luxury (and entire industries where your choices are to show up sick or be fired), and unlivable wages. We're expected to value work, especially if you're a young adult—getting your foot in the door, earning your keep, and proving you're worth keeping around. But work absolutely does not have to value us.

Luna, a twenty-five-year-old who described herself as a low-income, first-gen college graduate from a rural place, poured energy into the perfect grades and scholarships in order to get into "a good college" and a "good career," "whatever the heck those meant." Luna explained that, despite feeling she had no idea what she wanted to do, every time she brought up concerns to a teacher, a friend, or even her parents, their reaction was that she'd be great at whatever she chose. "Obviously they meant well, and everyone was so supportive," she said. "But I was so, so lost. I'd been told what to do my whole life and now all of a sudden it was *my* responsibility to figure out what 'exceptional' meant?"

Up until recently, Luna was working eighty hours a week. She had a full-time job in her field, and two part-time jobs on the side. Right when she moved, her housing plans fell through and her rent tripled. The house she was planning to share with two roommates, paying $300 in rent, went up for sale, and she couldn't find a rental under $1,200 a month. Thinking about what would best serve her future, Luna bought a house, a benchmark of young adult success. "I had the plan, and the savings, and it should have been enough," she said. "But then the basement flooded and all my credit cards got maxed out." Luna's story is an illustration of the part that gets left out when discussions of emerging adults, work, and finances pop up: You can do everything right and still find yourself at the mercy of circumstances beyond your control. There's never going to be enough money to solve *every* emergency; there's never going to be enough hours in the day to work *every* job at once. When Luna emailed me, she explained she was worried about getting all her "actual work" done before she had to go to one of her restaurant jobs, and spent her previous evening, her one night off, driving to the closest Walmart forty minutes away to get dog food and frozen food to get her through the week. "I'm worried about trying to pay off all the credit card debt I accrued when I first bought my house, moved in, and the basement promptly flooded with sewage in a nasty metaphor for what this whole year has seemed like," she wrote. She followed that up by saying she was also worried about keeping in touch with friends, something she hadn't been doing at all, because she has roughly an hour of free time each day to do "indulgent things like eat and sit down." It felt like a direct tie to the common theme I kept hearing: The lines between work and life are bleeding together.

The result is disorienting, and that requires us to suspend disbelief about what's possible. You've seen the stuff shared virally: "You have as many hours in the day as Beyoncé!" "Don't stop until you're proud," reminds another, never taking into consideration that you could work until you collapse and it still might not be enough to pay the bills, let alone harness the kind of self-worth we attach to jobs well done. Extraordinary people don't just work extraordinary jobs, nor are they simply extraordinarily good at them. They live them, they breathe them, and they embrace the gospel of "grind life," "no days off," and "you get what you work for." Or, the more skeptical view is these ideals are promoted as saving graces: Love your job enough and just maybe, you won't be let go. Work harder than everyone else and you'll save yourself from the financial horrors you've watched others judge. Of course, it's not true. It's how ordinary things, like days off without guilt, or doing one thing at a time instead of shoveling dinner in your mouth while responding to emails, become luxuries in the unruly web of work.

A few months after we first got in touch, I heard from Luna again: She'd quit one of her jobs shortly after her last message to me. "I had been coasting at work, and no one had noticed that I was working so much," she said. She left her part-time position after feeling she'd been "coasting" at her full-time position in her field of interest. It seems like an accurate summarization of our work culture: She was working three jobs, and concerned she was coasting at work. Adding another layer, Luna felt she had to keep the second job because she had a cancer scare, and her time on her parents' health insurance was expiring. We should question why something so ordinary, so very basic and essential—healthcare—is attached to an extraordinary feat of endurance that is keeping any job, and why so much of us hangs in the balance of work. The answer isn't about us at all.

Dismantling extraordinary expectations in work experiences doesn't mean rejecting the idea that work matters to some young people. But it has, in some cases, attached itself to our identities while making basics feel like a magnificent mirage—because even if you spend all your time working and "earning it," making a decent living and having a solid footing for your life aren't guaranteed. Work contains multitudes, which is the problem, because work contains us. The old adage goes that we are what we repeatedly do, and nothing captures that quite like work. I, like a thousand other peers who work harder and struggle more and are better, would like to be enough. We're not sure where that goes on our résumés.

# 3

# A WAITING ROOM

*On home, and how we build it*

"BUMFUCK NOWHERE," "PART OF THE COUNTRY THAT NEEDS to die off already," a "nowhere place": It was a jolt to hear how other people—from well-intentioned friends to bosses to random strangers I met in passing—referred to the place I knew as "home."

"Home" is writing these words at the long kitchen table that my grandfather built as a gift for my mother a few years ago. It's the smell of my mom's lemon cake and coffee wafting through the house and the cat running down the hallway; the neighbors I used to see every year at our childhood street-wide chili potlucks on Halloween, and family friends always offering to help in the face of struggle or loss; how I'll always get the key stuck in the front door, no matter how many times I've unlocked it. That's how I think of it now. But for the majority of the time I spent growing up there, I thought of "home" as a waiting room, the place I had to be until I could go somewhere else. It was as if everywhere else—everyone else—was waiting on me, and I kept being the cog stuck in the clock of the timeline on which we tell young people to move out, move up, and move on.

There was a pull to "city life," which I couldn't have described, that I had no idea how to articulate: I imagined it as every block being different, life being a revolving door of new people, new experiences, and new locations. Now that sensation feels less like an emphasis on moving to a "big" city, and more like an allure of leaving, in general: of forging a path on your own, embracing a sort of rootlessness we align with the in-betweenness of young adulthood, and moving somewhere new being a marker of a certain kind of success in growing up. Our popular culture is saturated with stories of leaving home, in movies and books, featuring thoughtful ponderings on a road trip to your new life against a background of scenic landscapes and backpacks and spontaneous adventures. Growing up, my adventures looked like parking in front of a fast-food joint or an empty field until three a.m., talking about how there's nothing to do and not realizing we were doing more than we knew at the time.

I'm lucky to have a home in the first place, one where my childhood books still grace my bedroom shelves, where I'd be welcomed back anytime I wanted. But the starkest transition in my own young adulthood was how sharply my perception of home pivoted: In high school, I wanted to leave so badly that in retrospect it's embarrassing—I imagined that my life would really begin once I was somewhere else. Yearning for belonging I believed could only be built elsewhere; I wondered whether new places would bring about new selves for me to try on. By the time I left college after my freshman year, I was humiliated, not because I'd left school, even, but because it felt like a glaring way I'd stumbled off the traditional path everyone I knew had taken: If you move away from home, you don't move back. That's not how young adults do it. We leave. We find our way. Imagine the ache when I felt, over and over, that finding my way was actually leading me home.

This so-called milestone, of course, leaves out so much, including cost of living and lack of opportunity to move in the first place, being a caretaker for a family member, and an individual's circumstances mattering more than meeting some milestone of when we're supposed to move out. Personally, it felt complicated, like I was behind in a race I wasn't sure I wanted to run. Friends who moved far away seemed to shift their lives so effortlessly that I was dumbstruck when it didn't happen that way for me, too. Meanwhile, people I knew from home were happy and fulfilled, carving out routines and buying houses and embracing the sense of belonging I couldn't seem to capture.

Feeling somehow broken and deeply behind other people my age, I tried to move, and keep moving. I moved like I was lost and trying to find myself—as if good things only came from searching, as if looking for something was the only means of mattering. It never lasted long. My first year of college, I stayed close to home, while replaying the well-meaning quips from family friends ("Oh, we really thought you'd end up somewhere far away!") in my head. After that, I lived at home for a while, the way more and more young people are doing now (which in and of itself is a privilege), trying to tune out comments on why I couldn't "handle" moving away by embracing precious moments, like coffee in the mornings with my mom and romps with the family dog, that didn't feel guaranteed to happen again in the same way. I listened as people wondered aloud to me why anyone would want to go back to a place like my home, even as I longed for it. Being in between places, leaving for so-called opportunity but longing for family, manifested in living with bags perpetually half-packed, pulling out a couple books for the nightstand and necessities like pots for cooking, and leaving the rest stuffed under the bed. And by the time I'd moved farther away than a couple hours in the car, I was aghast by the fact that what awaited me wasn't some new self or newfound capacity for adventure. It was homesickness.

The more I listened to how people described their homes, the more uncomfortable I became with the seemingly popular belief that metropolitan cities are just adventure grounds for people in their twenties, where you live for a bit on your way to elsewhere. And disenchantment with the idea that going from a "small town" to a "big city" was a rite of passage ran deep. Even when people I knew moved back to their hometowns, because the cost of living was lower or they needed to step in as caretakers, others talked about them as though they'd reached for the trapeze bar of young adulthood swinging you to the next thing and missed. If "wanting to see somewhere new" meant "getting out," it felt like "going back" got framed as quitting. Moving-as-a-rite-of-passage, especially to certain places exalted as the ultimate young adult experience, big cities and college towns, didn't make sense the more I unpacked it, even as it was spun as the allure of adventure. Nor, for that matter, did moving as a milestone, not subject to personal preferences or economics or circumstances, make much sense. It feels like a milestone made of leaving, this idea that there's a countdown clock on when you've "made it" on your own. It's important to note that this isn't *everyone's* tradition, which is why moving out and away as a milestone is so baffling. It represents this ideal that building your own life has to happen somewhere other than where you are. And all this made me wonder how on earth you build a home for yourself.

"Home" is a privileged conversation. I haven't had to care for a family member or sustain the family business, though what that looks like in the future informs every decision I make. Young adults who face housing insecurity[1]—which can look like homelessness, staying with friends or relatives, eviction and forced moves, or cost of housing burdens—are grappling with a lack of stability that can influence health, happiness, and security, and mean the loss of social identity and loss of self.[2] Living out of cars or bouncing to and from friends' couches isn't just some trope of young adulthood that glorifies the "adventure" of being unattached. It happens because of situations including abuse, inability to pay rent or even find affordable housing, or moving to a city specifically for a job and getting laid off and being unable to find another. According to the National Alliance to End Homelessness, roughly 550,000 young adults up to age twenty-four have experienced a "homelessness episode of longer than one week."[3] It's one aspect of home and moving that rarely pops up in listicles on what houseplants are hard to kill or what neighborhoods have the most bars, as if that's all moving is about.

"Moving," "going somewhere new," and "seeing the world" have a certain kind of nostalgia and cultural lore embedded in them. How else will you look back decades from now and be able to explain how your cross-country road trip, apartment on a great street with no air-conditioning or working locks, or house with the backyard where you strung little lights impacted you? But not every young adult moves for the same reasons, and not all of those reasons come at the absence of responsibilities and addition of adventure. In 2014, almost a quarter of emerging adults in the United States were first- or second-generation immigrants, and according to research, often faced competing social responsibilities like family or community obligations on top of the demands of work and school, which can make identity and sense of home and belonging more layered.[4] Not every young person has the luxury or time to feel "in-between" homes, and not every young adult has the ability to buy into the idea that achieving a certain kind of success means living in a certain place, be it a big city or a color-coordinated, well-decorated space with ample plants lining the walls.

According to Dr. Dalal Katsiaficas, in terms of how young adulthood has been traditionally defined, moving away from home has been one of the sociological markers of becoming an adult. But in her own writing about the idea of collective contribution and deeply held values of "reciprocal contribution between individuals, their families, and communities," Katsiaficas pointed out that giving back to communities and being able to contribute to family in new ways is actually *part* of this coming-of-age component for young people, especially those from immigrant backgrounds. So, there's this push and pull, where it almost feels part of what has to be given up to fulfill this Americanized ideal of being out on one's own, and forging one's own life—it comes at the real cost of contributing to families and communities in tangible ways, she explained. "I think for so many people, young people that I've talked to, they've kind of narrated that hyper-individualism as a real sense of loss," Katsiaficas said. This sense of loss—what young people have pointed to regarding lacking a village, or community, in the name of independence—is a reframe of something that's so highly prized, she added, and even glamorized in the media: the grand young adult adventure of solo living. It was the first time I'd heard it narrated like that: For all the adventure we're getting, it feels like a tremendous sense of loss to give up the feeling of home if we have it, even for the excitement of creating a new one. The aspirational part of new beginnings is highlighted over and over, pushing us toward the enchantment of the new. But rarely, if ever, had I heard that sense of loss, or even homesickness, described as anything other than something we're supposed to grow out of. It's not just the places, but the people in them, that create a meaning of home.

And it's important that we do attach meaning to wherever we land. Place attachment, or the "cognitive-emotional" bond between people and their important settings, has a significant impact on our well-being.[5] As some research points out, these places can include homes or communities, and "these bonds provide a framework for both individual and community aspects of identity."[6] Even more interestingly, the same research—on place attachment in adolescence, specifically—points out that we can't just think about "place attachment" as local places anymore, since some places can have a "tangible meaning," like neighborhoods or schools, and "occasional meaning," like a grandparent's home or natural setting, and even virtual meanings, like online social networks. But, the research explains, "local places, and the people one loves and depends on in them, provide everyone with the rootedness that is needed to survive in an increasingly complex world."[7] I read it a couple times, trying to parse why I felt a draw to places—the creek down the street from the house I grew up in; a bakery a few blocks up from where I lived in New York that felt homier than my apartment—that seemed almost illogical when, aren't we supposed to be roaming instead of rooted during young adulthood? Instead, it seems like that rootedness is what helps us navigate life transitions.

It made me consider where we're rooted, too. When the headlines are about young adults trading city life for the suburbs, there isn't much space given to the fact that not everyone from a rural place, or a small town, can feasibly live there, especially if it's not possible for them to safely exist. Nor do the zingers about young people not being able to afford homes in more metropolitan areas acknowledge that for some people, that *is* their home—not just a place they stopped, so why wouldn't they want to be able to afford to stay? The question shouldn't necessarily be "Why don't you just move to this place, or that one?" The longer the myth of only certain places really mattering is perpetuated, the harder we make it to let ourselves grow things that matter to us: roots, ties, and attachment.

All this to say: Home isn't just where your stuff is. Home is complicated. Because of the assumption that, as a young adult, you have more mobility and opportunity than you ever will, if you're not taking advantage of that, you've missed out on the golden opportunity of this age: exploration. And exploration, of places, of selves, of opportunities, is a good thing, they say. But it never gets presented as part of a balance—that you might also need stability and commitment *alongside* exploration and adventure. Newness, be it a text from a new crush, a new apartment, or a new city, gives us a hit of dopamine in our brains, which fades as the novelty wears off.[8] It's why our first times in a new place are often overwhelming and exciting, whereas your once-wonderful new neighborhood has likely lost that shiny luster going into year three of the same sights day after day and the same commute with the same coffee stop. When there are constantly new starts on the horizon—including new neighborhoods, new jobs, or new trips—it's not hard to see how the pleasure of new beginnings could become enticing. It's also a visible marker that life is moving forward in some way.

Laney, twenty-two, talked to me about novelty from her childhood bedroom—where she returned when her college campus closed during the pandemic, and has been working full-time in ever since. Talking about friends who, at the same time she transitioned into adulthood in her childhood home, transitioned to new graduate schools and new cities, she explained, "Especially in this coming-of-age story we write for ourselves, getting to that next chapter is so rooted in location." It's about the growth of a person, but she said it is "always contextualized by exploring and novelty." Now, she's wondering what happens without those external markers for change: "How can you measure up compared to all of your friends?" She knows there's lots of growth in her life but said, because she's in her childhood bedroom, from the outside looking in, it doesn't look like much change or growth at all. The idea that moving shows growth matters to how we think about this.

Building a home, building a life, is something else entirely, and it demands making real decisions on where you want to be and who you want to be around, logistics like what you're willing to fork over on rent or if you really want to share a bathroom with three people. All of these material decisions fly in the face of the excitement, anticipation, and novelty bubbling around fresh starts. And it's hard to overcome the messaging we're getting about settling into places. Connection between home and new beginnings is hardwired into a lot of marketing around what the "young adult experience" is when it comes to where and how time gets spent. From the jump, college gets presented as an opportunity for a young adult to make their own decisions, a presentation that often leaves out practicalities like in-state versus out-of-state tuition, familial obligations that might prevent someone from moving far away, and the fact that not every young person wants or needs the same kind of postsecondary education. I remember being told, by people who did not know my circumstances, college was "my shot" to start building a life for myself somewhere else, a chance to pick a new city, any city I wanted, because I had a reason to. In some ways, the college decision, assuming there is one, is a sort of promised land—the promise being you get to decide where you go from here (again, ignoring the very real barriers surrounding the reality of these moves).

Then, it builds, with where you go next depending on what happens next, another notch of newness: where you get a job, if you pursue more school, whether you *can* get a job, and whether you can afford the city in which said job is located. It also explains why postgraduation travel has become such a common trope, where the happy grad stuffs a backpack full of necessities and exits "real life" for the summer, using the time to see the world, and maybe grabbing that one last shot at newness before routine settles in. "Moving" is so intertwined with growing up, perhaps because we want to see tangible proof that we've made progress, we're doing it—we're changing, we're growing. "Why don't you move?" and "There's nothing for you here" were defining soundtracks of conversations about moving, usually offered up by people whose opinions I didn't ask. But the feeling that's come with me is that rootedness, feeling settled, is another means of growth, one that's just as worthy. One that felt an awful lot like a version of coming home; one of exhales, one of comfort.

Laney is the first person in her family to graduate from college, and if she moved out of her home state, she'd also be the first one in her family to do so. She applied to jobs all over; getting one that allowed her to live at home was a total fluke—and it's a cyclical job, one that won't exist in the same capacity in a few months. While her family will support whatever she decides, she said there's this tension within herself on being the first to leave: "It's a rhythm that, am I going to be the one to kind of disrupt?" On the flip side, part of that tension, she said, is between "not wanting to miss out, but not understanding if what you're missing out on is even important to you." And while she loves her home and considers it special, she also wonders if it's foolish not to seek something else out—if only to know, for sure, that she had it really good where she's from. But for now, she's there, and it's another example of how tightly tethered moving is to the general idea of *moving forward*, something we're always encouraging young people to do.

Rattling off Instagram posts, tweets, Facebook posts, and LinkedIn updates, Laney explained that the way we view each other's lives plays a role here, pointing to a dissonance between reaching a new step and how much value you actually prescribe to it. For example, she explained "It's really easy to show that you're in a new place," but it's more complicated to show how much meaning is actually attached to it. "Because I know a lot of people who moved cities, who did the whole next chapter, are really unsatisfied right now and feel really empty," she added. It's less a matter of meeting the external marker—the move—and more about the feeling and meaning it holds for you personally. Laney said the fixation on being able to show that you're growing and changing and moving on is a matter of validation. But the way she articulates it is the opposite of "doing it to get likes on a picture" that gets ascribed as young people's reasoning. Instead, it's like, "I've done what I need to do, in the time frame that I was meant to do it in."

Now, we're watching the moving marker get unraveled for young adults. As the coronavirus pandemic has continued to ravage America, the number of eighteen- to twenty-nine-year-olds living with their parents has surpassed the last peak of this happening, which took place during the era of the Great Depression (previously, white young adults were less likely than their Asian, Black, and Hispanic peers to live with their parents, the data reports—now, white young adults account for two-thirds of the increase in young adults living with their parents).[9] In other countries, in a lot of cases,

young adults living with parents or family isn't just socially acceptable, it's normal. And even in the United States, it's worth looking at
how the "traditional" trajectory of moving to college, followed by
a few years of renting, and then finally, homeownership, feels typically aligned with white, middle-class adults, anyway.[10] Relatedly,
there's no separating economics from housing—another result of
COVID-19's economic crisis was an eviction crisis,[11] and given that
nearly eleven million low-income households paid over half their
income in rent back in 2018, skyrocketing unemployment numbers
exacerbated already-stark disparities within who can afford to even
live.[12]

It makes the instability of emerging adulthood—an age in
which we frequently change plans, jobs, residence, or roommates—
look completely romanticized: Changing residences because you've
changed your mind or gotten a new job is one thing; changing residences because you can no longer afford to live there, are being
pushed out by gentrification or climate change, or because you're
not safe, is something else entirely. Sitting on the floor of your un-
furnished apartment eating cheap ramen noodles with your best
friends in a new city might be presented as a glamorous rite of passage, but true housing insecurity and a lack of affordable housing
are real barriers facing young people. And it was happening pre-
pandemic: Julia, twenty-two, experienced housing insecurity when
she left an abusive relationship, which included leaving the house she
rented with her then-partner. At one point, when staying in the living room of an apartment, she had no heat throughout the entire
winter season. And it remains a challenge to find safe, affordable
housing with working utilities that gives her the dignity needed for
renters. "I've been able to find that feeling of home through friends
and experiences more than I have been through physical spaces, just

because my space has changed so much over the years," added Julia, saying home doesn't have to be rigid. "I feel like there's so many sub-cultures nowadays that people find home in, rather than finding home in their own families." One of those subcultures, for Julia, was hardcore and punk shows, which she's been attending since she was around seventeen. At shows, Julia described meeting other people of color, being surrounded by young people who preached a drug-free lifestyle, and feeling safe. "[I'd] never met anybody else that liked the same things as me that looked like me," said Julia of the friends and community she's met this way. "And it just pro-vided this sense of . . . it just provided this missing piece." While Julia notes a lot of people her age live at home and have that con-nection with their immediate family, for those who don't, it can be easy to feel isolated. "I've had people just ignorantly ask me, like, Why don't you stay in one place? Why are you always trying to run? Whenever it's not really a run thing. It's just a survival thing," Julia said. She wishes people knew that young people are just as vulner-able to housing insecurity as any other person—and wishes people would recognize their internalized classism to the fact that this ex-ists, and isn't unique to a certain subset of people. The belonging created through an idea of home or community matters. Hyper-individualism, or the self-reliance we like to tell young people to de-velop by struggling through things alone, isn't just lonely—often, it's impossible.

Data from the US Bureau of Labor Statistics shows that "boo-meranging back" is—unsurprisingly—related to characteristics like income, race, education, and gender. If you have nowhere else to go, of course you're going to move home[13]—and that doesn't even factor in young adults who don't have a family home as a safety net. It got me thinking about what Dr. Katsiaficas had mentioned regarding socialization around cultural values: Immigrant-origin young people are getting mixed messages, where the dominant one is to "make it on your own," while the message that often occurs in the context of families and communities is "they've helped me get here, now I want to help take them with me," Katsiaficas said. Something she believes needs to be explored more deeply about emerging adulthood is how critical interdependence and social responsibilities are during this time. Caring for families, opening a small business in your childhood neighborhood, and saving to buy a house with space for parents to live were all mentioned in conversations with young adults about their aspirations for home, as were means of home being an opportunity for interdependence, taking care of others, and feeling cared for yourself. Community is a really human need we have, Katsiaficas told me. "But in the broader US society, we tell emerging adults that they should learn to stand alone, and that can be really painful." It's overlooked, she added, but "taking care of family or community, and in turn, feeling taken care of by them, has real benefits." At its best, home can feel like being held. It's why the quips about moving back in with your parents, or being thirty and still having roommates, are less a commentary on young adult failure than they are a commentary on how we sometimes prioritize going it alone above all else.

What gets spun as failure to launch, not leaving the nest, or skipping significant markers of adulthood is sometimes just the reality of circumstances in which we live right now. I watched my full-time job dwindle to part-time, then those hours dry up, right around the time my lease on an apartment in a city I'd moved to solely for that job expired. Discouraged, I packed up the car and drove back to my hometown, where I took on enough freelance projects to supplement my income until I found another job, nursed my wounded self-esteem, and tried to make myself a help to family who still lived there, instead of feeling like a burden. I wrestled with knowing how profoundly privileged it is to be able to "go home" at all while fielding comments from people who thought I was a lazy, unambitious failure for coming back. As someone told me, a comment etched in my brain, I'd given up.

That line of thinking felt fraught—your zip code can mean larger obstacles and greater structural barriers than whether you move away or not. For a lot of people, there's a fine line between wanting to venture elsewhere to gain experience and a deep-rooted obligation to serve the place you're from. And not every young adult is going to grapple with moving cities at all. For some, it's not feasible, and beyond that, not wanted. In conversations with twenty-somethings who had opposite experiences—one felt guilty for moving out of a big city and loving suburban life; the other felt her hometown friends judged her for moving far away—it dawned on me that there might not be any winning as long as we assign virtue to places beyond how it feels to be there—the worthiest, and seemingly most ordinary, pursuit in all this.

Research shows that Americans' values and attitudes could be geographically clustered—and one article from a researcher at the University of Cambridge explores three different potential factors that drive a place's personality: The hypotheses were selective migration patterns, assuming people move to places that fulfill their interests or needs (one example the article offers is, "People who are open and enjoy new experiences may decide to move away from their humdrum hometowns to places where their interests in diversity and their desires for varied experiences can be satisfied"), which supports the idea that people want to live in places they feel accepted; social influence, or how people's lifestyles and daily practices in a specific area impact social norms, leading us to take on personality traits valued in the region—like if your community is known for being cheerful, you might be more inclined to be so, too; and finally, ecological influence, where physical environment actually impacts the activities people can engage in and their attitudes toward them, like places where hiking is a normal weekday activity or living so close to the ocean that visiting the beach is built into your routine.[14] Other research shows that personality characteristics can be used to describe geographic areas in America—a study in the *Journal of Research in Personality* cites the example of Middle America being characterized as "friendly and conventional," while the West Coast, Rocky Mountain, and Sun Belt regions get characterized as "relaxed and creative." This research also points to the conclusion that people tend to migrate to areas where people share similar occupations, ideologies, and personalities.[15] The takeaway from this is that we don't exist in a bubble by accident when it comes to our locations, and especially in emerging adulthood, an age defined by identity exploration and a focus on what you want to do and where you want to be, who we are isn't entirely separate from where we are. So, this idea of moving as a marker of success for young adults becomes obvious: Who doesn't want to be ambitious, adventurous, spontaneous, and open to new experiences, as opposed to cautious, routine-oriented, and rooted?

But that might be missing it a bit, at least the way it's currently framed: You can be rooted in community, *or* you can be adventurous. While, ideally, these qualities can coexist, one is presented as a whole lot shinier. Being content isn't as sexy as newness. But always having an eye on the horizon, looking for the next opportunity, next place, and next big move is exhausting. It's almost the same commitment anxiety you hear about relationships: *What if I move, and miss out? What if I stay put, and a better apartment comes along later?*

"Ohio, where my school is, I don't have any connection to," Grace, a twenty-five-year-old law school student who is planning her next move, explained. "Don't want to stay, never wanted to stay." It's also one of the places she has stayed the longest. "My landlord is sending me a lease renewal," Grace said. "I've never been able to do that before. So it's such a weird feeling." While she described herself as an East Coaster, down to the way she walks, Grace moved frequently, including spending most of her high school years in Florida. Grace hates it when people ask her where she's from: "All I know is that I'm here right now. I don't know where I'm from anymore, but this is where I am." When I asked what she wanted home to mean to her, she said that when you're so transient, home is wherever you are—and you're in search of this "big meaning of peace." "I guess I'm looking for a new kind of familiar that I created," Grace said, explaining she doesn't necessarily mean creating her own family, but a sense of familiarity with routines and with people, and in turn, her being familiar to them. She described it as being "established" as a person, something it feels everyone craves in their own way. That familiarity sometimes feels like the unspoken part of young adulthood, something we're somehow supposed to want later, but feels precious and grounding right now.

Even for students, it feels like only one side of the equation gets addressed: the big questions about where you're going to school, and where you're moving postgraduation. The way those get amplified leaves little room for other, more ordinary, equally important questions: *Where do you feel safe, and like you belong? Are you homesick with so many places, like a hometown and a college town and maybe somewhere entirely different after the fact, in the mix? And is it possible to have roots in multiple places?* The dark side of that transience was especially highlighted in 2020, when, in an effort to promote social distancing to stop the spread of COVID-19, universities and colleges throughout the country forced students to move off campus—sometimes with less than a week's notice, leaving some to return to their parents' or other family members' houses if they were lucky, and others, who were reliant on campus housing, completely displaced, and separated from the communities that they'd built their daily lives around. Meanwhile, other young people were stuck in apartments in cities they lived in almost exclusively for work, quarantined with roommates they didn't really know, and missing family or close friends who were sheltering in place elsewhere.

Because moving is so ingrained in how we think about this time of life, despite whether or not everyone can "achieve" that milestone, it feels staying is rarely celebrated—with going-away parties to celebrate new adventures, graduation celebrations to mark the close of one chapter and the newness of another, staying in one place can feel like the boring middle part. The idea of "boomeranging" ties into our sense of home and identity, because, rather than moving forward, marching down the jetway between our average homes and our best selves, coming back can feel like an unwelcome confrontation with a self you have left behind. Thinking that newness creates meaning and value, or wanting a city to tell you something about yourself, makes it easy to fall into the line of thinking that if you move to a "better" place, you'll find a better self to go along with it.

Of course, some of this depends on what gets considered a "best place to live" in the first place. And just like industries that rely on us pursuing a better self—a fitter self, a smarter self, a better-looking self—home and housing aren't immune to being part of a marketplace that makes continual searching feel like the only thing we should be spending time doing. If you're not looking for a more convenient or cuter apartment, a lower cost of living, a neighborhood with more amenities, a city with more vibrance, are you really embracing this time of your life? To take that even further, what do the things that get overlooked in discussions on where young adults live and why—including financial disparities, familial obligations, and job markets—say about what gets popularly valued in how we think of home? What gets valued high or low is a factor in this conversation: Yes, that can look like the general "big city" versus "little city" that pops up in regard to young people, but it's smaller than that. Life logistics, like accessible transit or getting to be close to family if you want, almost feel quaint, whereas there seems to be a meaty cultural value placed on the ideals of youthful adventure and independence, a million buddy comedies in which finding yourself always begins with venturing somewhere new, with the background of Denver mountains or Nashville street art or the New York skyline.

The ordinary part here is that a lot of this comes down to personal preference, because there are some people who feel genuinely more engaged and excited when they're constantly on the move. But sometimes, because of the way we romanticize starting over while you still can, it comes across as though settling in automatically means settling down. Melody Warnick, journalist and author of the book *This Is Where You Belong: Finding Home Wherever You Are*, thinks young people go through a "FOMO period," or fear-of-missing-out period, when they're newly graduated from school and it "feels like settling to stay in one place very long." "There's this sense that you want to experience lots of different things," Warnick continued.

"And we kind of have this long history in American culture that to be upwardly mobile also means just to be mobile." There are entire industries centered on that idea of mobility, or rootlessness, including subscription-based services that offer furniture rentals, some of which market themselves from a sustainability lens rather than the obvious: Sometimes you might want nice furniture, but if you're not able to commit to your home or city, do you really want to be responsible for finding a way to transport your couch to its next destination? Some young adults described doing their own versions of this, passing furniture back and forth between friends depending on who had stuff in their parents' garage, who was selling their worldly possessions via social media, and who moved in with roommates where everybody brought one thing to the living room—think *The Sisterhood of the Traveling Pants*, but with a coffee table and kitchen set. That sense of one foot out the door is built in to the extent that home repairs, painting, or actually installing shelves feels not worth the effort. Permanence—unbroken dishes that match, a nightstand that isn't just a pile of boxes, framed art hung on the wall—feels like a luxury if you don't know whether you're staying, or if your landlord will hike up your rent next year and you're off to the next spot.

Grae, twenty-six, is a "person that leaves things in different places," an articulation of similar thoughts I heard from multiple people. She moved to her hometown after first living in a different state for college, followed by a few years in New York, where she left many of her belongings because she kept telling herself she'd move back. "I don't know if it's a roots thing or not, but it's also with the certainty that I'll be back, when most of the time, I know I won't be," she said. In other words, the door to elsewhere was still propped open—when you have friends or communities or even possessions in a different place, it creates the feeling of having options.

Keeping the search alive extends to other parts of moving, too. Apps like Zillow, StreetEasy, and Redfin make it easy to sit on your couch in one home and actively search for another, and even Airbnb seems to contain some degree of "finding home" wherever you go. Because traditional markers of stability, like homeownership, feel out of reach for so many young adults, it's like we've catapulted in the opposite direction: Being always on the move ensures you'll see everything, and miss out on nothing. That's how I felt: I wanted to see it all. So why, in retrospect, did that mean ignoring what was right in front of me?

In our conversation, Warnick pointed out that there is a stigma in America against not only small towns, but staying in the same place at all. We tend to think of it as representing "the abandonment of our big dreams," Warnick said, a feeling of escape that some young people feel acutely. I felt called out, and with good reason: I'd clung to the belief that life would really begin once I left wherever I was. It kept dreams I was too scared to say aloud at arm's length; it allowed me to imagine, and reimagine, the "best life" I'd finally find with a new zip code, conveniently forgetting that my real life, my life-as-is, was happening wherever I happened to be. I could participate, or I could wait. I could reach for belonging, I could build it, or I could wait for it to find me. And for years, I waited.

Some of the qualities that attract people to urban life—diversity of ideas, acceptance, and accessibility—are ones other people have found in smaller cities, too. The reality is, while it's impossible to separate conversations on home from logistics like job markets, gentrification, and accessibility, there isn't one single definition of what makes a "good" city for a young person. Like most things, our "good" places, moments, memories, and times are a combination of things—not necessarily textbook-perfect ideals, but puzzle pieces we move around, personal touches we add in, little routines we build, and people we build them with.

In emerging adulthood, we get the chance to redefine home. For Grae, that looks like thinking of people being her sense of home, as opposed to a physical place. She adores the sense of home she's created with her partner. "I love that home because I know that it has roots that will go where I go," she added. For others, there's a great sense of rootedness in a physical space—one created on your own terms, made up of things you chose. Amy, twenty-eight, said she learned the kind of environment she wanted to live in by finding the places she's lived, and people she's lived with. Getting out of her family bubble and having to coexist with strangers—roommates—made it clear what kind of place and habits she wanted for her own life. With what she described as a "pretty messy family situation," Amy said, "Just because I grew up in a place and had all of my formative years in a place doesn't make it *home*. My hometown isn't 'home.' It's a place where my mother lives, but it's not home." She thinks the pressure of "home" is difficult—over the holidays, it's hard to see everyone's family portraits and traditions, and just because she's able to compartmentalize doesn't make the choice not to go home easier to explain to others. "A lot of my friends and coworkers don't understand that I was happier to sit home on Thanksgiving with a book, a craft, and a Whole Foods turkey dinner than I would have been flying home to see my family," she added.

Now Amy lives in what she described as a beautiful, historic building, where she keeps the couch cushions perfectly fluffed and fresh-cut flowers on the table. Having a clean place full of all her personal things might be one of the biggest points of growth in her twenties, she said. "I'm fully responsible for it. It's decorated to my liking. I spend time and money to make sure it's exactly how I want,"

Amy explained, saying that her home feels like her identity, almost, in the sense that it is the place where she can experiment and decide the person she wants to be. "I never felt that growing up," Amy adds. Before, if Amy wanted to eat a certain way for health, she'd be criticized; she never wanted to have friends over because of her parents' drinking. In her own home, her favorite way to spend a Sunday morning is doing laundry, cleaning, and filling her fridge with what she wants to eat, things that never make the list of why we're supposed to move to a certain place. Usually, those go something like: nightlife, bars, outdoor activities, proximity to airports, museums and cultural opportunities, all of which make a place, and are significant parts of where they live for some young adults. But affordability, community, routine, and stability sometimes make a home, too. And not just after you've tired of the previous stuff. Maybe you want that in the first place.

It made me think of the places that people had mentioned as meaningful, either with the buoyancy of good memories or the heaviness of bad ones, when it came to home. It wasn't just houses and apartments and "Welcome to" signs when you cross a certain state line. It was airport terminals that meant coming home or escaping; front porches that held first kisses and prom photos and opening college acceptance letters; open fields where bonfires and beers made the party; blocks where the owner of your corner store knew you by first name. Simple things that it feels impossible to rank in a city guide, and too complicated to explain when asked why you moved, or why you stayed. And, as Warnick pointed out, there's an imagination element of certain places. If we're seeking reinvention or creating a new identity, moving somewhere we aren't known could make that easier. "But the new place isn't the thing that completely changes us as people," Warnick clarified. "It might change things about our circumstances. It might trigger some opportunities to change things about ourselves. But yeah, you have that moment of like, 'Dang, I am still the same human and I brought all my baggage, and now I'm going to have to move again.'"

I am wired for coming home in the same way it is assumed we are wired for leaving. Any adventure that lures me out is no match for the ties that draw me home again. I come home in the way you'd fall asleep after a day spent in the pool and the heat of the sun as a kid—before you know it's happened, before you know you want to. Home is a collection of pauses—the pencil marking my place in a book left on my shelf; rounding down the same stairs I'd tumbled down as a kid on Christmas first thing in the morning as an adult, sweatshirt and socks on and searching for coffee. Half the pang of growing up is realizing that I'll somehow have to create a sense of home wherever I go, that for all the effort I spent trying to leave, all I would ever want to do is figure out homecomings, ways of coming back to the place where I feel the most like me.

For many emerging adults, this is the period of moving away for the first time, and a first chance to really decide what your home will feel like independent of one you were born into. But it's as though we forgot those transitions don't have to keep transitioning. It can be equally transformative to stay put for a bit, giving us the chance to know ourselves in the context of stability, rather than just the context of *pursuing* something. When we're home, we can take inventory of who we are. It's not quitting the adventure early to just want to settle in and stay for a while—nor is it dismissing the ideal of exploring to remember we can explore in all kinds of ways, in our communities, in how we build our homes, in how we feel about ourselves in different contexts. It can feel like coming home to ourselves.

When we listen, we hear it in conversations we have with our peers. The terrible dorm room where you were too cramped, but where you learned to be on your own for the first time. The place you greet your loved ones when you walk in the door. The first place you locked yourself out of. The field—for some of us, at least—that held high school memories. The school you attended; the first city you moved to after graduating. The place your best friend or sibling moved to that you love to visit. It's the meanings we build, the routines we create, the people we love; the place we feel embraced and emboldened, wherever we can remove the weight of the world and stop searching, and sit with ourselves. It's the "at home" feeling, the made-for-Friday-nights-in sweatpants that have been washed the perfect number of times; not a search, but a sense of welcoming. It's not always wrapped up in a new start. The feeling of coming home so rarely is, and that is, it turns out, the part that makes it worth searching for.

# 4

# FINDING YOUR$ELF, COMMODIFIED

*On hobbies, experiences, and what creates identity*

So, what do you like to do in your free time?

In a job interview, on a college application, on a first date, at a networking happy hour that's never actually that happy: This question is supposed to be the human one, where we get to rattle off weird stuff that brings us joy or makes us curious or teaches us something without the burden of our having to be good at it, work at it, or feel bad if we decide not to do it for a week. It doesn't tie us to a job title or a school name; it can't be quantified in the way other elements of life can be. Experiences, hobbies, and outside-of-work activities are, ideally, ones free from the trap of betterment—no ladders to climb, no hurdles to clear. The old work-life balance adage goes that we're more than what we produce, but these days we are what we do, too.

Which is why, for a while, the question was enough to drop-kick me into an identity crisis. There's a pervasive sense that if and when we do have free time, it had better be spent on activities or experiences that are practical, or more likely to move us toward productivity. Picking up graphic design could be a cool hobby but could also make you a more competitive candidate at the ad agency you want to apply to. Running marathons, or playing a sport, can be an awesome activity but, depending on how it feels to you, could also be a strategy for getting in shape, whatever that means. Hobbies shouldn't be stressful, in theory, but given that time feels fleeting, how we spend it can result in constant micro-calculations about whether what we're doing is the *best* thing we could be doing.

It's easy to see how many of my own hobbies, daily routines, or small joys cross the line into "betterment" territory. A glance at the teetering stack of books on my nightstand is a reminder that so much of my reading is for work; the last time I read a book *solely* for pleasure was months ago—in fact, the line dividing "pleasure" and "productivity" seems narrower than ever. Working out, or just going for a walk, was mostly built into my schedule, but that often felt like one more Hail Mary grip on the steering wheel: Maybe the rigidity and regulation would keep me healthy, and thus enable me to keep it together (obviously, this is not how that works, nor an option everyone has). Movies and TV were now opportunities to doze off on the couch and stumble to bed as the credits rolled, just to say I'd had some "me time" or that I *had* indeed seen the Netflix show my coworkers were talking about. This realization was like meeting myself and being disappointed: *Oh no*, I remember thinking. *Not only am I not learning enough, exploring enough, or venturing out of my comfort zone enough, I'm also* boring, which is the worst quality you could possibly have in young adulthood, we're told, when opportunities glitter and our time is really our own.

Hobbies I'd enjoyed—knitting, as a teenager; cooking, which I was slow at and loved trying in my first apartment; seeing ballets from the cheap seats where I was up high enough to feel as though the entire theater was empty—floated away as idyllic has-beens that used to, at least I thought, say something about who I was. Now, they came loaded with guilt: It's hard to justify spending money on "extras" when you're staring down student loans or medical payments; it's impossible not to feel like you're wasting time when you've accidentally wired eighty-hour work or academic weeks as your baseline normal.

Then, there seemed to be a whole other swath of experiences I *should* have been having, and wasn't, a highlight reel of vacations or backpacking trips, yoga retreats where peers reemerged tuned in to their true desires, the kinds of adventures that get presented as ours for the taking in young adulthood that we might not have the freedom and flexibility to do later. But those small hobbies, knitting and cooking and ballet-watching—even videos!—were the ones I thought about and missed. What puzzled me was I couldn't pinpoint a specific moment, or even a specific reason, that I stopped pursuing them. Maybe they got overlooked in the hustle of responsibility, practicality, and abject fear that I'd drop a ball, or maybe I stopped paying enough attention—I took them for granted, and treated it as though the little stuff I did just for fun was too mundane to notice. Turns out, it feels like that's part of what counts the most: the new things we try, the small things we love, the little pieces of who we are and what we like and finding meaning in them. That shapes us. I found meaning in those things, but I didn't do them because I was *searching* for meaning.

One of the most critical things that happens in emerging adulthood is identity development, which, put simply, helps us get to know our place in the world, and allows us to establish a sense of continuity of who we are across different contexts.[1] Questions like "Who am I?" and "Where do I fit into all this?" might get dismissed as navel-gazing, but having a sense of identity creates a "sense of mattering," "a sense of direction in one's life," and "ideological commitment."[2] Exploration, including exposure to new experiences, new ideas, and new people, is indeed a key part of forming that identity. In a study on how emerging adults use leisure activities to develop their identities, leisure—which is defined as things marked by free time combined with the "expectation of preferred experience" (in other words, stuff you do for fun)—offers context where "emerging adults actively navigate their identity development through exposure to new experiences and relationships, as well as resulting commitments."[3] In this case study of forty emerging adults from eighteen countries, evidence was found "supporting leisure as a resource for individual development." But it also pointed out something a lot of young adults seemed to articulate, too: "Experiences, ideas, and people that seem foreign, uncomfortable, or unattainable could be missed in a leisure context where individuals can choose only what appears attractive or rewarding."[4] Without obligations associated with work, school, or family, the study suggests, leisure activities pursued in free time are an opportunity to define part of who you are, including creating an "identity label," an ability to say "I am a person who does this, loves this, and finds these things important."

It sounds like it could almost bounce into the kind of toxic positivity every young adult has heard, like "Just be yourself" and "Don't compare what you do to someone's social media!" It's often well-intentioned and sounds good in theory but overlooks the pressure to have every formative experience or time *look* that way, since it appears everyone else is. But while it might sound silly to say, it's true: The small ways we choose to spend time might shape us more than we realize.

It's obvious why this would be so important in this era of life. Hobbies can be carried with us, regardless of what we do or where we live—it isn't that those things don't seem to play a role in our identities, but in a way, hobbies feel like the safest and lowest stakes. In young adulthood, when so much is in transition, it makes sense to want things in your life that remain steadfast: You're a person who loves long walks, likes to paint, is a devoted dog owner, concertgoer, an expert cook, Ping-Pong champion, or home-repairs master. One way I thought of it, personally, is: *Who am I if everything else—work, places, appearances—were to fade away?* It was comforting, in a way, to find tiny meanings in things that didn't outwardly seem overtly powerful or meaningful or significant. That's where the whole "search for meaning" comes into play. Nowadays we are hyperaware of what it means to create our own meaning, and what the activities we pursue and experiences we have say about us. It's not a bad thing to want to be more well-read, more cultured, well-traveled, or more athletic. But it's easy to see how leisure, just-for-fun experiences, and hobbies become tasks to excel at instead of things we do because we want to do them. It makes the hobby something precious—a part of who we are that we get to define on our own terms.

The reason experiences—those we pursue, those that are marketed to us, and those that are held up as cornerstones of young adulthood—matter is because they help create meaning in our lives and contribute to how we see ourselves. But what happens if you spent your entire teenagerhood doing a certain thing, like playing basketball, only to realize you don't have time for it as an adult? Why does everything we enjoy doing or are good at have to be turned into the guiding ambition for our lives? Why is there pressure to have hobbies that are specific and neatly defined, rather than just stuff you enjoy? And where do things that get spun as rites of passage factor in—if we're doing things "for the experience," as the saying goes, shouldn't they be ones we choose, and not just what we think we ought to be doing?

If experiences, hobbies, and activities are ways to create at least part of our own meaning, then there's no wonder extraordinary, infinitely Instagrammable experiences top the list. Who looks at the range of experiences the world affords us (if we can, you know, pay for them) and chooses ones that don't reinforce the best of you—that you're tough enough, adventurous enough, spontaneous enough, curious enough, cultured enough, brave enough, or ambitious enough, to have this experience? Really, it's incredibly difficult to be who you are when who you *could be* plays in the back of your mind, movie-montage style, with an itinerary of moments-to-be-had already outlined for you.

But the discussion of any of these experiences must be had in the context of accessibility and affordability. Sometimes it feels like the deeper we get into adulthood, the more "free time" pursuits get crossed off the list. They aren't something that comes up on the list of things we need to teach ourselves to do, like paying taxes or changing a tire. They get lost in a flurry of résumé-building, rent-paying, and all-out efforts to establish a stable, secure, successful life that leaves little time for reminders that we're also human beings who might enjoy doing things purely for the sake of enjoyment.

There's a cost to having hobbies, and if an activity happens to be free, it demands some freedom of time that a lot of young adults simply don't have. The pursuit of experiences requires elements that leave a lot of people out of the equation, because of cost barriers, because of ableism, because of lack of time, because of family responsibilities. And the so-called significant experiences that get billed as uniquely young adult—things we won't have the freedom to do later in life, theoretically—are even more exclusive. It's a strange line to straddle, when half your friends are booking Airbnbs for a road trip or are at a music festival and the other half are trying to figure out the last time they had time for fun.

The term "experience economy" was coined by B. Joseph Pine II and James H. Gilmore, who wrote in a 1998 piece for *Harvard Business Review* that "an experience occurs when a company intentionally uses services as the stage, and goods as props, to engage individual customers in a way that creates a memorable event."[5] They explained that while services are intangible and goods are tangible, experiences are "memorable." In a lot of ways, it's as though they were predicting what we'd want to Instagram. Now the concept of the experience economy is embedded in our consciousness, impacting how we gather and what we participate in. Live sports, music festivals, theme parks, escape rooms, meditation seminars, yoga retreats, ax-throwing museums—these are all experiences we pay for and pursue because we think there's something to be had within them. It made me wonder why there isn't much space given to the idea that the small things create the story we tell about ourselves through the experiences we have, too.

There are entire industries crafted on the idea of having an "experience," even beyond live events or gatherings that have been popular across generations. "Instagram museums" have become a staple, like the Museum of Ice Cream, 29Rooms from Refinery29 (which, according to Eventbrite in summer 2018, sold sixty thousand tickets and reached one out of every two Instagram users), the Color Factory, and the Museum of Pizza. All with snappy art installations made to grab our attention—and with the pop-up element that adds a "Do it now or forever hold your peace" urgency—the experience of the museums almost demands to be posted. These for-purchase, of-the-moment identity markers are everywhere: There are dance parties where hundreds of people gather to groove, freeform, in order to get out of their heads, as well as silent discos or even flash mobs. There are wildlife tours that let you take selfies with the animals, escape rooms that take problem solving and team building away from playing board games in your living room and into a scene with a script, and yoga workshops that come with swag bags.

It isn't that experiences within the "experience economy" are inherently negative—a lot of them are just plain enjoyable, and especially if someone is genuinely excited by the idea of planning their vacation around a festival or saving disposable income to go backpacking, they're important. They matter because someone chose them. The problem only unfolds when these experiences-for-purchase are presented or understood to be the only ones worth having, and that without them, you've somehow failed part of adventurous young adulthood. And, of course, not all of these experiences are inherently new. Like cross-country road trips or camping at music festivals, some of these have existed for our parents and their parents, too. But it's hard to imagine a significant perk of the experience economy—shareability—being such a strong marketing tactic in any era previously. Just like it's worth examining how what we do impacts who we think we are, even beyond the flagships of work and school, it's worth looking at how much of the time we have on earth is devoted to things we think we should be experiencing, rather than what we are experiencing or want to experience.

"On social media, I will see profiles, and people will be like, oh, you know, I just won this, I just got that, I got to travel here, I got accepted into this, I got this job," Melissa, twenty-two, told me. "It makes me feel like, oh, well, now I gotta work harder. I gotta have just as many things happening in my life, and then sometimes it's like you're striving for something that you don't even know you want." Melissa, who also spoke with me about college and the pressure to achieve as the daughter of immigrants, mentioned that between an honors program, jobs, fellowships, clubs, and internships, she didn't even have time to watch the new Netflix shows her friends would talk about. Thinking about the experience economy, she mentioned traveling and studying abroad—something she heard peers talk about constantly in terms of it being a formative experience, one she couldn't afford until she applied to a grant and won a scholarship. While she discovered she loved to travel and that was a positive experience, there were other activities embedded in campus life— ones marketed as critical to the experience of college, including bars and clubs—about which she said, "You feel pressure to do them as a young person and I had almost no interest in doing it." After realizing she was devoting time to a lot of experiences just for the sake of having the experience, Melissa began "meaningfully choosing," picking projects to take on more selectively, prioritizing time with family and friends in a way she'd been too busy to do in the past, and opting for less optimization. She has a couple hobbies: a bullet journal, watercoloring, reading. "And I don't do that with the goal of, like, I'm gonna sell these watercolors. I'm gonna write some book reviews and get money out of it," she told me. "I just do it because I like to do those things. And they bring me happiness, and sometimes that should be enough for us."

Even when an activity begins as a tiny hobby, with no larger ambitions attached, we now have the ability to broadcast it into something bigger, turning snippets of who we are into major features under the spotlight of social media. Muriel, now thirty-three, started a challenge for herself several years ago: She learned to bake pies, and decided to bake fifty pies in a year, a fun challenge after hitting rock bottom with severe anxiety. At the start of her challenge, she began posting fun pictures of the pies on Instagram. By the end, she said, she was putting far more effort into the pies, the photography, and the captions, being cheered on by followers urging her to get more creative with ingredients. "All these different pressures came out of nowhere when it was literally just me baking pies," she said. "It just became a different kind of anxiety." She even turned recipes and essays into a zine, collaborating with people she met online. She sold them online and donated all the proceeds to a local food bank. But by the end of the project, people were asking whether Muriel was going to bake pies and sell them—a classic pivot young people know all too well, when a hobby makes the transition into a side hustle. "I actually haven't baked a pie since," she told me.

My conversation with Muriel captured so many nuances of the experience conversation: the amplification of life on Instagram, the pressure for every hobby to be taken a step further, and the stress-scroll your brain does when someone asks what you do for fun. While she was interviewing for jobs, Muriel explained, "What do you do for fun?" became a dreaded question. Despite having a full-time job, Muriel spent evenings on freelance work—something she genuinely loves, but she realized potential employers weren't responding positively to that answer. "So then, I started being like, well, you know, I like to cook, and I like to watch Netflix with my dogs . . . but what else?" It was never enough. Muriel even polled friends on Instagram, asking them what they like to do, so she could have a list of hobbies at the ready to fulfill the question, even if they weren't hers. It reminded me of college applications' seemingly innocent essay questions; it's in every introduction to new colleagues, where you have to "share something about yourself," the kind of gimmick that automatically makes you feel boring; it's on the date when someone asked, "What do you do for fun?" and when I mentioned reading, I was told that didn't count. Recently, someone else described telling their friend they started running, and the friend wondered aloud why they would spend time on it if it wasn't to train for a 5K or marathon. It's the perfect extraordinary spiral: You spend all day attempting it at work or at school or as a friend, and then, in your spare time, it's not enough to enjoy the activities you engage in—you also need to excel at them. A survey by the Harris Group in 2014, "Millennials: Fueling the Experience Economy," said that "living an epic and meaningful life is about creating, sharing, and capturing memories earned through experiences that span the rich spectrum of life's opportunities. Experiences, for millennials, are about identity-creation."[6]

Fair enough, but in young adulthood (and likely throughout adulthood, more generally) *all* experiences seem to be at least somewhat about identity-creation, whether that's intentional or otherwise. What gets left out of that conversation, though, is that this includes the less sexy experiences that aren't marketed as the game-changers that are supposed to transform us, make us breathless with exhilaration, or enlighten us. "Epic" and "meaningful" aren't the same thing. What about ordinary and meaningful?

According to that same Harris Group study, 78 percent of millennials would choose to spend money on a "desirable experience or event" over buying a material object, with 72 percent saying they want to increase spending on experiences instead of material things over the next year, which the report said points to "a move away from materialism and a growing demand for real-life experiences." Obviously, they're real-life experiences, given they're happening and people are participating in them, often with enthusiasm. But it seems like the emphasis on young adults having experiences that take them out of their normal, everyday lives is important. They are opportunities to not be the person who goes home from work on Friday night and falls asleep watching their old favorite movie while leftovers heat up, but being the person who goes on adventures, does things not everyone else does, and has the coveted experiences we're told define this period of our lives. It's our only chance to do them, we're told. Enjoy it while it lasts. Sweet freedom of youth!

Perhaps because of the prevalence of the "you only live once" approach to these kinds of experiences, they still get treated as universal. Because young adulthood is wired to be the time for exploration, there's an urgency about it—to pack everything in before real life swallows you whole. But the "big experiences," or even big activities, don't apply to every young adult the same way. Marie, twenty-three, moved to the United States from the Democratic Republic of Congo when she was young, and is the middle of seven children. Living in a home with so many kids and not feeling she fit in, she said, made her push herself to stand out. Growing up, ballet and contemporary dance were huge parts of her life, and she was able to find a sponsor to afford most of it. But as she got older, she realized the amount of time, family involvement, and money needed down the road wasn't a good fit for "someone who needed to give all their focus to building a life." Dance, she said, was the only thing that gave her an identity and purpose outside of academics—once she was in college, trying to make friends without the "safety net of dance shaping my personality, my time, and who I felt I was" was difficult. At college, she started to value having money and, after working for the university and getting a scholarship refund, felt rich. "I did not have a lot growing up, so the idea of having my own room, being in college, and being in charge of my money felt amazing," she explained. "I remember saving up my first $1,000 of spending money and blowing it on a nice trip." She kept thinking of all the emergencies she could need that money for. Now, she enjoys taking trips and spends money on self-care, though she notes it still makes her feel anxious to spend large amounts of money at once. Big experiences, like traveling abroad, a hobby like dance that culminates in performances, or a concert or show or event you paid a ticket price for, can't be dismissed as lacking value or meaning—they have the value we apply to them. That's also why it is critical we not think of them as necessary milestones for having a fulfilled, worldly young adulthood. What we do with our time depends on the access we have to it.

That feels especially important to keep in mind when you consider that the activities we pursue are part of the stories we tell about ourselves as people, which is another reason we shouldn't be ranking or qualifying what gets counted as meaningful or formative. "Other researchers have shown that compared to stuff, we feel as though experiences make us who we are as people," explained Michael I. Norton, the Harold M. Brierley Professor of Business Administration at the Harvard Business School and coauthor of the book *Happy Money: The Science of Smarter Spending*. "When we buy an experience, in a way we're kind of buying a new version of ourselves and we get to try it out and build it into ourselves," he continued. A good example, Norton explained, is that no one ever says "I want to tell you about the first time I ever bought a TV." That's typically not what we do with stuff.

It's an interesting way to think about emerging adults and what we're drawn to. Maybe because we're making less money, maybe because it's better for the environment, maybe because we're burnt out on hyper-consumerism; the heaviness of material possessions sometimes holds less appeal. Experiences seem to carry more heft, if we're picking and choosing things that define us. You don't have to pack those up and move them to the next apartment if you decide it's not really "you" anymore.

In contrast, he told me, you could absolutely tell someone about the first time you left your state, or had sushi, for example. It's one way to consider how we understand the experiences we have in regard to becoming who we are: *What's the story I want to tell about myself?* The experiences are examples, the "show, don't tell" of our lives, that pop up in those stories. If we want extraordinary selves, then we can search for examples that prove we're extraordinary. There's some element of us wanting, needing, to prove it to ourselves, too. "Those experiences are the stories we tell to other people, but we also tell them to ourselves," Norton said. "What kind of a person am I? I'm a collection of my experiences, not a collection of my stuff."

And when we invest so much in hobbies or experiences as markers of our identities, especially in our childhood, the moment we stop spending our time doing them throws us into flux. Many young people spend the majority of their early life working toward something—getting good grades to get a scholarship, making varsity soccer, performing in choir—only to realize those things don't turn into careers for most. But finding a place for former passions in the adult world of working all day, trying to exercise, cooking dinner, and doing life maintenance in the evenings sometimes proves challenging. It feels like a certain kind of identity crisis, one that occurs when suddenly your life doesn't have room anymore for the thing you spent *all* your time doing. After I quit dancing, people would still meet me and say, "You're the dancer, right?" I had no idea what to say in place of it, or how to articulate: "No, now I'm just me." It was a weird, teenage realization that I'd dumped the heft of my identity into a thing I did, and I made that thing who I was. It dominated my weekend schedule, my future plans. It was *everything*, and without an answer to that "Who are you?" question—that I heard peers respond to with "I'm in choir," "I'm an athlete," "I'm an honors student"—I felt like nothing. Avid runners discussed being unable to afford race entry fees; others mentioned trying to join a recreational sports league and eventually falling off the schedule after they missed so many games because of work. Some mentioned how puzzled they were to see something that was once a favorite activity or a dream they chased fade from view, either because they lost interest, discovered they enjoyed other things more, or simply ran out of time for it—and nearly everyone classified it as "quitting," giving up, or failing, as if the activities we spend our lives pursuing aren't supposed to grow and change as we do.

One person in their mid-twenties messaged me about being a competitive athlete in high school: She was talented, revered by the community for her skill, and was "known for" being a star in this sport. Then, she got pregnant in high school and struggled with postpartum depression, toggling between the grief of losing her identity as an athlete and her new identity as a mother. "I literally didn't know who I was without it," she wrote. "I felt like a no one." We underestimate how gutting that sensation—of not knowing how to define yourself—is. The idea that we shouldn't crave markers for who we are defies everything we know about this time of life. Of course you want to be able to say you're a photographer, or a painter, or someone who gardens and grew those tomatoes. It feels like it helps put ourselves in context, a context we choose—not things we have to do to some degree, like cleaning the house, going to class, or working. There's a self that exists beyond all that.

So much of these aspirational experiences, this identity seeking and building, is about wanting to be noticed for things that make us unique or special, acknowledged for the experiences we've had as we make our way through the world, and armed with specific examples of exactly the kind of people we are. We all want to feel like someone. More important, we want to feel like *ourselves*; we want definers and descriptors and proof that we're in the world, doing things that matter and mean something to us. And maybe what the emphasis on certain kinds of experiences tells us is, actually, we want to be our *best* selves. When I found myself at a party where somebody asked a version of "Besides work, what do you enjoy?" the answers were

fascinating: Other people went scuba diving, got their yoga certifi-
cations, tried new restaurants every weekend. I remember thinking
about my honest answers: that I like reading the same books, like
Nora Ephron's *I Feel Bad About My Neck*, over and over again; that I
watch ballet videos on breaks at work; that my only athletic achievement is teaching myself to do a handstand that I still only practice
when I feel like it. They are tiny and unimpressive and, mercifully,
things I do not have to strive to be good at. They are ordinary, and
mundane, and somehow likely tell you more about who I am than
any single accomplishment or Instagram post. Doing things "for the
experience" has long been a standby of young adulthood, but it's impossible to ignore that there's something uncomfortable about being able to curate your own experiences, and inadvertently rank and
weigh them, *this much*.

Income inequality, lack of time, and privilege in access are critical parts of who gets to do what, and in some ways, the experience
economy, and even hobbies and activities beyond it, further disen-
franchises people who don't have access to these things: If you're
worried about paying rent each month, you likely aren't going to
ponder whether to take up painting or pottery; if you're supporting
your family, standing in line for the latest museum exhibit may not
be within the realm of possibility. When decidedly optional things
become "formative" or "meaningful," you have to look at who has
time and access to them in the first place. We might all choose
things that we feel build our identities, but the selection pool isn't
equal. Who is to say that the little routine where you take a walk
after work isn't more meaningful than the big event you spent five
months waiting for? Can't they both matter? Can't they both be part
of the collection of things that make us who we are? Having a variety

of experiences or activities or interests, it seems, can help figure out what matters to you, what feels relevant to your life, and what carries meaning. That process of elimination becomes virtually impossible if we're only engaging in what we think we ought to find fulfilling, instead of what actually is.

When I talked to young adults about the experiences or activities that felt formative—not milestones that they accomplished that might be part of their identities, too, like graduations or moving for a job they love—the breadth of experiences was astounding. The milestone clarification is important because sometimes, these identity markers feel similar: When you graduate from college, secure a job, or move into your first apartment, you get to identify as a person who has done those things. When you explore new places and travel, or make a habit of going to museums, you get to claim yourself as someone who does those things. Somehow, it feels all these elements create the kind of person we imagine ourselves to be. Emerging adults described organizing, being involved in activism, and volunteering as pieces of their internal puzzles—the first time they felt connected to their community or realized that service felt like part of who they are. Someone explained their only hobby was going out to their grandparents' house on the weekends and listening to them tell stories from their young adulthood. People characterized the loss of certain activities—like basketball, chess, being a member of certain clubs—as a sort of grief, a real loss of a former self as they moved on to something new. Most conversations were peppered with the questions experiences actually warrant asking: How do you balance time between what you have to do to live and what you want to do in order to feel you're living fully?

If leisure or just-for-fun experiences can form our sense of identity, then it's not a small question to ask how you want to spend your time. When I posed the question that opened this chapter, answers ranged from playing with pets, taking baths, embroidering, baking, grocery shopping, composting, singing in a choir, and hiking, to playing video games, milking cows, following a certain sports team, taking weekly dance classes, learning languages, watching specific genres of movies, organizing events in their communities, and cleaning as things people felt were part of their identities that didn't involve work. It struck me that so many of these were simple, not grandiose. Even individuals who mentioned seemingly "big" things, like marathon running or traveling, articulated how these things were built into the fabric of their lives in some way. No one, it seemed, pointed to the gorgeous one-off where you sign up to have your life changed, like those "under thirty" international trips guaranteed to return you to shore as a totally new person. In fact, most of what was mentioned wasn't described as transformative so much as it was affirming: People described things that made them feel more like, well, them.

During the coronavirus pandemic of 2020, that came even more sharply into focus: Events people spent their years looking forward to, like festivals and vacations, among others, were put on an indefinite hold; the ability to adventure and travel and carefully outline plans to go to wineries, take tours, and participate in organized fun disappeared. For some, it meant catching up with old friends during Zoom happy hours; a surplus of banana bread swarmed social media; going out for a daily walk felt like the same level of novelty as boarding a flight for an international destination. Not everyone had these luxuries—including the luxury of staying home, or the pleasure of wondering how to occupy their time as the world caved in around them. People died and said goodbye to loved ones via FaceTime. Tragedy and layoffs ran rampant, and lack of federal response left too many without relief needed to pay rent, medical expenses, and safely stay home to begin with. "Fun" wasn't high priority, and what did "fun" even mean, anyway? The defining mundanities we experience every day, and small things, were what was left, if you were in a position for it to even enter your consciousness and how your life felt at all.

In my dreams, of course I'm the kind of person who travels the world and tries everything once, from skydiving to scuba diving to learning how to make wine. I dance on rooftops in the hot and sweaty summer; I cherish novelty and am the first to say yes to anything that could be classified as an adventure. In reality, I am boring. And those boring, silly little things I enjoy spending time on have been every bit as formative—if not more so!—than the big stuff. My own list of small activities that feel formative are breadmaking, which I'm often terrible at but enthusiastically eat the crumbs of anyway; curating long emails to my grandparents featuring the appropriate number of photos of the family dog; and taking walks down the same couple blocks while talking on the phone, the part of the day I savor as feeling as though everything switches off.

Just like the demands of work that leave time for little else aren't likely to slow, it feels unlikely that experience economies and experiences marketed as milestones will fade from young adult consciousness, and they shouldn't. The opportunity for transformation will always be there, in things big and small, and there will always be a version of those "15 Things to Do Before You Turn 25" lists. I like to think we'll have things to savor, new things to try because of curiosity and enthusiasm, and a million little experiences throughout the course of our lives that are meaningful, not just one narrow opportunity to cram them into *right now*. Choosing what you do is important; knowing why you want to do it, more so. If anything, in emerging adulthood, there's an opportunity not just to be the kind of person who does a certain thing, but to use the experiences you have and activities you pursue to inch a little closer to who you really are. It's worth the time. Just because.

# 5

# CRACKS

*On perfectionism and being enough*

HERE'S A BRIEF LIST OF THINGS I'M NOT DOING ENOUGH OF: cooking at home, creating healthy and Instagrammable dishes cribbed from the *New York Times* Cooking Instagram account or the family cookbook we keep on a bookstand, open to the chosen page, garnished with the fresh herbs I keep alive on the always-dusted kitchen windowsills; socializing in ways that are memorable and thoughtful, and always being the friend who remembers to send a just-thinking-of-you card and is always the first to order a gift off the wedding registry or birthday wish list; working out to show I'm pushing myself and not getting complacent and boosting my mood; sorting out why I feel guilt for the evenings I don't want to do anything at all; scheduling entire days devoted to laundry, cleaning the toilets, finally updating my computer, and reorganizing the closet; calling to set various appointments: for my eyes that have definitely changed since my last glasses prescription, my hair that's overgrown, filling the prescription that's long overdue, and scheduling the medical procedure I'm supposed to be having that somehow never seems urgent enough to follow through on. Instead, I am cracking.

There are all the kinds of "enough" we could be, if only we were a little more of this, a little less of that, talked a little softer, worked a little harder: smart enough, cool enough, pretty enough, responsible enough, calm enough, organized enough, *good enough*. We're eaten up by enough, and our lack of it. Even the word itself sets the goal of doing *more*, hinting that a threshold exists somewhere, that elusive finish line. To define what "enough" is implies that we'll *be* enough someday—we'll fill the well and check the boxes and live up to the potential that's ours to waste. It's been renamed to the extent that it almost sounds noble if you don't think about it too hard: "making the most of every moment," "paying your dues," "the hustle," "ambition," "living up to your potential"—but in every single context, it means: *Have you maxed yourself out? Have you done your best?* As if "doing your best" means "operating at 100 percent all the time, in five different areas of life at once, regardless of circumstances or reality or energy or resources," instead of "this is the most I have to give with what I can right now."

When I think of being enough, I imagine fullness. Of feeling whole; of finally stopping for a while. Of knowing that, if this is all there is, this is enough for me—enough to know I woke up today and did what I could, to know I called my friends and felt the wind whip through my hair on a quick bike ride to see the sunlight, to know I went to bed when I wanted and that sometimes, taking of care of myself means just ordering takeout. And instead, on a loop, like an old VHS tape you watched as a kid, I run toward enough as if my lungs are on fire, as if it's something I'm meant to live up to, not something I inherently am. I always thought I'd eventually outgrow it: that an approval-seeking little girl would become a woman who didn't weigh her worth by the number of people she managed to please, often to her own detriment. I heard that from other young people, too: that they imagined there was a threshold somewhere and they'd drop perfectionism like a bad habit. They described getting the right job, getting the right raise, being in a relationship, making new friends, finally having their apartment organized and furnished, changing their eating habits, developing an exercise routine, or completing big projects as points where they'd finally stop worrying so much about things being perfect—or not meeting expectations. All these things were sort of like benchmarks: Once we meet them, we'll ease up. It never seems to be the case, because there is always something we should be more of.

And we start measuring early. Young adulthood has been engineered to feel like this constant competition, with standardized tests and GPAs and extracurriculars, and success stories that paint a certain kind of triumph awaiting us atop a hill made of our self-sacrifice and struggle and striving. The myth is that perfectionism exists because we want to be perfect, just like the myth persists that we're obsessed with work because we want to achieve. It assumes a level of freedom of choice and financial security that doesn't exist for a lot of people, and ignores a bitter truth: So broken are things, doing it all perfectly feels like the only shot at things turning out okay. It isn't hard to track this, but perfectionism feels like such an individual, personal problem that it rarely gets brought up in conversations about societal shifts, beyond pressure to get good test scores or sarcastic one-liners on participation trophies. As expert perfectionism researchers wrote about these shifts, "Over the last fifty years, communal interest and civic responsibility have been progressively eroded, replaced by a focus on self-interest and competition in a supposedly free and open market place."[1] What does that look like for us? Well, a lot like being measured, in school and for jobs, for sure, but also in less obvious ways, like how social we are (is it enough?), how healthy we eat (enter an endless array of apps designed to track this), and even our lifestyles (what city you live in, how you spend time, and what your apartment looks like are all visible now). Social media gave us the opportunity to look over everyone else's shoulders and see what we could be doing better, and sometimes life feels as though it's turned into one big outperformance: When we're all being ranked as commodities and products who exist to produce, it's not difficult to see why we'd interpret every mistake, flaw, or weakness as something insurmountable, not a part of being human, but instead, something we immediately need to fix.

"This is a culture which preys on insecurities and amplifies imperfection, impelling young people to focus on their personal deficiencies," wrote the researchers.[2] Perfectionism is a lot of things: a buzzword, at this point; a synonym for "ambitious" or "hard worker" that sinisterly assigns value to what you accomplish or produce; a result of capitalism that makes us think this is all *our* problem anyway, that it's our fault we can't keep up. Even when you google "perfectionism," that's a lot of the framing around it: how to "overcome" it, a feat of your own will and work ethic. That's the lie perfectionism tells you: That this is about *you*. That you're out here alone, the only one lagging behind, the only one unfulfilled. The only one who has ever missed a big work email or blown a test you needed to pass, forgotten a birthday or important anniversary, failed so consequentially it feels like it's going to alter the course of your life, or forgotten to brush your teeth before bed. The only one who feels like they're one wrong move away from everything falling apart.

Today's young people aren't the first to experience this, but there has been a generational shift: In the first study to examine group generational differences in perfectionism,[3] Thomas Curran, PhD, of the University of Bath, and Andrew P. Hill, PhD, of York St John University, the researchers mentioned above, found that more recent generations of college students reported much higher scores for each form of perfectionism they examined than earlier generations. In other words: Perfectionism increased between 1989 and 2016.[4] Self-oriented perfectionism, when you hold unrealistic expectations for yourself, increased by around 10 percent; socially prescribed perfectionism, when you believe you have to be perfect to gain approval and acceptance from others, jumped by an estimated 32 percent; other-oriented perfectionism, when you impose unrealistic standards on others, went up about 16 percent.[5] What these numbers tell us is that, first, it isn't just you, and in some cases, it's a structural issue that has specific ramifications on our well-being: The study states that socially prescribed perfectionism has been shown to be positively associated with body dissatisfaction, eating disorders, and suicidal ideation, and had the largest relationship of all other dimensions of perfectionism with depression and anxiety.

Squaring that with how perfectionism still gets discussed, especially for young people, is disorienting. Think of the well-meaning times you've been called "composed," "poised," or "such an overachiever," or the instances "you're such a perfectionist" was brought up as a celebratory thing, in job interviews or when you went above and beyond to plan an elaborate surprise party for a friend. Then, there's the inverse, the systems, like work or grades, that reminded you of all the ways you weren't doing enough to meet your potential, even if it wasn't necessarily potential you wanted to meet. The feeling you'll never be perfect enough, or have accomplished enough, is dismissed as obsession with "specialness" that exists for entitled young people in a vacuum—like we woke up one day and decided the only way to be happy was to be special, and being special required being perfect. Some young people don't have the luxury of not being perfect—or, at least, trying to be. For marginalized young people, the stakes are higher, and they're judged more harshly; perfectionism functions like oppression, another systemic pressure that puts the onus on the individual not being "good enough" instead of existing in a society that works against them.

When perfectionism worsens the mental health of young people, it's an additional barrier: Back to that "growing out of it" idea, other research[6] found that, as perfectionists grow older, they unravel, becoming more prone to guilt, envy, and anxiety and, surprisingly, less conscientious, reliable, and disciplined.[7] It doesn't get easier one day, which is why it is so horrifying to hear so many young people self-describe as perfectionists and listen to how they feel it's flattened them already.

I'm only a little ashamed to say that perfectionism feels like a greater force in my life than my dreams or failures. It's an overwhelming presence that pops up in small things, like acting as though a typo in an email will end my professional career, to large ones, the largest of which is my own mental health. The challenge I'm still unpacking—in my opinion, amplified by perfectionism—is that part of me still believes I should be able to "fix" it all myself. It feels like something that trapped me early and has managed to persist. The first time I stared into a foggy mirror in the bathroom after a shower and counted the bones in my sternum, each of them defined like mountain ridges protruding from under translucent skin, it wasn't because I wanted to be perfect. I didn't know it then, but it was because I wanted to be enough. For a long time, that looked like whittling away at my body until leotards hung off me and I clutched the ballet barre as if it was the only thing grounding me to the earth, holding me upright as the room spun. But when I left ballet, the urge to work toward enoughness didn't leave me. I felt it every time my chronic illness flared and kept me from being the appropriate amount of fun and spontaneous. Every time in a crowded bar I took a shot that I'd begged someone not to order for me, even as a familial history of alcoholism dwelled in my mind, because that's what being cool and *belonging* felt like. It was in every boy I kissed but didn't want to, because I thought that's what it meant to be a good girl—unflappable and unfazed. When I don't have the energy to be a good girlfriend or friend, when I don't read the stack of books on the nightstand, when I forget who I am at all—the thing I am supposed to know for sure. I chiseled, and cut, and edited, looking for where I could be more and where I should be less, tucking the reality of emotions and experiences under neat and breezy *I'm fine*s and *It isn't a big deal*s.

This is just a small slice of the constant balancing of "enoughs" facing young people: balancing being responsible enough to be a family caretaker *and* enough of an irresponsible young adult at the same time; young people in marginalized groups having to do twice as much; hiding your real identity, for safety, while trying to grow into enough of that person to eventually be your true self; having chronic illness or a disability that impacts your daily life and balancing that; negotiating power dynamics that tell us only certain kinds of voices deserve to be heard; dismantling the standards that tell us our worth can be housed in ACT scores or saving $100,000 by age twenty-five.

I think about perfectionism and extraordinariness all the time—

*What are we really striving for? Does this really all come from social media, as some seem eager to suggest? What about all the factors that made enoughness unattainable, just out of reach? Should life feel like more than just trying to stay afloat?* These extraordinary lives we reach for, these extraordinary selves we take ourselves apart to be, are less about wanting to be exceptional in every way, and more about craving security and stability and feeling seen—ordinary wants that feel scarce and complicated. Being special is just the scapegoat. And in general, "specialness" feels less about a calculated desire to be unique and heralded as exceptional, and more about a yearning for security that only seems possible if we're doing better than our best. Perfectionism gets applauded as a virtue, and we categorize things like pulling all-nighters as markers not just of achievement, but of goodness. But what happens when it feels like the definition of "good" has been warped so much that it became exceptional, and now, exceptional is always expanding in accordance with new ways to be good at, and good for, things? Enough: It's such an ordinary thing. But the extraordinary pursuit of it feels like it is cracking us open.

"Right now, in our culture, we continue to precipitate messaging and celebrate the alleged achievement of just absolute perfect superstardom," Jessica Rohlfing Pryor, PhD, psychologist and faculty member of the Counseling Program at the Family Institute at Northwestern University, told me the first time we spoke. "The way that it is embodied in American culture is at the absence of messaging that while that's a great motivational aspiration, it is an illusion," she added, when talking about the culture of success and what has contributed to it.

Cross-legged in my childhood bedroom, I could see the bags of old pointe shoes, tattered and dusty and taking up space, in the corner of the closet, relics of a past life when I'd tied my worth to my weight and sought control wherever I could find it. Pryor said researchers collectively refer to fear of being average as "fear of failure." What they've found, she said, is that the messaging is getting louder, and more specific—that you have to be extra-extraordinary and extra-special. Now, it feels, not only are overt "failures"—like racking up credit card debt, taking out hefty student loans, getting fired, failing a class, misunderstanding something, dropping the ball in a relationship, not living up to your parenting ideals if you have kids—considered unacceptable, but being average itself feels like a failure. Anything less than the best we could possibly be simply isn't enough.

When I spoke to other emerging adults, they told me perfectionism felt like the thought that if only you'd studied harder, you could've gotten an A instead of that B; if you'd worked enough to keep your side hustle afloat in addition to your day job, you would've saved enough money to take that nice vacation or pay a security deposit on a nicer apartment; if you'd worked out a little harder, you'd feel more confident in your swimsuit; if you'd woken up earlier, you'd be inherently more virtuous and get more done, even if your body needed sleep. Many articulated additional pressures that get eye-rolled away when we talk about young adults wanting to be perfect, including literally not being able to afford to fail, because they can't pay to retake a class; meeting the expectations of their parents; trying to hold it together so they don't burn out at work because they're terrified they'll never be hired again. No matter what we do, there is always a bit more we could've done, and so much of it orients around going it alone—these are things that are within our control to do better, to fix, to change. In young adulthood, the repeat of "It's your life to shape!" is freeing and a gutting amount of pressure at the same time. What if *everything* is dependent on you doing it perfectly, and you fall short of your own expectations? The only person to blame, when it functions that way, is yourself.

And it starts early. Pryor's work focuses primarily on millennials, but she pointed out that children, preteens, and teens receive these messages from the minute they start growing up, about how "perfectionism is this perfectly normal, achievable, acceptable goal."

"We have all of these American, aspirational messages about going all in and being the best and sacrificing everything for that sweet, sweet success," Pryor said. The other half of the message is totally missing—that mistakes are necessary to learning and to growth, that mistakes aren't inherently failure, and that failure isn't a referendum on you as a person. "And so growing up in a society where we're told that you need to sacrifice everything for these great accolades and the ultimate success story, and grit your teeth harder and grind deeper, without the balanced other half—which is, of course, you're going to fail often and hard—is an absolute disservice to the psychological development and intellectual development of our whole society," she said. Personal growth might be necessary to young adulthood, but at what point is "growth" just another synonym for accomplishment or improvement, and at what point should the entirety of our lives not be built on achieving?

Pryor explained that it is setting human beings up for absolute failure—devastating failure, she clarified, not a mistake here or there—to imply that they alone can combat their own perfectionism, because they didn't create it themselves. "The society, our culture, the messages they are inundated with, the ways they're shaped by our education systems, by families, by communities," Pryor named. "All of these parts of society are players in the creation of the perfectionism that's eating that person alive." In other words, the fixation on your own inadequacy didn't just spring from your own mind. The pressures are real; they're tangible. If anything, it feels like perfectionism, or chronically feeling like never enough, is designed to keep us feeling small: We don't talk about it, because it hovers too close to shameful. We're uncomfortable with it, because who *really* embraces failure like an old friend? So, of course it feels like a problem with you and you alone, that only you can undo some of the qualities that brought you here in the first place—working hard, grinding, striving, and fixing. If younger generations really are struggling with perfectionism at higher rates, Pryor pointed out, she believes the question needs to be changed: "It isn't, 'What are these young generations not doing right or doing differently?' It's, 'Whoa, what have we created that they are now manifesting the symptoms of?'"

It's hard to track when "average" became a bad word, synonymous with "failing" instead of "just fine." Some peg it to social media, the rise of having others' achievements and lives and shiniest selves carried with you in your pocket, ready to be reviewed anytime you're waiting at a bus stop or struggling at work or home alone with too much time to think. But the focus on development-as-achievement and future success stories at the expense of your current, personal well-being has ramifications. We can hide under it. If I was thin enough to look like a ballet dancer, I theorized, no one needed to know I was having an identity crisis about what I wanted to do with my life. If I always seemed to have a plan, I would be impervious to the stress of deciding what I really wanted deep down. Perfectionism, in that way, felt like a mask. When you see young adults holding it together, or achieving "highly" according to the standards by which that gets measured, the pressure that might be within all that gets murky. You can be objectively successful and still unhappy, or worried. You can appear perfect and feel like you're crumbling inside. I had a hard time holding in my mind that I could be imperfect and still deserve happiness; that my flaws, things I could do better, or stuff I got wrong did not automatically cancel out moments of joy or those that felt meaningful—nor should they. "Earning it" felt so ingrained in how I felt about myself, there was no space for me to exist as I was. I was always a work-in-progress, someone who wasn't worthy unless I'd appropriately self-sacrificed and self-flagellated to the point that I felt undeserving and anxious over happiness anyway. What a profound waste of time.

"There's this sense of self-sacrifice and grueling punishment for reward that has triumphed right now in our society, like the ultimate example of a worthy human," said Pryor. "And I can't imagine what it's like to grow up, to develop self-identity, in this kind of incredible hornet's nest." I mentioned that I knew self-focus was a big part of this time of life, and wondered aloud why the idea that we're supposed to just magically "fix" ourselves didn't quite track. Because it doesn't: If success or failure has been a significant part of your life experience, Pryor pointed out, then how people respond to that informs who you think you are. She used the example of a kid who finds school easy, or excels in athletics: *Who am I if I start making mistakes? How could I possibly know who I am when I'm not always making the final shot in the game and pulling it off?* It feels like the questions interlock: *What happens if I fail?* and *Who am I if I fail?* I thought of young adults who told me about crashing so badly their physical health tanked to the extent they had to take time off work, and felt lost without the identifier of always being the person who showed up early and stayed late. Others talked about being burnt out from always being the friend who planned surprise birthdays, brunches, and themed holiday parties for their friend group, and also the loss of control they felt when their well-meaning friends attempted to take that off their plates. Injuries from over-exercising also came up, leaving people feeling guilty and out of sorts for not being able to keep moving. It's hard to separate your sense of self from being the person who is always *on*, always has it together, and is always doing their best at all the things, at all times. It feels a little bit like letting yourself down, the self that you made.

And that's not to mention letting everyone else down. *What if people only care about me because I'm successful? I don't know who I am if I'm not running X number of miles per day. What if people think I'm a bad friend, parent, student, or person if I don't do X, Y, and Z? What if I take a break and find I can't get going again?* All of these questions echoed back and forth across my conversations with young adults who tied a certain level of performance to their self-worth and self-acceptance. Dr. Pryor mentioned she'd found in her work that if you think others only care about you because you're successful at a given thing, you start minimizing your mistakes from everyone around you. "If I'm failing at all the things, I need to minimize how many of those things I'm going to fail at, because the people who love me or the people I want to love me, their tolerance is pretty low, and if I fail enough, they're just going to leave," she explained. So, if you're succeeding, you have to keep succeeding; if you're failing, you have to squash that into a secret. It's what she described as a "huge social fear of abandonment." It's fear of rejection that makes being anything less than exceptional feel like such a risk. We want to be loved as a whole person; we want to be secure as a whole person. And increasingly, it feels like that wholeness means deleting any of the flaws or missteps, as if it's as simple as dragging an eraser across them, rubbing them out of the story we tell about ourselves.

Once, in the ballet studio as a teenager, a teacher took their stick and thwacked it across my knees to straighten them up. It bruised the bruise already there from their last visit. And I thought about leaving. I thought of collecting my little pile of pointe shoes and sewing kits and walking away. I thought of ordering a whole pizza, a food I'd convinced myself I hated. And then I thought of what that would say about me: That I couldn't handle it. That I was a quitter. Never once did I reverse it to think, *What if choosing not to pursue this is setting me free, not failing? What if failure isn't the heft of me anyway?* It's unnerving how many times I've had versions of that conversation with myself since then, trading eating disorders I was in denial about for not walking out of an academic situation where I was being harassed by a classmate, not leaving a toxic job, or even not saying, "No, I cannot take on that extra task." In every scenario, I invented an imaginary reason that was stopping me: *If I don't come back to this class, I'll be considered hard to work with. If I quit that job, I'll never find another. If I say no to that extra thing, someone else will say yes.* Looking at it a little closer, I realize it was all wrapped up in versions of enough: easygoing enough not to raise a fuss, grateful enough to be glad I had a job in the first place, eager enough to say yes to whatever came my way. This almost sounds like martyrdom, until you factor in that it made me miserable, guilty, and paranoid— not exactly an exemplar of being your "best self." Just like I thought being thin enough would ensure I didn't fail at a career that, at the time, I wanted more than anything, it was a theme of making my way in the world as a young adult afterward, too. If I was the perfect friend and daughter, I could never feel the ache of loneliness. If I was the perfect employee, I could never be fired or fail.

It's a structural problem, but there are structural inequities built into the problem, too. "There are so many young women of color, people of color, queer young people; anybody who's marginalized, you end up bumping up against it," said Dr. Alfiee M. Breland-Noble, whose work focuses on engaging marginalized youth and empowering them to care for their mental health, said of perfectionism. "Because there's this myth that, 'If I just get it right, if I just do something different, if I just do something better, people will stop discriminating against me. If I show up early for class, if I stay after class, if I let the teacher know that I'm invested, if I go to office hours, all of those things outside of just doing the work, that's the stuff that will ensure that this teacher is going to give me this A that I deserve.' The sad part is that's not true." This idea of perfectionism gets ingrained because "you gotta be five times better to be considered for half as much," Breland-Noble said. That's "the double-edged sword of racism and discrimination," she told me. "It is there to convince you that who you are fundamentally is wrong." There is no room for mistakes, she added, because any mistake is attributed to your race, ethnicity, or culture. In a study that focused on maladaptive perfectionism in African American adolescents, young people who reported higher levels of experiences with racism were "more likely to be in maladaptive perfectionism classes."[8] A separate study, on personal and familial aspects of perfectionism in Latino students, reported that results support the idea that maladaptive family perfectionism is associated with the negative mental health functioning of young people, and suggested assessing feelings surrounding not meeting the family's expectations.[9] Tokenization, microaggressions at school or in the workplace, and being maligned as less competent or less capable than white peers all add to an entirely different kind of stress. Perfectionism might exist for everyone, but privilege offers a buffer layer between perfectionism and oppression. It is not the same. Discrimination persists, and includes warped standards of what it means to be good, beautiful, articulate, proper, productive, competent, and yes, even perfect. "The structure is telling you that you need to be better," Breland-Noble said. "And then what you run up against is even when you're better, it's still not good enough. You are still facing discrimination."

"If my identity is cisgender woman, which mine happens to be, or Black male or Latinx immigrant, or queer lesbian, there are social messages about what I'm expected to be or do, or what the perfect version of that looks like," said Pryor. So, perfectionism isn't confined to its own bubble. It plays out across different aspects of your identity. And we assign value and virtue to chasing perfection, even in spite of toxic context. Perfectionists, or strivers, or hard workers, or whatever we're calling them, are typically considered reliable and deadline-driven, resilient in their desire to try until they get something right, and are perceived to have it "together." It signals we have a certain kind of value, to ourselves, to other people, to the ideal of what it means to be "good." Maybe that's why guilt melts us when we fall short. It turns us into an "if only" that has real consequences for our self-worth, and that touches every part of our lived experience. In chronic never-enough culture, every single thing, every decision or circumstance, contains a "what if": What if you'd pulled that all-nighter—would that have made the difference at work? What if you'd gone out that time all your friends managed to, and you met the perfect partner, but instead you chose to stay in? What if you had a different body—surely you'd feel better about yourself? Oh, and by the way, what if you made peace with all these demons on top of doing everything else, because can't we perfect *not* being perfect, too, in the era of enlightenment and do-it-all self-help?

If I had any worth at all, it existed in "if." It's a dark kind of hope; placing your worth in your future self assumes that one day you'll be someone worth being. No one wanders around *truly* thinking they are invincible against failure, but we do seem to collectively believe if we try hard enough, if we're good enough, we should somehow be able to avoid it. Young adulthood was once presented as time blocked off for making mistakes and being imperfect, because how else were you supposed to know you were trying things and experimenting and putting yourself out there in a meaningful way? For today's emerging adults trying to craft a stable, fulfilling life, caution and precision and perfection feel like the qualities closest to a guarantee that you won't fall short of the standards you set. It's trying to put out a million little fires at the same time: How do you outrun your most ordinary self? How are we actually supposed to embrace ourselves as we are? How do we let it go?

Obviously, the social structure factors heave perfectionism up and make it the foundation for everything else we do. Hyperindividualism tells us not only should we be seamlessly managing all this alone, but we certainly shouldn't speak about perfectionism and its impact out loud. Capitalism instructs us that there is always more we can and should be doing. We have the feeling that the only person who is going to catch us, should we need it, is, well, us. While structural change is integral, I wondered what we do in the meantime: sit with this? We can't undo perfectionism with a bunch of happy-go-lucky reminders to embrace our flaws when society still doesn't accept us making mistakes; we can't unravel structural inequities by telling people marginalized by them that it's their job to rise to the occasion. And that advice—"Accept mistakes!" "Embrace flaws!" "Lean into failure!"—feels like feeble platitudes. Fail, but not so much it becomes insurmountable or you need *too* much help. Be flawed, but in a way we can comfortably understand. The only thing that kept coming up was that we should talk about it—which sounds simple, too—but in a more practical way: being open when we're struggling, about what standards are inequitable, and being willing to look twice at what we consider worthy, and why. The eerie silence around perfectionism, unless it's being used as a humblebrag, isn't doing any of us any favors.

Self-compassion is challenging to put into practice, but it feels like a critical skill to develop when we're all trying to do more and feeling lesser. That also feels important because, while achievement and work are one facet of perfectionism, there's an emotional and self-esteem component, too, not necessarily tied to work: Where do we get our value if we're having a hard time or fail? How do we actually let ourselves off the hook? It's not all gold stars and pressure to score big at work. Perfectionism can make you question your own worthiness to exist in the world, and that's a major thing. It was one of the reasons I was interested to hear how young people were attempting to loosen perfectionism's grip. For some, it meant deciding to get rid of their five-year plans and goals lists, because logging them felt more detrimental than aspirational, or trying to stop reading emails ten times before hitting send. Letting their guard down to their therapist, posting job rejections on social media and finding solace in know others were experiencing the same thing, and trying new hobbies they knew they'd be bad at all came up multiple times. Others cited designating calls with friends specifically for "brag sessions," where they talked about what made them happy or feel good, and making lists of things that they felt brought them to life that didn't involve buying or accomplishing anything. The examples were reminders that, maybe, if this really is the "time of our lives," it's worth reconsidering who gets the privilege of making mistakes and messes, and how much of our time goes into rehearsing what we know we can get right.

So much about perfectionism feels like it is about trying to protect us, like a guardrail. *What if I feel too sick to go out one too many times, and they decide I'm more trouble than I'm worth? What if I tell someone I'm struggling, and they tell me I should be able to handle it?* These feel like more specific versions of a similar question: *What if I'm not enough; what if I haven't done enough?* At points, I've tried so hard to be perfect that I may as well have not existed. I was a figment of a million people's imaginations, disappearing into whatever I was supposed to be. The impulse to make myself smaller in order to make my life bigger—more significant, more perfect—still exists, but in a way that's quieter. What perfectionism looks like now is subtler: Not thinking my feelings are valid enough, or *big* enough, to warrant sharing. Thinking I have only earned something if I'm bone-tired and burnt out at the end of it, or else I didn't sacrifice enough. Rehashing mistakes over and over until I've analyzed every second from every angle, and developed alternative responses for each. Failing to call friends as often as I should and falling into a guilt cycle about that instead of just making the call. Opting out of making hard choices about my life in order to defend myself by keeping *every* option on the table.

It feels like wandering around naked to say it out loud, but sometimes I have to repeat it like a mantra: *I care a lot, I am messy, but I'm trying.* And then, I stop and I try—somewhat counterintuitively— to try *less*, to let that be enough. What that looks like: taking little things I "saved" for special occasions, or until I had earned them— baking a boxed chocolate cake at six p.m. on a Thursday night for no reason; taking a nap on a Sunday afternoon—and deciding my life is worthy of them *now*. Letting rest exist without it being earned. Reframing "I'm behind" as "I'm where I need to be right now." Reminding myself that there's a difference between thoughtfully listening to other people and seeking their approval as the governing force of my life. As scary as it sounds, asking myself: *What if this is all you are?*

It brings me solace. Is being imperfect, making the mistake, worse than being mean because I'm hungry, or being so tired I can't hold my head up to listen to a friend who needs me? Is it worse than paying all my attention to the next chapter of life when so much is still happening on this page? It's a process, again and again, of finding that the answer is no. It's looking at *this* self, not the one I could be, and sitting with her, through the messy parts and the mishaps and the things I said wrong. The times she dropped out, the hearts she broke, the routines she messed up. And noticing: Even with cracks, an ordinary life—not glossed over by glory, not absent of mistakes, not as great as it could be—has felt awfully full, as is.

# 6

# GOOD LITTLE CATHOLIC GIRL

*On asking big questions: Do I have meaning?*

THE LAST TIME I WENT TO MASS, IT WAS ASH WEDNESDAY, the first time I'd spent Easter away from home, and it felt about as pious as the dentist appointment you cram in during your lunch break. Sandwiched between a morning class and a meeting later that afternoon, I ducked into an Ash Wednesday service, following a pull that seemed to come from nowhere, especially considering I hadn't been to an Ash Wednesday mass in at least four years. I was, at best, a lapsed Catholic; Catholic born, raised, and abandoned. I went through the service on autopilot, carefully checking that my sign of the cross matched the pattern the person next to me was making, reciting prayers I'd learned a decade ago with the kind of absentminded ease with which you recite a favorite takeout order, or your address. To this day, I have no idea why I felt compelled to go into the church: A strange sense of obligation that overwhelmed me more in that moment than others? The fact I felt I was struggling in other areas of my life and wanted comfort, even if it took a form I was no longer used to?

Mass was a Sunday ritual in my family when I was growing up. We would drive twenty minutes into the backroads of Kentucky to attend the service with my grandparents in a little church sitting high up on a hill the way it would be on a Christmas card. Church was full of memories and most of them weren't great: my First Communion in the second grade, when I wore the pristine white dress that looked unnervingly bridal; when I was the youngest lector, the person who reads passages from the Bible during Mass, and the priest took me aside and, with a kind of solemnity I'd only seen at funerals, asked whether I comprehended the responsibility of spreading the Word of God—I was eleven; the moment teenage me sat in the pew and decided I'd never go to church again, when a priest condemned the suicide of a young person, only a couple years older than me, instead of providing comfort to the congregation. That felt like a confirmation that there had been a moral split between me and this religion, and I didn't step foot in a church for years after. What made it slightly more complicated, as a young adult trying to figure out what it meant to do the right thing in practice, not just in ideals, someone trying to discern the line between what we believe and what we're told, a person balancing the comforting presence of something higher with the practicality that modern life demands, is that I didn't stop believing in God.

Questions of spiritual identity and meaning aren't uncommon during this period of life. "We know that cognitively, [emerging adults] are in a much more elaborative state than they were even in a middle school or high school," Mona M. Abo-Zena, PhD, assistant professor of early childhood education at the University of Massachusetts Boston explained. The prefrontal cortex is thought to mature anatomically during emerging adulthood—meaning that young adults can engage in problem solving, planning, and reasoning on a deeper level. This ties right into spiritual considerations happening during this time of life, when emerging adults are engaging in "metacognition, planning, and abstract thinking, all of which support a more complex understanding of religious and spiritual issues."[1] This stage of development coincides with the time in our lives when we start to stray from, or at least wonder about, the beliefs our parents had put forth for us—for a lot of people, it's when you might move beyond the family home, if that's where you lived prior, or be exposed to new people or friends through work or school. Suddenly, young people who may have been locked into a religious routine that was repressive, or wondered about other beliefs and practices, are exposed to roommates and professors and bosses and colleagues, all of whom come with their own ideologies and existential questions. These different contexts trigger self-reflection, or "self-inventories," as Abo-Zena phrased it, creating tiptoes between questions of the purpose of life and opportunities to create that purpose on our own terms. "I think that for some people, they feel like it's not so important what they're tied to but that they are tied to something; that they have some sort of purpose," Abo-Zena said.

It's not unique to this moment that young adults are asking big questions like "Who am I?" and "What does it all mean?" It feels nearly like a rite of passage to crave meaning, and understanding of your own meaning. Research on meaning in life and well-being among late adolescents showed that "while facing new situations and events, young people try to interpret and organize their experience by identifying significant aspects of their personal and social life, and discovering deeper meanings in their lives."[2] It makes sense, then, that young people would be seeking communities or opportunities in which to explore that.

Religion or spirituality can intersect with multiple parts of someone's identity, familial structure, or personal belief systems, including those related to morality and relationships. For some young adults, any conversation on religion and spirituality is going to have more tangible ramifications, largely because, just as these elements of life can be comforting, community-building, and life-affirming, they can also be dismissive, destructive, and alienating. Young adults have been discriminated against based on their faith, including the fact that 82 percent of Americans say Muslims are subject to "at least some discrimination" in the US today, and 64 percent of Americans say Jews also face discrimination in the US.[3] Others have experienced abuse or discrimination within the context of their own religion, or been made to feel that there's no place for them. A study on religious affiliation and prayer for lesbian, gay, and bisexual emerging adults found that young people who are attracted to the same sex are twice as likely to "disaffiliate from organized religion than their heterosexual peers, but there was little change in prayer."[4] Prayer could be done in the safety of one's home or a comfortable environment. It's also worth noting that religion, spirituality, and meaning-making are going to be defined differently based on who you ask, since different practices hold different meanings for people (and, here, I tried to use the terminology young adults applied to their own beliefs or practices, realizing that others might have different definitions of the same terms). It's one reason that figuring out how we create meaning or develop what we believe in young adulthood felt relevant: The process should be happening on our terms, with the practices, circumstances, and language someone feels comfortable and safe with.

It felt somewhat grounding to know that the questions that suddenly felt more urgent in young adulthood—*What am I doing here? What's my meaning?*—are actually signs that we're maturing, and not that I was the only one without a compass. It's also why we should be deeply skeptical of mocking young adults for this brand of existential curiosity (think "teenage angst"), shrugging off crises of meaning as today's young adults being self-centered. It's like saying they're paying too close attention. It's about meaning-making, and while religious or spiritual practice might be a more structured way to do this, it's not the only way anymore. "We're trying to answer central questions of, 'What does this mean for me? What should I be doing next?'" Abo-Zena said.

Part of that, then, it seems, means reflecting on where we go to ask those questions, because it doesn't always feel built in, by design, to our lives. As a churchgoer, my focus flitted more to following rules and balking at the idea of absolutism—the idea that my religion was supposed to be superior, a talking point that seemed to pop up as often as the rosary was said—than it did to really unpacking any of the questions I had about myself or my life. In childhood and as a teenager, when experiencing what I know now to be grief, that never came up in youth groups, where I would stand awkwardly against the wall and watch others bond over inside jokes about Bible study. The older I got, the questions almost felt too self-focused to even let them enter my consciousness: *Was I a good person, and how did I know for sure? What was all this supposed to mean? For that matter, did I mean anything, and did it even matter if I did?*

For other young adults, they described not looking for answers to questions they had about themselves, but practices that brought out what they already knew was within them. Rather than another pressure to figure out your life, Deana, twenty-two, told me that their spiritual practices, which include journaling and tarot, "tap into things that I feel like I already know, but [I'm] able to articulate them better." They're new to figuring out their relationship with spirituality: While their mother is Pagan, Deana grew up in a household where religion wasn't discussed, and they were an atheist in junior high. Then, between having a terrible experience their last year of college, and graduating into a pandemic and recession, "I've just kind of been figuring out, like, what am I doing? What is the point of doing all of this?" As someone who is anxious and scared of failure, Deana explained, just being able to step outside other people's gaze is significant, creating an opportunity to focus on "Who am I, who is the kind of person that I want to be? What am I like? What is my life purpose?" Deana is part of reproductive justice and abolition movements, and points out there's a tie between spirituality and liberation work for them: Both are movements that focus on others, but Deana said at the end of the day, there's also an element of whether you're in the "right relationship" with yourself. That's the best way you can do this work, they said, and they have realized that's what spirituality means for them. Just like there seem to be precious few opportunities to ask questions we don't already know the answers to, especially introspective ones, what Deana described felt like creating space, time, and practices to allow you to sit with what you *do* know.

Society, in general, places high emphasis on self-reliance and already knowing the answers before the question has even been asked—think: *What do you want to do when you graduate? Where do you want to live? You mean you haven't figured out what you want your future to look like?* Answers that aren't concrete get dismissed as too sappy or too flimsy, which doesn't create a ton of opportunity for us to ponder things that, by default, feel more abstract. By the time I was in my early twenties and firmly out of church, life felt loaded with too much fear: of losing my job, of losing friends, of failing at such a consequential scale I was unredeemable, of being unworthy of the life I'd been given, and thus, incapable of living up to it. I was fascinated by peers who found sanctity in spirituality. I wasn't searching for a Band-Aid, something to slap over my life and call it fixed, or flawless. But I wondered about the idea of grace, or patience, or being able to trust that I could keep going. Something to pull me out of low points when self-motivation was failing me? Something to inspire me beyond just trying to do and say the right thing? It felt almost beyond my comprehension, which, it turns out, is the point.

It seems I wasn't alone in my uncertainty or my search—I wasn't looking to replace church, per se, but I wondered about elements I was craving in my own life that I thought people associated with religion. Over the past several years, surveys[5] have shown that younger Americans are "less likely than older adults to attend church, believe in God, or say religion is important to them," and roughly a third of US teens identify as religiously unaffiliated.[6] When researching what I'd heard other young people reference as "like church" for them—including tangible spaces, like workout classes and gyms, as well as habits, like hosting weekly dinners or scheduled walks in certain parks—I came across research from two Ministry Innovation Fellows at Harvard Divinity School, Angie Thurston and Casper ter Kuile: It sought to look at the organizations millennials, specifically, were moving toward in search of the belonging or spirituality traditionally aligned with religious practice.[7] Specifically, it mapped six recurring themes—community, social transformation, creativity, personal transformation, purpose-finding, and accountability—and looked at organizations including CrossFit and SoulCycle, in addition to groups like The Dinner Party, a community of twenty- and thirtysomethings who bond over significant losses they've experienced while enjoying homemade food together. The organizations, the report said, use secular language *and* mirror much of what a religious community would provide, including "fellowship," "confession," "worship," and "pilgrimage." I'd technically be one of the young people who are religiously unaffiliated—or religious "nones,"[8] according to the Pew Research Center—the report references: Based on birth year, I'm a millennial, and the language used was wording I was used to seeing on sleek website layouts and in email subject lines, usually trying to convince me to buy something that'd change my life. Some of the organizations mentioned immediately reminded me of organized religion by virtue of the fact that, yes, lots of people are finding goodness and community in it, but at least several of those organizations or companies have been accused of some form of misconduct. That factored into the "religious nones" idea, too, that young people might be questioning the institutions themselves, and how their conduct squares with what they literally preach. Six out of ten religiously unaffiliated adults reported that questioning religious teachings is an important reason for their lack of affiliation,[9] and the second-most-cited reason was opposition to positions taken by churches regarding social and political issues.[10] It obviously depends on the church and the young person; plenty of young people mentioned feeling in alignment with what they heard in church, or their spiritual communities, and how inclusive their institution or community itself was. Intrigued by the idea that young people might be creating their own spiritual practices, but still skeptical about some of the communities that housed them, I wanted to know more about the importance of this kind of connection for young adults—and how they might be shaping their own alternative practices, communities, and experiences.

It didn't feel like a question of worship, because we have plenty of that: work, working out, significant others, family members, locations, political ideologies, travel locations, bank accounts, and even social media have become altars at which we can lay ourselves bare and wait for the almighty whatever to fill us up again, to make us whole. We don't have to look far to find something to believe in. Belonging in it, though, felt like a different matter. "We are human beings who crave connection as deeply as water and air and die without it," Angie Thurston, cofounder of Sacred Design Lab and Ministry Innovation Fellow at Harvard Divinity School, told me. "The need for belonging is as profound as it's ever been." People used to be able to participate in a religious community that was a one-stop shop for everything, Thurston said, pointing to things beyond worship and prayer, like finding a babysitter, meeting your partner, and having an immediate community upon visiting or moving to a new city. "Especially young people, who for whatever combination of reasons no longer belong to a religious community like that," she said. "They still need all these things, but they're having to go out and scavenge for them on their own."

Unlike following a formula for belonging, fulfillment, and prayer, it felt like young adults I spoke to were deeply invested in customizing what practices they engaged in, and in turn, how it made them feel—and range itself was a reminder that this should all be a personal process, not an obligation. Harper, twenty-seven, said her mother had a saying: "Everything in life is trivial, and that's why the trivial things matter." Her spirituality helps her pursue that meaning, and what matured her sense of spirituality was actually the study of psychology. "You learn that we have an inborn proclivity toward ritual, and that symbols and mythology are important for us to function as individuals and as societies," she added. "I'm of the belief, and psychological research backs this up, that everything has meaning if you choose to seek it, and pursuing that meaning is what leads to fulfillment." When attending Sunday school while growing up, she felt like the Bible was another book of mythology, something she likened to fables, and has felt that she was a witch since she was a kid. She explained that she tries to keep her spirituality "flexible" because she doesn't believe there is "one truth that works or that we are capable of understanding," which is something that turned her off from the Christianity she grew up with.

Assessing practices or belief systems that were part of your child or young adult years—and how they factor into your life, if at all—is an important part of the equation, too. Curtis, twenty-four, said there's been a "lot of renegotiation" he's been thinking about: He feels the foundation of his own, personal faith is still fairly centered, but he's been considering the application of what that means, how to live that out, and why other people claim the same "foundation" and arrive at very different conclusions about the world. Especially for people who are in their teens and twenties, Curtis said, "you're starting to look at the things that you were raised with, and seeing how much of it you agree with, how much you don't, and how much you're willing to identify of that, how much you eventually want to impart on other people in your life—how much you want to share, and distinguishing those things from each other." Growing up, he described having a very limited perspective of what Christianity was: He was raised in a Chinese American Southern Baptist church, and as he got older and began looking at things more critically, "I started to recognize a lot of the more nationalistic and racist tendencies within American Christianity, and I had a lot of questions about that," he said, including why the extension of grace and love, the crux of *his* Christianity, are only extended to certain people. In a lot of cases, he said, he thinks it goes overlooked that young adults are recognizing that spiritual truths they grew up with aren't being upheld, and are trying to correct them. "In the hyper-capitalist society that we live in, I think so much is placed on our ability as individuals to succeed, essentially economically, personally, emotionally; you're supposed to have all that controlled and handled so that you can produce," Curtis said, and pointed out that lack of rituals can make you feel adrift, like you don't have anything in your life anchoring you besides work. He still attends church once a week (virtually, during the pandemic), and said it has been helpful to have a "place of rest, recoup, and re-centering" every week. It's another means of building that reflection, or process of renegotiating meaning, into our routines.

On one hand, spirituality feels like another extraordinary demand, one where everything has to mean something. But these ponderings can be powerfully ordinary things. Sometimes, who we surround ourselves with when we ask those questions matters as much as the questions themselves. One of the pitfalls of creating your own spiritual practice is actually that lack of community, so, while we sort out what spirituality means to us, *if* it means something, the spaces we bring that to are significant as well.

One of the challenges of what Thurston described as "that context of shallow community and isolation" is that of the interrogation of self (including, Thurston said, *What are my gifts? Who am I? What am I for?*). Those questions have to happen in deep relationship and deep community with others who are doing the same. Otherwise, Thurston said, "it can drift toward a kind of spiritual narcissism." He continued, "That's what we get accused of a lot, generationally, or just narcissism in general, self-involvement." The absence of "containers," as Thurston described them, in which to hold, build, and grow relationships in suddenly has people bringing their deepest questions, most profound pains, and uncomfortable fears into places not traditionally designed to house them. It's why you might find yourself having a deeply personal conversation with your workout instructor, or finding yourself asking a professor whether you should try to begin therapy. These containers also help hold us accountable, another critical element of this kind of community. Life is a lot to handle alone, and it's like we seek out spaces to lessen that whether we know it or not. "This is the only deep community in their lives and they start bringing all the highs and lows of their life to this space," Thurston said. These "deep communities" can look like a lot of different things, it seems. Friendship, yes, but it can also exist in spaces where we gather to be part of something bigger than ourselves. Several young adults I spoke to thought of the arts, including their improv or pottery classes, as their "deep community," and tons of people referenced exercise groups—a walking group, spin, yoga classes, and kickboxing all popped up as places where people had unexpectedly found themselves experiencing a profound sense of community.

Harper said the internet, in general, has been a primary source of community. She explained that she has felt so "alone in the world" since she was a child, and felt belonging had not been granted to her, but instead was something she had to fight for. "I've always done that by asserting myself and taking up space that is generally not afforded to QWOC [queer women of color]," Harper said. "Having an online community through things like blogging and Twitter have become real-life, deep connections. The internet has also helped me learn to explore my spiritual beliefs and find a coven." Among the places she has found that sense of community is PostSecret, a collaborative art project where individuals send in secrets anonymously on postcards. "New ones go up every Sunday, and reading those every Sunday felt like what church feels like for the joyously devout," Harper said. "It's an anonymous, public confessional, not only of our mistakes, but also the pain inflicted upon us, our anxieties, and other things ranging from silly to heartbreaking." What draws her in is that there's no request for absolution, or even forgiveness. The point is being heard. "That is soulful," she said.

Especially during COVID-19, when we became reliant on the internet for everything from work, in some cases, to socializing, the idea of digital communities became more pronounced: Weekly services, communal prayers, and holidays and holy times, including Ramadan,[11] Passover,[12] and Easter, were impacted. Eid al-Adha was celebrated differently for some, including with socially distanced prayer services.[13] Rosh Hashanah and Yom Kippur[14] happened for some via Zoom or livestream. If digital communities are one of our "containers" for finding and fostering this deep community, it seemed that sometimes, this occurs in an ordinary place: on our phones. Some young people described GroupMe chats with their classes or colleagues where they found themselves opening up more than they would have in person; others described reading Reddit posts, which can contain crowdsourced answers to real-life questions, as making them feel less alone. Others talked about Facebook groups, online fan clubs, and Instagram communities they joined based on factors like age or a specific niche interest. At times, unpacking the difference between what was self-care and what was a spiritual practice was complicated, because for some people, they're inherently linked. Needless to say, the line is thin, because turning inward to reflect on our meaning or beliefs sometimes doesn't feel substantially different from turning inward to reflect on how best to care for ourselves. Depending on how you feel, there could be elements to both that feel they involve the soul in some way. In some cases, it's about the meaning we bring to these spaces, even meaning others may not necessarily see.

"I find belonging in finding groups," Alexi, twenty-three, shared. She's one of the lucky people who enjoys spending time with her coworkers, and lunchtime walks or errands with them gives her a sense of community during a boring workweek. As an avid gym-goer, she said she uses "workout classes as church in a way." She described the moment at the end of class—where you stretch and everyone feels a little better—as noticing you spent an hour solely focused on what you were doing in the moment. While she believes in God and considers herself spiritual, she has a "bit of a problem with organized religion." As a born-and-raised Catholic who grew up in the Bible Belt, she felt she witnessed a lot of bigotry and double standards when it came not only to Catholicism, but Christianity in general. "I believe there is a God, but I think religion, since it is created and run by people, is inherently flawed," she said. "I think I really flipped my switch on religion when my dad died. I had prayed for my dad for years and years and years and it was still not enough to heal that relationship or to keep him from dying alone." She understands the comfort of a church community or shared spirituality but doesn't believe in the tried and true Christian mantra that "everything happens for a reason." Particularly for young people who have grown up seeing "thoughts and prayers" scrolling across their timelines as a flimsy response to ongoing tragedy and oppression, this feels like an urge for something more specific—yes, something to believe in, but also ways of manifesting those beliefs and bringing them to your life. That's why the community aspect matters so much.

"Spirituality, I believe, literally cannot be an individual pursuit," Thurston said. It feels a bit like dismissing the solo journey to finding yourself that we've been marketed, where self-reflection often gets spun as wishing to live deliberately in the woods (not a bad thing to want). But what's fascinating is the link between finding our opportunities for meaning-making, which feels like an inherently messy, trial-and-error process, and realizing these deep communities can actually be messy, too. In our conversation, Thurston remarked that it was funny to hear how some people talk about community as if it is this "glossy, sexy thing." Community has to do with the experience of being deeply known and loved—which is often different from the commercialized version of community. "It is mundane, and it is most of the time not sexy; it is messy, uncomfortable, vulnerable," Thurston said. People who have experienced deep community, she said, know that it is "the worst, and it is also the very substance of life."

When speaking to Thurston, I wondered about the last time I'd experienced "deep community." I had friends and colleagues, but wondered about a space that felt like a singular opportunity just to reflect with others who were doing that, too. Instead, I found a log of incidents in which I tried to fix myself through being the appropriate amount of spiritual, present, and good: I thought going to Mass that Ash Wednesday would make me feel better; instead, it made me feel shallow and confused. I thought of the meditation class I took a few months after I first moved. Fifteen minutes in and with every embarrassing thing I've ever done using the silence of my mind to suddenly roll itself on repeat, I was overcome with the same sensation I'd felt all those years in church: Everyone around me is taking away some profound realization, and I'm not. It was as if I was failing at profundity, and by extension failing to forge connection with all the people who were excelling at it.

We turn to spirituality or community or connection for understanding, which makes sense, because we want confidence that everything—including us—is going to turn out all right in the end. But it's more vulnerable than that. "We have, in at least American culture, a very truncated definition of success or what it means to succeed as a human," Thurston told me, so these other things, like a philosophy of living or finding meaning, feel like something we're supposed to explore on our own, if at all. The circle of belonging, she said, is what nurtures us to grow; it halts us from putting the need to succeed in front of worthiness. "Right? That you're not worthy until XYZ," she said. "It's like you start with worthiness, and then you grow from there." I'd even managed to bring that sensation *to* communities that felt designed for centering and reflecting. But it struck me how often young adults described their own practices as exactly that: the absence of striving for worthiness; that whatever practice they held dear, and whatever community they practiced it in, ran deeper than anything that involved effort, aspiration, or a best version of themselves. It's where they were broken and felt safe to show up anyway, where they didn't have to have answers, or even want to find them.

When I heard other young people talk about their own spirituality or belief system as the steadiest thing in their lives, instance after instance, the ways they described spirituality, or rituals, or traditions felt practical. At the heart of it, it seems these things—workout communities, church, tarot, astrology—are tools to get to know ourselves better and encourage a kind of identity exploration.

And as we've seen, those tools appear in all kinds of places. Type "religion" into your phone's app store, and not only do apps on religious history, religious practices, and religious dating pop up, but so do apps more generally aimed at self-care, including yoga, anxiety-reduction strategies, soothing sounds, goal-setting and manifestation journaling, astrology, and palm-reading. Self-awareness, self-knowledge, and self-reflection all sound a lot like searching. But maybe that's what is so illuminating about the focus on searching for meaning in young adulthood: So much of the rest of our lives relies on external markers, guideposts we want to meet to consider ourselves on track, fulfilled, and successful. We're looking for instructions, and maybe instead, figuring out what combination of "tools" makes sense to you in the context of your own life is an opportunity to turn inward and define what matters to us on our own terms. It made me wonder how many of these tools aren't just about bettering a self, but being seen in your own meaning.

Kenyatta, a student and activist, sees meditation as an opportunity to connect to their ancestors, something they explained they haven't figured out how to put into words. "I feel a very deep connection to them," they said. Kenyatta remarked that being near water, grass, or on the ground while meditating draws out that connection, and "it makes me feel almost guarded and safe, in a way." They use the Headspace meditation app once in the morning before scrolling through their phone, once around lunch if their schedule allows, and once before bed, as the app lulls them to sleep by ambient sound. Beyond meditation as being merely an opportunity to hit pause on a Google Calendar filled with school, an internship, and a variety of activism work, there's a decidedly spiritual side to the practice. "I think, especially within communities of color, we're always thinking about being independent and self-sufficient and, like, relying on ourselves," Kenyatta explained. "I think it's okay to be vulnerable. I think it's okay to not be okay. It's okay to cry. It's okay to need help." In their activism work, Kenyatta mentioned constantly dealing with discussions and incidents of racism, sexism, and homophobia, and believes "having a force to lean on is really critical, I think, to staying sane." But recently, Kenyatta has struggled to find time for self-care, because "part of self-care now is taking the time to grieve because we have to spend so much time being on Zoom calls for eight hours a day and pretending to be normal." The only time to really let their guard down is time ordinarily taken for self-care. They broke down crying running errands with a friend upon seeing pictures of George Floyd and Breonna Taylor—that was a moment of self-care, they said, because they hadn't taken time to feel sadness and grief over what happened to them. It's a worthwhile question: Where is grief held? Why is there no space for that, even in the midst of tragedy? About what they wish people were talking about more within this spirituality conversation, Kenyatta said that spirituality is connected to everything else in life. "It can be very easily connected to our race and who we are, and being Black within itself can be a very spiritual experience. And being in community with other Black folks is a very spiritual experience," they added. It's a critical point that still goes overlooked—we are not in a bubble when it comes to our feelings, experiences, and connections; they're interconnected, through different aspects of our identities and different needs we have. Perhaps that's why those containers matter so much: We need spaces to hold the heft of us.

Considering our belief systems in emerging adulthood gives us the capacity to notice that, and reflect on how it shapes us as we make our way in the world. It doesn't have to be overtly sacred and spectacular. Sometimes what's mundane is precious, and what's transformative is small and contemplative rather than explosive and overpowering. There's not a single takeaway, not even "All young adults should form a belief system!" The point is unpacking that—and meaning— for yourself, it seems.

The factors that have gone into my own introspection on spirituality or belief during this time of life, the more I examine them, really aren't big questions to which I'm seeking answers. It's more like: *Can I be small, nothing in the scheme of things, and still matter out there? Can I do good and still be a flawed human being?* When I pray, it sounds less like a recitation or something I know for sure, and more a thinking-out-loud about things I'd never actually say aloud. When I try to build that muscle, or explore communities that allow for some space and self-reflection, I think less about where they fall on the scale of religion, and more about what they bring to my life— where I don't have to have the answers, where I can still be figuring it out. I think of my decade of perfect prayers on bent knees in church pews, recited words uttered in nervous reverence against a backdrop of stained glass. And then, I think of all the other places that have borne witness to my messy prayers that I didn't even know were prayers at the time: bathroom stalls with a broken heart, childhood bedrooms when my future life scattered into pieces, times of terror, moments of joy so overwhelming it was terrifying, on backroads and in open fields, in times I questioned the worth of everything, including myself. Maybe just saying them is enough—maybe that's the point.

# 7

# ONLINE IN REAL LIFE

*On being—and broadcasting—yourself online*

WHAT'S IMPORTANT FROM THE JUMP: THERE ARE EMERGING adults who have never known a life without social media. Posting, storying, captioning, and curating have become part of the dialogue of growing up. It means that social media feels more like a thing to learn to live *with* rather than an ongoing debate on whether we should be on it at all, given that people exchange Instagram handles instead of phone numbers sometimes, entire communities exist in online-only spaces, and some job applications even have a section to list your social media profiles. You'd be hard-pressed to find a young person who doesn't know the toxicity or stressors of social media, and it might be harder still to find someone who doesn't think those dynamics play a role in their online experiences. We know that social media has the capacity to impact how we see ourselves, in addition to how we see others. We also know that what we're seeing often is its own form of reality, existing in a space that can be carefully curated, cropped, and collected in a way lots of other aspects of life just can't be. When talking to young adults about how social media impacted their self-perception, what jumped out wasn't that they feel pressure to post certain things, to show they're having a good time or living a certain kind of way. What was more interesting within the conversation on the so-called digital age was hearing about how some people shame themselves for caring about what others think at all, for not knowing how to be completely honest or "real" online, and whether they're feeding into the negatives of social media by just being on it in the first place. That felt like the heart of the question when it comes to swiping, scrolling, and self-perception: What does it mean to be yourself online, especially during a time of life when we're building those selves?

Social media brings up uncomfortable truths about how we go about the world, in real time: It warps our self-perception, for certain, and not just the perception of toned bodies and flawless skin, but the perception of what life could be—maybe we should be filling them with fluffy bouquets of peonies on coffee tables that never seem to have drink stains, and sweaty and scenic adventures every single weekend while wearing activewear that always matches, and candle-lit bathtubs that never have rings around them. We know there's another side of the story, that the breakups and breakdowns and dusty corners never make the highlight reel, but that doesn't mean it's easy to hold both truths in your mind at once: It seems impossible that there's a less-glitzy version of these people's real lives that we aren't seeing. And since they're posting it, this *is* a version of their real life, at least a crumb of it. So often, social media is punctuated by pangs of "self," and all the things that can encompass: self-awareness versus self-consciousness; self-enhancement versus self-compassion; comparison and self-analyzing and seeking validation all can pour out of our double-taps and shares at various times.

And when it comes to posts we see from others, maybe sometimes it is actually less about what they've posted and more about how you feel looking at it.

After all, in any kind of communication, it's a two-way street, Danielle Ramo, PhD, clinical psychologist and senior director of research at Hopelab, said. "There is what one person intends, and in social media, you can call that what's being posted," she added. "And then there's how someone on the other end interprets that." There are countless interpretations we can make based on a social media post, given filters and social strategies and the fact that social media *makes* money off all of this, and that means young people seeing social media posts are "much more apt to interpret their friends' or others' postings to mean that others might have a life that they don't," Ramo said. This social comparison is so common in adolescents and in young adulthood, anyway, and it seems social media adds another layer.

And it's true that comparison culture has always existed: Maybe for previous generations, whose lives weren't quite so subject to documentation, it looked more like nice cars and ritzy houses, a kitchen to match the Joneses'. Now, it looks like a certain kind of "aesthetic" that manifests in the color scheme of your Instagram grid, the way you pose your body, and a spontaneity that doesn't betray that you posted the photo it took you twenty-five takes to get.

While social media has posited original challenges around privacy, abuse, and the tech world's all-consuming grip on us, it's amplified others that existed before. Beauty standards—mostly thin, white beauty standards—have been around for a long time, but now they follow us around in our pockets *and* on magazine covers. The idea that a certain kind of glamorous life is impressive has been omnipresent even offline, but now, we're able to document every scene, moment, and memory we want to share. It could even be argued that we always want to present our best selves, but isn't that what all of the above is sharing, anyway? When you think of the words that tend to pop up in conversation about young adults and social media—"highlight reel," "likability," "pressure," "sharing," "performing"—the talking point that what happens online isn't "real life" makes sense. But for a lot of young adults, social media is an extension of their real lives, including where they find opportunities to connect and explore who they are and what versions of themselves they want to share with others.

But how much truth should we assign to social media? How much of our "real life" even needs to exist online, and why is there so much pressure to ensure you're real and authentic, especially when you're still figuring out massive parts of your life and identity? Do we actually owe followers and friends real-time documentation of our realest and rawest versions? We're in it and on it, but we're also supposed to be above it. There's this idea that if you care about what you post, or care about what other people think, you've failed to rise above the need for validation that only people with low self-esteem look for. But caring about what other people think is actually a human impulse that doesn't vanish when we log in. "I think we often miss the nuance in the way that young people communicate on social media," Ramo said, explaining there's popular messaging coming from primarily older adults that social media is bad, and young people should simply stay off of it. While people should be aware of the dangers of social media, Ramo said, this is completely unrealistic—not only because social media does actually have benefits, but because "social media is so deeply ingrained in the lives of young people." Social media, and the standards of bodies and lives and selves on it, may be giving us a chance to figure out, and broadcast, what type of person we want to be—something necessary to young adulthood, and more complicated than just logging off.

"In the digital world, emerging adults communicate online with others and portray themselves in ways that can be temporary, facilitating moment-to-moment alterations in one's persona or shared self," Chris A. Bjornsen, author of the chapter "Social Media Use and Emerging Adulthood" in the book *Emerging Adulthood: Current Trends and Research*, wrote.[1] There's no denying that social comparison is built into social media, the research says, but it also notes that those "qualities are also inherent in real-life social relations." On social media, it's happening faster, and on a larger scale of audiences, but as the research states, social media during this age period "serves as an important socialization context in which emerging adults assert their developing autonomy, explore their identity, and initiate or maintain social relationships." We can create selves and perform them; we can embrace who we are and amplify it. Social media, in those ways, gives young people a sense of agency. They are *choosing* to share a piece of themselves, their story—their life is no small deal.

Emerging adults today grew up with a unique consciousness that what we do on social media is absolutely connected to real life. Sometimes, your public persona reveals who you really are—resulting in lost jobs or college acceptances as a consequence of toxic attitudes or unacceptable behavior and abuse coming to light. Some of us have gotten job offers *because* of social media, or received help with medical bills, rent, or picking up the pieces following a tragedy. We've made and kept friends online, and, in some cases, found community in ways we didn't in real life. Multiple people I spoke with talked about addressing a physical or mental health issue they were experiencing on social media, and said that the outpouring of solidarity boosted their self-confidence, while others mentioned feeling liberated by the ability to be honest about their body image or insecurities online, finding solace in networks they didn't know to search for.

Nearly everyone I spoke to about social media expressed a desire to be "authentic" and "real," which runs counter to the idea that young adults *want* their online selves and feeds to function like a highlight reel. Figuring out what that looks like in context is more challenging. "We can paint a very specific picture of our lives," said Lexi, twenty-one, noting that not everybody can have the lifestyle projected on Instagram as the "only lifestyle worthy of having." It's gotten to the point, she said, where she'll only post something that fits a specific, self-curated image. "I want to be perceived in a certain way," she said, adding that apps like Instagram make you think you can control how people perceive you. "I think that a lot of what I struggle with is that a lot of it doesn't feel very authentic. And I think that I'm really aware of that when I post." Shortly after she had a tweet go viral, she hung out with a friend she hadn't seen in a while, and when he mentioned the tweet in real life, she said it was a "jarring" feeling. "I think if somebody was to show me my Instagram on their phone out of context, I'd be taken aback because I think it exists in a very separate part of my brain," she said. Lexi explained she knows it's naive to think she can keep the internet and real life separate, but that it's almost easier to have "those two personalities" when you're picking and choosing what segments to put out where.

For others, the idea of curated imperfection has also become a weird pressure to navigate: Sure, we all might feel pressure to share our "best selves," but what about the pressure to share your behind-the-scenes, to show that you're "real"? "Perfection posts say one thing about you, and vulnerability posts say something else about the 'type of person' you are," Alanna, twenty-seven, told me. Posts sharing vulnerabilities make the poster look "more grounded, raw, relatable, and not so self-centered anymore," she explained, likening it to the *Stars! They're just like us!* feature in tabloid magazines. It makes sense. These perfect moments we see lose some of their charm when we see them so often that we can make jokes about doing something specifically "for the 'gram." But there's a flip side. "The sharing of vulnerabilities that still seem pretty perfect is very real," Alanna said. So, we start to feel a different kind of pressure: the ability to be open and honest and genuine, but in a way that's manageable and understandable enough to fit comfortably on grids and in character counts. Now we don't just have to worry about perfect pictures. The questions get deeper: *How vulnerable can we be while still being protected? What kind of messiness makes us relatable instead of just a mess?*

On the surface, being more honest about our average, ordinary, or even deeply flawed selves in our online presence seems like a no-brainer—the social media equivalent of "get more sleep and drink more water if you're tired." But it's never quite that simple. Sophia Noor Kiser, doctoral student at the Hussman School of Journalism and Media at UNC Chapel Hill, who researches diet culture and the mental health effects of social media, said that when it comes to content, this is the worst: curated imperfection. Many privileged people, often women, pretend to be "super relatable," while having resources and connections most people can only dream of, she told me. "It sets the bar at an unattainable level," she said. "Guess what? I am never going to have skin like that because I will not be spending hundreds of dollars a month on a ten-step skincare routine; I have a kid and I have to buy diapers." The sad thing is that this ideal is really narrow, Kiser said. "If you spend any amount of time on social media, you'll find that the ideal is thin, white, rich, young, conventionally beautiful," she said, adding that when it comes to mental health, all of this is a perfect storm. She uses the example of how this ideal targets young moms, in which everything is cute and perfect, you get your body "back" within a few months just by breastfeeding, set to a color palette of neutral colors and bright light. "Having these ideals to live up to, especially during stressful periods of your life, can result in inordinate stress and exacerbate anxiety or depression that may already exist," she told me.

Even the captions themselves—"Such a mess," "Not perfect, just real," elaborate confessionals detailing the chaos behind the scenes—aren't particularly helpful for combatting the stressor of comparison, it turns out. "I think what's important to think about with disclaimers is that they always accompany an idealized, enhanced image," said Dr. Jasmine Fardouly, a research fellow at Macquarie University whose research focuses on social influences on young people's mental and physical health. This differs from the body-positive movement, she said, because body-positive posters aren't attaching comments on generalized imperfection to still-idealized images; they're promoting body acceptance and challenging narrow, unattainable beauty ideals. "I think that sometimes those things that kind of get promoted as being real are kind of still enhanced versions of people's lives and people's selves, but just not as enhanced as they would usually be," she said. "As enhanced" is the part that's missing from a lot of these conversations: How often have you looked at someone's allegedly fresh-out-of-bed photo and thought, "Whose skin looks like *that* first thing in the morning?" or read a tongue-in-cheek caption about hijinks behind the scenes, like flat tires on road trips or the glossy blue someone is painting their apartment walls staining the floor, matched to an image engineered for effortlessness? Even as vulnerable or imperfect as a post might claim to be, we're still deciding it's shareable. But what we share and how we share it can actually be part of undoing the disco ball effect, where we're glittery versions of whoever we want to be, reflecting the standards and glimmers of authenticity and likability no matter what direction we spin. "I think that if we're really wanting to make change, then people have to be genuine and really show different versions of their appearance, different versions of their lives," Fardouly said.

Sometimes, those different versions can feel impossible. "Since working in social full-time, I've pretty much halted posting on my personal account," Georgina, twenty-four, said. "Curating perfect-looking feeds is exhausting, and to be honest, I don't really have the energy to do it for multiple accounts anymore." Because her job relies so heavily on metrics, she couldn't help but track the success of her personal accounts, too. For many of us, there's no more separation between our "online selves" and "real-life selves." You can order groceries or takeout with a few clicks, then connect with your therapist in a chatroom, and talk to friends on Twitter you speak with daily but have never met in real life. And that can be an incredible thing. But it's also a disorienting one. "Outside of the influencer world, we're told how to present ourselves if we're going to apply for jobs," she said. "You hear of people being rejected for posting bikini pics, rejected for things that an employer sees as undesirable qualities." And yet, she said she's worked at places where individuals were hired, in part, *because* of lives and qualities they presented on social media. "Our profiles now say so much about us, they push past the realms of social media and extend into our lives, too," she added.

Georgina wasn't the only one to bring up that distinction: that "influencer culture" is a split between social media as part of your real life and social media as a fantasy stomping ground for illustrating only the best of you. "Everyone's like, social media is not real," said Brie, twenty-four. "But it is, because it gives you that space to be an actual person." Where it can be harmful, Brie said, is when people are selling you an idea of how you're supposed to be. She thinks social media has changed our lives and what it means to experience the world around us regardless of age; it just looks different across generations. "I've noticed that older generations seem a lot more focused on needing to portray the perfect family and financial stability on social media, for example, than younger generations, where I think we're expected to focus more on travel, romantic relationships, trends," she explained. But that doesn't dismiss the value of it. "It can be like a space where you really discover so many things about yourself," she added.

And it does feel like real life: We use social media to share and communicate and document, including true feelings, thoughts, and insecurities. We have shades of who we are, and just like we bring those shades or versions into real-life interactions, we can bring them to social media, too. Maybe alongside encouraging everyone to take screen breaks and social media cleanses, accepting that it is part of our lives, to be navigated like everything else, good in some ways and terrible in others, might help it feel less overwhelming. Telling young people social media isn't "real life" is supposed to draw the line between reality and what's been photoshopped, edited, and tweaked to protect our self-esteem, but I wonder how much it downplays real, emotional reactions and responses to something someone *is* really seeing, and real connections. There's no doubt our reactions are real, Ramo told me, meaning that if somebody is on social media and it makes them feel bad, that's a genuine feeling. "And if young people are connected to how social media makes them feel, meaning if they're mindful about times when they might be more likely to be depressed or anxious after scrolling through news feeds, it's important that they stay on top of it," Ramo continued, including going through periods of not using it at all or unfollowing people or accounts that make them feel bad.

But that doesn't undercut the fact that young people do use social media to have real, meaningful interactions with each other. "I hear often that young people are able to find a real community and express themselves in a very authentic way on social media, sometimes even more authentically than they would in the offline world," Ramo said. Similarly, Ramo said that she works frequently with the queer community of young people, and while there are risks like targeted bullying of those who are queer, or targeted bullying around ethnicity, there's also a lot of community to be found there. In some cases, social media afforded opportunities to share personal experiences, find safe spaces that may not exist in person, and get support for being who they are. Other people articulated versions of the same thing. Alanna described herself as not having a huge circle of friends in "real life," but said she enjoys "social media for creating little spaces where we can find like-minded people. For some of us that is life changing and can make a world of difference from feeling all alone, to knowing the world has people who are like me and [are] bonding even from a distance." The distance part matters, too. Lexi said she knows Instagram was not built to be good for her mental health, but during the pandemic, without her phone and laptop, "I wouldn't be staying connected to the most important people in my life." And what you see online can have emotional impacts: After all, the sting of betrayal you feel when you see a picture and realize your friends are hanging out without you and the flash of self-doubt when you see someone else's happiness that *looks* more real than your own feels are real emotions that can influence the choices we make and our self-perception.

In my late teens and early twenties, I was horrified by how much I cared who liked whatever I posted. Even while it was happening, it felt embarrassing to grow up online, creating a dated diary of things I'd almost certainly regret later, including photos: underlined lines of *The Great Gatsby* I thought were profound, oversaturated sunset photos, photos of myself I dumped heaps of effort into taking, all for the appearance that I hadn't tried at all. I recall seeing—and frankly, still see—selfies of friends looking like the kind of cool where you strike a pose that doesn't look like a pose, the kind of photo that looks like you got it on the first try. Meanwhile, turning the camera on myself felt so uncomfortable, I tried to make it into a joke, even adding "bad at selfies" into the bio of a dating app I used forever ago, all while regretting not being comfortable enough in my own skin to share moments that felt significant. All the birthday photos I ducked out of, all the group shots where I hid in the back. It's a sheepish admission, in a culture where not caring what people think often feels like the most empowering thing we could do, but I *did* care. Where is the line between not caring what people think in the sense that what matters to you, your comfort in your own body, what you share, stops with *you*, and one more unrealistic expectation that we're supposed to be too cool, too "real" to notice what others notice about us?

"Caring what others think of us is normal," explained Dr. Ellen Hendriksen, clinical psychologist and author of *How to Be Yourself:*

*Quiet Your Inner Critic and Rise Above Social Anxiety.* "I don't find that to be pathological. I think when people rely on others to define their self-image, then that becomes a problem because that is fraught." When we rely on others to define how we see ourselves, Hendriksen said, we give away our power and let them decide who we are based on what they pass judgment on. We have to strike the balance between not-caring-at-all psychopathy and worrying-too-much-what-others-think narcissism. "I think it's totally normal to wonder what people think of us, to want them to approve of us." What a relief that is, to know we aren't alone in wanting to be liked, in wanting to be seen. We can define what we share. But ironically, "being ourselves" online might work best if we all do it together, sharing all our different versions.

Because we can see bits and pieces of the lives of so many others, we can constantly analyze what labels, identities, and appearances might work best for us. It can be comforting when you see a glimpse of you reflected in someone else—a reminder that you aren't the only one—but stressful when you're trying to determine who you are, too. "Don't compare yourself!" falls a bit flat when you can read résumés on LinkedIn and see vacations on Instagram, and "some personal news" announcements of engagements or promotions on Twitter. When we're seeing everyone's best lives and selves so seemingly up close, it's easier to do the backward sort of self-assessment that goes: *Well, everyone is special, and I am not. I should be more of this, and less of that.* And depending on who you are and what you're seeing, that can slide your self-perception under a magnifying glass.

Brie told me she wishes she could remember where she heard the sentiment, but that when she thinks about "what things I feel like I'm supposed to be and how I'm not them all the time," she thinks of the phrase "My edges aren't always gonna be laid." It's partly because, she said, she rarely actually lays her edges down, but also because "a lot of 'Black Girl Magic'" that she sees in the mainstream media is "Black girls with laid edges with little to no frizz in their curls or braids or twists and the dopest makeup and outfits. I want to be Black Girl Magic, but the concept has been commodified in a way that feels like Black girls have to put in more work than I think a lot of us have time for every second of every day, just to be it," she said. "And just being a Black girl is also a lot, because everyone has these different expectations for what they want from you to be an 'acceptable Black girl.'"

A study published in the *Journal of Black Psychology* in 2014 stated that "young Black women continue to feel held hostage to white beauty standards that essentially deem them unattractive and unfeminine."[2] These beauty standards, and life standards, both of which focus on a largely white, "aspirational" image of success in both categories, remain a bulk of what we see in ad campaigns, online in promoted posts, and in what's considered jealousy-worthy lifestyle content. It makes those standards damaging to see over and over again, especially when you're concerned about being your real self and wondering where that's included. Some experts say women are more likely to be judged on their appearances than men,[3] and more specifically, research shows Black women are more likely to be objectified than their white peers.[4] It's impossible to discuss self-image and social media in emerging adults without acknowledging that we exist in a society that discriminates against many, encourages a specific idea of attractiveness and able-bodied-ness, and routinely works to displace people who don't fit the preconceived ideas of what it means to be "attractive" or "competent." We make it profoundly difficult to exist in the world if you don't fit this "ideal," and so many people are left out of what gets seen as valuable or worthy on social media—and real life.

That matters, because social media isn't a one-note experience, and sometimes it feels like there's only so much authenticity you can squeeze into a post you're making the decision to share publicly, so of course you want it to represent you. "I have to remind myself to put that grace onto both me and others, when I'm looking at their posts and what from their lives they're choosing or not choosing to show," Brie added, pointing out that she doesn't think we're entitled to know everything about someone's life, though social media has blurred that line. She thinks knowing she's not required to show her whole life on social media helps ease the pressure a bit.

It should be a given, by now, to know there's more happening behind the scenes—multiple versions of real—than what we see squeezed into a post. It made me curious about what we leave out of what we share. Just on a small, personal scale, I remember posting a picture from a performance I'd waited months to attend, excited to be dressed up and Instagramming a picture of my favorite thrifted teal heels. It was coming off a dark time that had compounded grief and already-existing anxiety, and I'd been eager to do—and post—something that felt light. Upon seeing the post, someone I thought was a friend informed me that if things were *really* that bad, I would've been sharing them, instead. And of course, when you do post about grief, heartache, trauma, or just having a bad day, there's the flip-side narrative: If things were *really* that bad, wouldn't you be too busy navigating it, taking it seriously, to post about it? In either direction, we're sharing too much and too little, all at once.

There's a lot of reasons someone may not post about their "real life." The expectation that if we don't post every single thing that happens to us we're hyper-curating our lives or telling half-truths seems outrageous. It's just reality: The outside, including social media, doesn't always match what is happening within. Alanna has serious health issues that have been on-again, off-again since her teens, despite an outward appearance that was always praised as "perfect and healthy." "It's hard to hear all of this when you're in a constant 'invisible' battle with your body and you feel like it's failing you with all of its issues," she admitted. "It all feels impossible," Alanna said, explaining that she spent a lot of time in her teens and early twenties experimenting with the different ways she was, and could be. She said it's like "one big, impossible, fake, perfect, male-made dream." "I think I was really desperate, in some ways, for someone to really see me, versus just seeing this shiny girl who could be that sort of perfect melting pot of desirable ideas we paint onto women," she added. Getting to see people beyond the "shell," as she called it, is a struggle.

All of this is rooted in an aspirational notion rather than a self-accepting one. And it really is *everywhere*, it feels: in diet culture and fad diets spun as healthy-eating kicks, so prevalent that sponsored ads for an "intermittent fasting" program scrolled across my Instagram feed last week; in the influx of pictures of people beaming at music festivals or posing at after-work drinks, causing you to wonder why the bags under your eyes are so much more apparent than those of everyone in the picture, or why you can't muster the energy to go out after work; in reminders that if you follow this plan or follow these people, they'll show you how to live your life in the same spectacular fashion they do. Body image obviously plays a significant role in this pressure, but the idea of "best lives" broadcasted online doesn't stop with how we look. It's also the feelings we present, the best life we choose to share, and a whole lot of external comparisons that leave us wondering why we're messy, impossible, and unfixable when everyone else seems so *flawless*, or, at least, manageably flawed.

What we post does matter. And what we see matters, too: While comparison creates chaos, representation can go a long way in helping people feel seen. Though the hyper-visibility of our online lives might suggest otherwise, feeling seen is a big deal. It doesn't happen all the time, and it doesn't happen for everyone. Social media can be an outlet for making that happen.

We know online representation—seeing people who look like you— plays a role in how we see ourselves, Kiser told me, adding that we know seeing people who look like you can affect feelings on belonging or safety. But the question researchers are asking is whether that translates to social media. "The dichotomy between how you see yourself and how society sees you is always present. From a psychological perspective, embracing flaws, or better yet, ceasing to even think of them as flaws, can be good," she said, noting that it's discouraging to see how segregated the process is online. Kiser said when it comes to embracing flaws, what may determine if you perceive something as relatable versus performative is the degree to which you relate to the person posting: "A plus-size model posting about her cellulite is going to hit different than a random friend of yours . . . The model has already gained validation for her body in other ways, so posting her 'flaws' doesn't really diminish her worth in the eyes of society." Whether those "flaws" are acceptable depends on how the person fits conventions in other ways.

Seeing elements of other people's lives and reflecting them onto your own doesn't have to be an inherently negative thing, just as caring what people think isn't automatically a character flaw. Seeing people who look like you, or looking at other's posts that capture a feeling you've had or something you've experienced, can feel comforting, and even freeing. As a trans woman, Norah, twenty-two, explained that a lot of her experience in regard to her transition has been figuring out how to present herself to other people and to the world, including taking bits and pieces from the styles of other cis or trans women and incorporating them into her style. "I feel like it says a lot about social media," she added. "Because it's kind of like, I feel like my own construction project sometimes." That construction has felt necessary just in order to survive, Norah said, explaining she does post some stuff on her own identity and self-image, because she feels seeing trans beauty on social media is important for people beginning their own transitions. As Norah pointed out, images have historically portrayed an ideal of white and class privilege that can be detrimental, especially in terms of body image. "I think that a good solution or just way out of that line of thinking in representation is just more visibility and representation for Black trans women, for fat fem trans women, and drag queens, just people who kind of defied the norms of beauty standards," she said. It's about the freedom to be and illustrate who you are, and it should count for more than pressure to confirm to a certain ideal.

That means having the freedom to define yourself, too. "The older I get, the more I see on social media, I'm like, 'Oh, okay . . . it's fine to say Black,'" Brie told me. "It's fine to say I am a Black girl. It's fine to give these identifiers and also not have that be the only defining trait that I have." As an example, Brie cited growing up watching Tia and Tamera Mowry on *Sister, Sister* and being able to think, "That's probably what it's like to a fourteen- or fifteen-year-old Black girl," she said. By the time she actually made it to that age, she said there were far fewer Black girls on TV, so she had fewer opportunities to imagine what being twenty, and so on, would be like. What she did have was Tumblr. So much of her understanding of other Black girls, she said, beyond herself and people she went to school with, came from "looking on social media and seeing how Black girls were interacting with each other. It was exciting for me, because it felt kind of [like we were] figuring it out together," Brie said. It felt like social media at its best: not pressure to be a single, standout version of yourself but a reminder that you're not alone.

For as much as there's community in it, what came up repeatedly about social media wasn't just the idea of feeling seen—it was the opportunity to illustrate how we're different. It's so much of the young adult experience: *What makes me me, and what can I share about myself—online or off—that shows you that?* Especially when so much on social media feels like versions of the same thing—the same joke on Twitter about Oxford commas, the same Instagram picture of a certain café—what we share online can also serve as a definer in the sense that we're *different*, something I heard about repeatedly, from the kinds of photos someone posts to the Spotify playlists they share. While there's certainly beauty and life standards that dump on the pressure to conform and meet them playing out online, it also feels as though there's pressure to be unique, something our digital presence gives us an opportunity to thumb through and handpick. Because the "Young people want to be special!" talking point always seems connected to Instagram likes, at least in popular discourse, looking at the ways we project versions of ourselves felt necessary. Because maybe the whole impulse to stand out can come from a vulnerable place of wanting to be seen.

"'Special' implies standing alone," Dr. Hendriksen told me.

"It implies different, or apart, or otherwise set apart from others. And the flip side of that is isolation. So, I think that when we put so much emphasis on individuality and setting ourselves apart, we also set ourselves up to be quite lonely." When the hierarchy is flat, Hendriksen explained, where we don't have to scratch and maintain our elevated place, we allow ourselves to be part of the community instead. "When we just allow ourselves to be real as opposed to being impressive, then we actually connect so much more easily," she said. "I guess the silver lining of being average, or the positive of embracing average, is that you build in your guaranteed community." While Hendriksen noted we have to choose our audiences carefully and consciously, sharing our average or flawed selves can be met with support and validation, and that disclosure—the spoiler to shame, which threatens us with staying locked down and locked in—not only can help us feel better, but also help us connect to people.

It feels like, as long as we're using it, we might as well reconsider how social media can help us merge the two. If we can realize our problems aren't unique or horrifying, Hendriksen said, and we can bond with somebody else over our shared insecurities, that's a basis for community. It's why the body-positivity movement continues to grow, why subcultures continue to gain steam, and why online communities, centered on everything from hair care to navigating chronic illness, expand. Why movements have been organized online. Why fandoms have been built via Instagram and Tumblr accounts. Why the answer to unpacking societal beauty, image, and life standards (and the facets of online life, including abuse, harassment, and whose voices and images get highlighted that perpetuate these standards) that unfold on social media doesn't always mean dismissing it outright. Instead, it deserves critical examination with an objective eye about what we see and why it could be the way it is.

There are a dozen ways social media can make us feel lesser, a million means through which we can distort ourselves, hiding what holds shame and stepping into the selves we have the unique power to alter, filter, and present. It's bigger than "Just be authentic." Social media, home of the #bestlife, might be an opportunity to try on the kind of people who inhabit what life truly looks like—a spectrum of things. Messy; funny; some days an open book, other days quiet; vulnerable not because we feel pressured to spill our secrets online to prove we're deep or real, but vulnerable because it's a means of connecting with each other. Buried beneath the comparisons and FOMO, social media can be a means of showing yourself and others who you are, and feeling it echo back. It seems like a worthy opportunity to evaluate who you're following, what you're seeing, and how it makes you feel. That's what demands to be noticed.

# 8

# HEARTSICK

*On dating, choosing, and love*

MY SOCIAL MEDIA FEEDS WERE PEPPERED WITH PEOPLE MAR-
rying their high school sweethearts, swaying under fairy lights in a
converted barn lit with mason jars, when an ex-boyfriend from high
school texted me from a number I'd long deleted to see "what I was
up to these days." While some people were talking about "swipe fatigue," or dating burnout, others were pondering if they'd ever meet
the right person, and what the "right person" even meant. A stranger
someone met once liked six of their Instagram pictures in a row, an
action we have to pretend not to decode. A long time ago, when I
told a friend, who was living with her significant other, that I was
tired of breezily acting like it didn't hurt my feelings when the person
I'd been "talking" to for months popped up on Instagram with their
arms around someone else, or brushing it off when I was someone's
lesson—the Big Thing they had to learn about how to treat people
before moving on to find their One True Love—she leaned forward
with urgency, offering up the standbys of "You're still so young" and

"Now is the time to focus on yourself." Meanwhile, elsewhere, old family friends were stopping me in the grocery store to ask if I was "seeing anyone special," which is code for "Are you anywhere close to getting married?" Ah, modern love.

Particularly with dating apps—which have become somewhat of a lifeline for meeting new people for a lot of young adults during the pandemic—we have the ability to broaden our social circles, a marvelous opportunity for freedom in choice and one that stings if you fall into an endless sprint of swiping you don't want to be in. Somewhere in the middle of a thousand headlines and dating tips and vague references to "sowing your wild oats" versus "settling down," there was a lesson on dating I wish someone had told me back when I went on a first date at sixteen, to a Panera Bread, where I unashamedly picked up the bread bowl and bit directly in. The messages I heard most about dating centered around one idea: *We don't control our hearts*. It's, as a million scenes have described it, bigger than us and all-consuming and overpowering and worthy of chasing someone through an airport, logistics of luggage and making it through security checkpoints be damned. And it sounds like relief—like if we're going to have soul mates, it'd be so nice to have them assigned to us. We could avoid bad first dates, like the one where a guy argued for twenty minutes that my name isn't a real first name, or true heartbreak, the kind that makes us wonder if our feelings are really fixable, or if we'll be stuck staring at the empty space where the person used to lie in our bed forever. But the most startling realization about dating and love and relationships I've had in young adulthood is how much of it *is* about our choices. "You can't control your heart" may be a romantic notion, but it's not always helpful, nor is it realistic. We *do* control our hearts, or at least, where we want to direct our hearts' efforts. That's the ordinary part, the terrifying part: naming what we want, whether it's a relationship or dating multiple people at once or even that, yes, we might want to "settle down," whatever that means. Having the power to say, "I'm choosing this person, I'm choosing these circumstances," is unnerving, especially in a dating culture where entire business models have been created specifically to convince us we have an endless array of options, and that if we just keep looking, we'll find *it*. Epiphanies about what you want in another person don't feel as profound as having epiphanies about yourself, especially during the time of life when you're supposed to be discovering who *you* are, as an individual, not as a partner or a significant other. But why aren't those things parts of us, if we want them? Who is to say our choices—and learning what we want and how to ask for it—about who and how we date *aren't* as critical as choices made about cities we'll live in or jobs we interview for?

For young adults, falling in love, or even wanting to, is sometimes spun as leaving the party early. It puzzled me as a teenager, whenever I heard (some, obviously not all) older people remark that these relationships didn't matter anyway; it was practice for later. Maybe they didn't matter in a benchmark sense—because marriage is still seen for so many groups as a sort of milestone, a finish line, there's a particular line of thinking that if you don't end up marrying someone, you wasted your time dating them. (Never mind that, you know, not everyone wants to get married, and marriage doesn't necessarily make a relationship more significant.) But the experiences we have in relationships during young adulthood seem unquestionably important. That includes the positives—like fond memories of awkward kisses in the parking lot of the movie theater, learning to ask for what we want, or figuring out how to care for someone while caring for ourselves—and the negatives, including heartbreak, shaming, and abuse. The relationships of young people aren't immune to these things.

The significance of relationships carried into my twenties: It didn't matter whether something was classified as "serious" or not (whatever that means); the impact was still there, whether it was a cathartic conversation with friends after a dismal first date or a big realization about what you want out of dating in the first place. Rose Wesche, PhD, assistant professor in the Department of Human Development and Family Science at Virginia Tech, said that in addition to influencing well-being, there are examples of how relationships influence our development. In her opinion, one of the most important functions of romantic relationships is developing romantic competence—a term I wish I'd known at least five years ago. According to Dr. Wesche, it includes insight, or knowing what we want and need; mutuality, knowing both partners have valid needs; and emotion regulation, being able to regulate our responses to events. "We learn these skills from interacting with our partners, and we carry these skills into our future relationships," she added. When I looked at a slide Wesche shared, one presented in her lecture on dating in a Middle Childhood and Adolescence class, on what developmental purpose dating serves, it became obvious that dating in young adulthood shouldn't be dismissed as superficial or secondary if we're choosing to do it. Among those purposes were autonomy, self-concept, intimacy, and companionship. "Many of these apply to young adulthood, too, such as learning about your sexuality and becoming a good sexual partner, developing a concept of yourself as a romantic partner, and connecting to new peers through your romantic partner," Wesche said.

It's hard to rattle off all the misconceptions surrounding dating, but there's a myth that if love doesn't effortlessly find you it won't be as good as it *could* be, and that if you aren't always looking, there's something sad about you. We hear a lot about people choosing *us*: Particularly for women, this "training" of how to be the perfect-seeming choice still persists—how to be polite and the right amount of funny and not too loud, but also not too quiet, because then you're a wallflower, how to be cool enough to "catch" a date and serious enough to "keep" him (because, in these heteronormative, gender-stereotyped tropes, it is *always* a him, apparently). Having the agency and resolve to find a partner on your terms is getting more airtime now—because people are refusing to do it the other way—but this pressure persists. That includes in young adulthood, where no matter what you do, you're either taking dating *too* seriously, or not seriously enough. Even among all the well-meaning advice on putting yourself first, there's a thought that deserves more attention when talking about dating in young adulthood: that we have agency as we search for our partners. The idea that love is a choice is powerful, not just in terms of how we date, but for how we carve out our worlds and feelings as young adults, too.

Swiping, scrolling, double-tapping, messaging, ghosting, catfishing, breadcrumbing: It even sounds exhausting. Dating and relationships have become choices young adults make instead of milestones to be chased and met, something we define on our own terms rather than labels of relationship statuses we are defined by. And that's why they matter so much. One of the issues at the heart (pun intended) of dating in this phase of life, it seems, isn't whether or not we do it—whether you prefer being single or in a relationship—or even how we do it—meeting in person, via apps, or some combination of the two. It's the dismissal of focusing our time and attention on relationships during this stage. When we become our extraordinary selves first, we'll meet someone extraordinary, the idea goes. There's a sense that there's still more we need to know—about ourselves, about our needs, about what we want—before we can *really* commit to someone else, whatever that version of commitment looks like. It can feel like you have a lot to lose: your independence, your precious time, your sense of self, even. What a terrifying thought: to lose yourself in another just as you were figuring that self out. For a long time, that's how I thought about it: I needed to be entirely self-reliant before I could earn love.

Turns out, that wasn't just me. In the US, there's this kind of individualism where "you have to figure out who you are as an individual, and then you can be good in a relationship," said Ellen Lamont, PhD, an assistant professor in the Department of Sociology at Appalachian State University, whose research examines how gender and sexuality shape people's hookup and relationship behaviors. Research[1] comparing the United States to the Netherlands showed a striking contrast, Lamont said, in regard to how individual self-interest versus being interdependent manifests in relationships, because there's a difference between balancing self *with* other, and in the US, it tends to be "self versus other."

It's as if you're an individual in opposition to others as opposed to being an individual in the context of your community and your relationships. "It's almost like Americans don't learn how to [say], 'Yeah, you can do things for yourself. And also you have to consider the effect of what you're doing for yourself on other people,'" Lamont explained. That felt like more nuance in what's often presented as an all-or-nothing: We've all had the friend who seems to abandon their friend group and interests at the start of a new relationship (or, if we're being honest, have slipped into that ourselves), or felt the pressure to get everything about our lives situated before letting someone in. But it felt to me like a good reminder that how we date (and who) can make us more of who we are, not less. Lamont said one solution to this would be teenagers receiving more guidance on this idea of balance—and how you have to learn how to balance competing needs versus "this idea of, 'Oh, during your twenties, you concentrate on yourself. And then during your thirties, now you're married and what are you going to do? Self-sacrifice the whole time?'" That's expected of women in particular anyway, Lamont said, and so we never learn how to do both at once. Yes, focusing on yourself, your needs, and your life is important. Focusing on how you feel in relationships, your likes, dislikes, and preferences, how you operate in relation to other people, how you navigate conflict and compromise, and how you love and want to be loved matter, too.

Knowing ourselves well is critical to the choices we make, including about partners and relationships. Some research actually cites the "achievement" of intimacy within a romantic relationship as a developmental task of entering adulthood,[2] and one 2018 study in particular found that young adults who were able to maintain positive, intimate relationships tended to be better adjusted later in life. The study focused on two aspects of young adult romantic relationship competence: developing of "strong, loving bonds" with a partner, and relationship problem-solving skills.[3] Even with the romance element taken out, it's a slate of skills important to navigating relationships of any kind.

But what's complex about dating in general is there is no single "right" way to do it. And during emerging adulthood, amid so many significant life transitions, dating definitely doesn't look like just one thing: Half your friends are debating whether the person who refuses to meet in real life is catfishing them, and the other half are getting married or picking out furniture together. Depending on cultural, religious, or social and family expectations, relationships can come with an additional layer of pressure for young people who don't feel their formative relationship choices are being made entirely on their terms. While research[4] points out that dating during the early adult years enhances identity formation and offers socialization experiences necessary to maintaining interpersonal relationships in life, that doesn't happen the same way for all young adults. Expectations surrounding premarital sex, public displays of affection, cohabitation, or even choice of partner are often intertwined with religion and culture. Not every young adult views dating as aspirational, or even explorational—for some, it's a means of upholding familial obligation; for others, it exists entirely outside their control. Some experts say[5] that shared values, culture, and traditions are critical parts of sustaining relationships, not unlike how it seems determining what values matter to you is a key part of young adulthood. And some aspects of one's culture, ranging from how you'd raise kids, if you ever want to have them, ideas about gender roles, finances, and broader values, like religious beliefs and familial involvement, can directly impact who or how you date. Relationships and dating relate to our identities in more ways than one, including that the different factors of your life, beliefs, and what you want aren't separate from how you might perceive dating or relationships.

In a study[6] that looked at parental factors' influence on interracial relationships of emerging adults, which looked at a cohort of individuals from 1994 to 2002, one of the things authors of the article found was that, in some dimensions, parents can continue to influence their child's relationship choice via closeness and control, which was "most evident for white men, Black women, and Hispanic women." The idea of young people being "independent" from their families—and making relationship choices not influenced by factors that are part of your family dynamic—ignores young people who continue to reside near or with their families, including the fact that "as family co-residers are disproportionately racial or ethnic minorities, immigrants or the children of immigrants, and from working class backgrounds, the assumption of family independence ties to reliance on predominantly white middle-class samples in emerging adult research." In terms of family, some young adults described other elements of involvement: that their familial relationships illustrated examples of the kind of relationships they didn't want to have, or that distancing themselves from their family, and developing a chosen family, gave them the confidence, freedom, and support needed to explore their sexuality or dating preferences. Dating apps have changed who we can meet and where we meet them, but the communities we're in can also influence how we date.

Just personally, I dated in my hometown, where you knew *everyone* and probably their parents, too, and it was a challenge not to feel left out and left behind if you didn't end up engaged to your high school sweetheart by the time you both graduated college—even if you weren't entirely convinced that's what you wanted. I dated in bigger cities, where it seemed like a feat of endurance to meet *anyone*, let alone see them twice. It became a sort of routine: I'd feel sorry for myself that I was going to end up all alone, then guilty for being sad about that instead of empowered, then justifying all the reasons I didn't need a relationship and repeating the cycle. Irritated by my own yearning for partnership during a time I should be riding solo, I threw up excuses—my introversion, my independence, even my chronic illness—for talking myself out of the dating game. *I love my career*, I'd tell friends, as if you could only love one thing at a time.

*I don't need anyone,* I would say to myself and puff out my chest, because I wanted to prove it was true.

But it's possible to not *need* someone, and still want someone. It stings to say aloud, for fear of sounding desperate or seeking or clingy: *I want love; I want to be loved.* And it's loaded, in young adulthood, when so much feels subject to change and letting someone into the most vulnerable parts of your life can feel risky, impractical, and immature. In reality, the cultural pressure to have a partner is strong. It feels as though in your teens or early twenties, dating shouldn't matter at all; by the time you've shifted into the early-mid-twenties range, you need to have this locked down—and some people mean that literally. It seems like part of where all this stigma really manifests: that if you're single, you're "behind," or that if you aren't dating, surely you're *looking.* The dichotomy is confusing and manages to gloss over what feels like a simple but significant truth: Dating can matter without being a pass-or-fail thing, and the most important timelines we set for how we date, how we love, and how we grow together are the ones that feel right to us.

Joining me on Google Hangouts from the place she shares with her partner and their dog, Maggie, twenty-six, told me she thought feeling guilty, or even superficial, for wanting a partner and not being entirely independent all the time was a "total thing." She has a successful work and academic life, one that provided her the opportunity to live abroad for a year, a choice her partner enthusiastically supported. One of the biggest realizations Maggie had abroad was that she wanted to move home to be with her partner after the year was up. "And it, actually for the first time, felt like I was following my own path and my own kind of destiny that way," she explained.

For so long, young people—especially young women—were told that ending up with someone was the ultimate goal and, much like moving out of your parents' house (which, for a time, was also related to dating and marriage), needed to happen in a certain time frame. In an attempt to correct that messaging, sometimes it feels like picking the scenario for your life that prioritizes a relationship is failing in reverse. Young adults I spoke to cherished more nuance in terms of their relationships and dating practices—namely, that a relationship could be significant without having to be *everything*. It's okay to want someone to lean on, to share the hard stuff and good stuff with. For some young adults, their partner plays that role. When Maggie was negotiating her job and was unenthused about how those negotiations were going, her partner said they'd support her if she wanted to search for something else. "And that was an incredibly adult kind of moment for me, that I was like, 'Oh my god, someone's going to help take care of me,'" Maggie said. She is financially independent from her partner, but the support felt like someone believing in the decisions she was making. While Maggie said dating may not be for everyone, dating was a "radical form of self-love," which, in part, is "admitting you need other people and admitting you want someone to care about you."

Though it doesn't get discussed as often as the perils of pithy opening lines or enough dating terminology it warrants a dictionary, Maggie touched on something equally important: making a decision based on what you want out of a partner, or out of a relationship. To her, choosing to move back home and move in with her partner *was* a form of finding herself, of pursuing the path that felt right to her.

"Sometimes I would be in my relationship, and I'd be like, should I be looking for something else?" Melissa, twenty-two, shared with me. The follow-up came swiftly: She was happy in her relationship. "Why do I always have to be thinking, oh, maybe there is something else, maybe there is something more?" There's this sense that when you reach your twenties, or a "self-exploratory phase of your life, where you're figuring things out," as Melissa described it, that means reconsidering your partner, too. But she said she and her partner had grown together—she made a choice, she explained, to be in a relationship with someone, and love someone, and over the years, that commitment has changed. But "getting to explore phases of our lives together is new, is exciting. It is not boring," she added.

Speaking of choices, some young people are choosing not to date altogether, focusing on fostering their other communities or their friendships. Others expressed that being able to safely date who they wanted for the first time—free of bigotry or harm from family, peers, or communities that judged them because of their sexuality—was a form of freedom, in which experimentation felt like getting to build who they really are. Because emerging adulthood is a time of heightened self-focus, Wesche said, the idea of multiple possibilities could explain why emerging adults feel pulled in different directions with their romantic relationships. "People's lives diverge in many ways—some people go to college, some start jobs, some get married, some move, some experience emotional, relational, or financial struggles," she said. "For many people, forming a committed long-term relationship represents a transition to adulthood, but given the many paths emerging adults take, it may not be a practical or desirable choice for everybody." "Choice" feels like the key word in all of this. There are internalized personal pressures and societal pressures, and they make navigating expectations around dating confusing.

Some of those pressures are deeply embedded into our heteronormative, highly gender-stereotypical perceptions of dating. Riley, twenty, said she identifies as gay, and for the longest time, she felt there was a pressure to be in a relationship, like you have to be dating somebody. "But then, when you aren't dating somebody it's like, 'Oh no, you should be experiencing, like, all these people and going out in your twenties' and that's just so not fun, either; it's not realistic." Then, Riley noted, if you're in a relationship, there are ample expectations of how it is supposed to be perfect. Media, including how film and TV portray relationships, make it difficult, she thinks, because they assign so many expectations and leave so little room to show that relationships can be messy and difficult. "With my own relationships, since they're queer, I just don't know how to navigate that, because there's no representation of that, either," Riley added, noting the lack of representation of queer relationships in media. Before she came out, Riley used to date men, and while being with women or nonbinary people feels right to her, "The gender dynamic is gone. Like, what do we do?" Riley wondered aloud about who is going to hold hands first, who is going to make the first move in terms of asking "What are we?" and making introductions to families. And there's a whole other layer of pressure Riley described— safety. "Will somebody call us a slur? Will somebody make a face at us?" Especially when the couple is back in their conservative hometown, Riley said it's scary.

At the structural level, Wesche said, "relationship and sexual education typically focus on heterosexual relationships, and there are few media representations of same-sex relationships," an echo of what Riley had mentioned of not seeing her own experience reflected in so many media-based presentations of dating. Dating is linked to the exploration of identity, which is critical, but as Wesche pointed out, discrimination creates additional stressors that can make LGBTQ+ young people vulnerable in relationships. Dr. Lamont noted LGBTQ+ young adults experience things their cisgender peers may not—notably, she mentioned research she is currently working on, in which some young adults expressed not having the chance to experiment in high school the way they wished they could have, and a lack of social spaces designed for LGBTQ+ people that aren't centered on activism. Some of her other research, which she wrote about for *The Atlantic*, also explained that because many "LGBTQ relationships do not rely on well-established ideologies, norms are often considered, questioned, and then rejected, with the aim of making space for egalitarian practices instead."[7] In contrast to the pressure on heterosexual individuals to date, marry, and do it all in a certain order or certain way, Lamont's piece in *The Atlantic* outlined how LGBTQ+ people she had interviewed wanted a different model for partnership that didn't follow social scripts connected to gender inequity.[8] That's huge, and can be seen in everything: who pays for meals, who does more of the housework, whose schedule takes priority when planning things, the "timeline" for getting married—as if that's an end goal for everyone. "So what I'm stuck on is, how do we shift what people feel love and commitment looks like in practice so that it can then reflect more egalitarian values but still feel romantic?" she said. Lamont explained she thought the LGBTQ+ community is doing better with that, the idea that it's romantic to come together equally.

Finally being with someone who makes her comfortable with herself is so rewarding, Riley said, because she was so anxious with other people. "I think that's because I knew deep down it wasn't right," Riley added. They mentioned it's different in queer relationships, in regard to firsts and milestones, but the physical and emotional aspects feel much more comfortable for them. "There's pressure, but that's coming from a very heteronormative spot," Riley added. "Stopping and thinking about that and then throwing it away is freeing." The element of having the autonomy of choices—doing what you want to do, not what you think you should do—feels like one of the single most important elements a young person could have in a relationship. Love, or wanting someone to take care of you, to be in the boat with you, takes myriad forms: Romantic relationships don't look just one way and we know that a significant other can't fill every need we have—even your "perfect" partner cannot be your friend, your financial advisor, your therapist, and your parent. Equality isn't a box check where you swap times paying for dinner and consider it a done deal, but an ongoing assessment and commitment. And the pressures facing young adults and dating aren't all self-created. Acknowledging that should be a chance to reimagine how we want dating during this time of our lives to feel.

"I believed in soul mates the way I used to believe in God, because I was told it was real at a young age and just took that as fact," Caroline, now thirty-one, said. She had a string of mostly long-term, monogamous relationships from her teen years onward. Some years back, when she was in a fraught relationship, she found herself in the back of a rideshare with a married friend whose spouse had previously been divorced. Her friend mentioned she didn't believe in soul mates. "She said it was about being open and in the right place in life, the other person being in the same or a similar place and headspace, and choosing to be together, stay together, and put in the work," Caroline explained. When the relationship she was in ended,

Caroline said that outlook helped her look at relationships with less pressure. "I didn't feel like my one shot at true love was over—I realized I could have many true loves in the future," she said. "Many true loves" felt like heaving a sigh of relief: The idea that this isn't a single-shot love story, that our loves can be as diverse and complicated and ever-changing as we are, feels freeing. Riley echoed a similar feeling: "I've heard a lot of doubts surrounding your 'forever person,' which I think I agree with a bit," they said. "I think overall people are meant to come into your life to teach you things, and if they leave then that's meant to be, but if they stay, that's all the more rewarding, because you know they're worth it."

On the flip side, hearing about people's dating app experiences, and how so many of them felt there was always someone else to find, made me wonder about when dating and the idea of many loves transitions from freeing to exhausting. It's where terms like "swipe fatigue," "dating burnout," and "relationshopping" stem from— that addictive idea that there's something, or, in this case, someone, better. It doesn't seem all that different from other pressures to become our "best selves"—it's not necessarily that a good date or good relationship isn't enough; it's that a *great* one could be just around the corner. If relationshipping, or serial monogamy, gives people chances to work through things, relationshopping is about "picking out the right person," Skyler Wang, a sociology PhD candidate at UC Berkeley, explained. One way of thinking about it, Wang said, is "relationshipping is about making someone the one, whereas relationshopping is about finding the one." The term seems to ring true in places ranging from academic research[9] to Urban Dictionary, but anyone who has dated within the last few years has likely felt a version of relationshopping. You date a person for a month or two, and realize something is not quite right, or you start wondering if there's someone out there who knows where you want to eat without being told. "Your immediate orientation isn't to be like, 'Okay, I need to work through these disagreements or differences with them,'" Wang said, adding that the reaction is to restart the search. "It's almost like treating every person as an object," Wang explained, likening our dating culture to fast fashion. "If your shoes are broken, you don't go and get it fixed now. You just buy another pair."

There's a world of difference between working through problems in a relationship and staying in a relationship that is fundamentally incompatible or abusive. Staying isn't always right or mature, and that needs to be said over and over. Generally speaking, the advice is about not succumbing to the idea that "good" isn't enough if "great" is a hypothetical option. The idea that we're always looking—or always have to be—is stressful, and it creates a neverending search that often reduces our ability to choose what we want to do, even if that choice is not dating anyone. And sometimes, it becomes easy to forget that what you're looking for can change.

If your reaction to "What we're looking for can change" was "Good lord, I hope so": same here. When I was in my late teens, what drew me to someone were the titles of books on their shelves and what music they listened to and whether they wanted to "travel," whatever that means for a teenager. I spent way too much time pretending to feel some deep love of Radiohead that I misguidedly thought pointed to depth, and fell, multiple times, into the trap of thinking someone knew who I was better than I did. I spent a lot of time listening—because I wanted to be listened to; I spent a lot of time pretending I could walk through my life, following someone else, and holding up a mask of what I ought to be. Now, books and music are like icebreakers to the ordinary things I feel strongest about: *How does this person treat other people? Are they hearing what I'm saying when I talk? Who makes me feel more like me—not better than, not changing shape for?* I don't want rooftop dinners and spontaneous Airbnb bookings for a vacation where you've got the ocean on one side and a pool on the other. I want a partner who puts on music while we do the dishes together and remembers that lemon VitaminWater is what I like to drink when I'm sick. And yet, how would I articulate that's what I was looking for? Even asking myself the question made me feel sheepish, like I was putting too much thought into it. After all, we're supposed to be casual and unaffected—an amped-up version of "When you're least expecting it, it will happen!" as though the only real kind of love worth having is the kind that falls in your lap out of nowhere. That emphasis on effortlessness has always been more of an extraordinary aspiration than a reality of dating. Dating has always involved some element of reaching out, of work. But now, we can almost see the work in real time: the amount of time we spend swiping on apps, the different ways we edit ourselves via photos or bios, the manner in which we're taught to constantly analyze whether there's someone better out there for us, or if we should want anyone at all. The risks of "Just put yourself out there!" or "It's not you, it's them!" feel more loaded when you're still in the process of negotiating yourself with yourself: *Am I funny enough, or cool enough, or personable enough? Am I a loser for feeling lonely instead of self-governed and self-sufficient in my solitude? If I admit I need, or want, someone else, what does it say about me?*

Dates aren't just a thing we go on, and relationships aren't just experiences that happen to us, the way you might get caught in the rain. My lightbulb moment came in the midst of Bumble swipes and trying too hard to convince boys who knew my name in high school

that they'd love the person I grew up to be: I wish I'd known that
*me* choosing someone, choosing who to date, choosing who to love,
mattered every bit as much as being chosen.

The fantasy of the "perfect match" also implies a sort of meet-
cute kismet that could heap onto that effortlessness. The "boring"
ways of meeting someone decades ago seem romantic to us now,
maybe because they're simple—bumping into someone in line at
the grocery store, meeting a friend of a friend at a dinner party, and
catching the Frisbee someone threw across the campus quad all
seem to lack the level of analysis, calculation, and conscious choice it
feels like dating now requires. But I also wonder about the idea that
true romance just "happens" to us. Now, even amid stressors on how
quickly dating has changed, and technology's role in that, choice
feels more out in the open. It's not that we aren't meeting people the
"traditional" ways; it feels like our perception of "normal ways" of
meeting people has expanded.

But still, the allure of effortlessness persists. Dr. Rachel A.
Katz, a digital media scholar, did research on Tinder that showed
"impressions of authentic effortlessness" were important to young
adults, even if that "effortlessness" was curated. Katz's research
shows people spent a lot of time and effort creating dating profiles
that were reflective of authentic versions of themselves, but "ironically, this sometimes involved making a conscious effort to create
a seemingly effortless profile," she added. Now, because so many of
our interactions in young adulthood do happen online, it makes
sense that meeting or talking or getting to know someone would
take place in that sphere, but it's fascinating that the pressure to
appear effortless, even while putting in the conscious work to create
the profile, remains.

Katz doesn't think dating apps are any more commodifying

than reducing yourself to another social media profile. She pointed out that while people might perceive image-based dating apps as superficial, "much meaning-making and identity formation occurs on these apps." Dismissing dating apps as "not really dating" or "not trusting fate" were among the most puzzling things young adults described being told, like it's not just about meeting the right person, but meeting them in the "right" way. Not only is there importance in dating apps—as Katz pointed out, as people increasingly find partners through the apps, that leads the apps to influence "family formation and therefore future generations," too—but some elements don't feel as far from "real-life" dating as one might expect. "Even though technologies can sometimes reduce the richness of interactions, they bring their own new ways of interacting that can be convenient and meaningful," Katz added about interacting through media generally, as well as through dating apps. We get to choose both how we interact with people we're interested in and where we do it. There's agency here: in choosing to approach the person you keep making eye contact with at a friend's wedding and asking them to dance; in swiping on someone to get to know them better. While the big, traditional markers of romance—spontaneity, searching, and soul mates—bring about a certain image of dating and love, young adulthood feels like a good time to reorient ourselves to what it actually looks like in practice. It's a spoiler that real life is sort of boring.

Despite extraordinary expectations surrounding dating, what so many conversations with young adults boiled down to was choice, which seems obvious, and yet somehow underdiscussed. Far from *The Bachelor*–adjacent fantasies of love and romance—"Will you accept this rose?" jokes notwithstanding—love and dating felt like practical parts of living, ways of building the kind of life or partnership or family that mattered to you. While it's anecdotal, for all my dating app awkwardness and hours I spent making the case for my worth to people who saw me as an afterthought, I met someone I fell deeply for unexpectedly, beginning with a message I sent on social media to tell them I liked their cowboy boots while I was eating Chipotle on the floor of my bedroom in sweatpants on an ordinary night. One version of my probably-too-nostalgic heart would call it fate, but the other wonders if it just being a slightly messy, kind of brave choice to reach out is just as romantic. And it started with a choice, not kismet, not divine intervention. Probably.

Nobody really says it aloud when we talk about whether young people are dating too much or too little, whether they're killing the marriage industry or rushing into everything: In emerging adulthood, we aren't *just* creating the people we're going to be. We're also developing the relationship skills to learn what we want and ask for it, and awareness of who we want to be *with*. In its most twee version, this sounds a bit like "Everyone you meet is a lesson!" which we know isn't necessarily fair. But I like to think the idea of choices runs a little deeper than that: Sometimes, choosing to be with someone, choosing not to, or deciding whether or not to date at all *is* a version of choosing ourselves—which, when you think about it, is pretty rooted in love.

# 9

# WHEN SELF-CARE DOESN'T CARE ABOUT US

*On self-care as self-reliance, and what it means to take care of yourself*

I HAVE YET TO MASTER CARING FOR MYSELF THE WAY I CARE for other people—if you need a baked good, a pep talk, or a reminder to close your computer and go to bed early, I'm your person. But when left to my own devices (literally) I log too many hours on screens, never remember to buy Epsom salt at the grocery store to finally soak in the bath instead of sprinting through the shower to scrub my hair, and have never done a face mask. When I get emails with subject lines announcing a new product designed to make self-care easier, like a subscription kit, or scroll through an article on self-care outlining new strategies to help us slow down, take care of ourselves, and clear our skin all at once, I'm impressed and slightly overwhelmed. If we're being honest, my "self-care" looks like calling a friend, getting carryout, and sleeping—usually not all at the same time. I never remember to schedule it; I don't really count exercise, because though it makes me feel good and, thus, probably *is* caring for my physical and mental health, it feels like it strays too close to self-improvement for me. Maybe that's the problem: I'm increasingly uncertain what self-care actually is. It feels as though self-care, in this context, gives us one more thing to do, promotes the idea that everything is a personal problem we can fix on our own, and encourages a deeply commodified version of self-care that's not accessible to lots of people, anyway.

To me, the word "caring" conjures something tender and kind, but the million things marketed as self-care to us these days—from apps that track our breathing patterns to self-care journals that give you daily assignments—feel like they're straddling an already-thin line between tending to our needs and improving ourselves. Self-care, the phrase, has origins as both a medical term, a means of patients building healthy habits, and later, a political act.[1] "We often think of self-care as a little bit of a frou-frou marketing term because it's often used that way, but that really obscures a really important history," said Natalia Mehlman Petrzela, PhD, an associate professor at the New School. In the 1960s or '70s, Petrzela explained, you saw people talking about wellness and self-care "to refer to a kind of reclaiming or claiming of bodily self-determination and self-possession in a culture that deprived them of such." That included, she said, radical feminists and Black activists, including Black Panthers, talking about bodily reclamation and self-care, empowering yourself, and the idea of knowing yourself best.

Now, it's hard not to feel that the term—and the practice itself—is diluted, as if it's a lavender mist we can spray over everything: natural makeup products and a skincare routine; homecooked meals and green juice; artsy motivational posters, Instagram posts, temporary tattoos, gratitude journals and "mindful positivity planners" bearing messages, with florals and cursive font, like *Care for yourself first, You are enough, Who are you when you feel your best?* and *Create your own magic*; flowers you bought for yourself; fitness routines on YouTube presented as *Taking fifteen minutes to care for you*; a whole lot of bath bombs; habits like waking up early enough to do yoga, have tea, and meditate, or running several miles. Obviously, some of these things are enjoyable and for some really do feel like self-care. And, also obviously, they assume a level of privilege that allows you to dip your toes into a certain aesthetic of what it means to care for yourself, something that, in a lot of instances, seems to touch more on luxuries than basic needs. There's an argument to be made that, in a world that ties our worth to our productivity and renders rest a prize to be won, whatever makes you feel good, held, and cared for is worth doing, whether it's a practice or a product or a combo of both. What felt intriguing about self-care for young adults is how many people described it as stressful—not that they didn't want to care for themselves with intention and substance, but how overwhelming different ideas of what that could be depending on your circumstances.

According to some, we should practice self-care because it makes us more productive. To others, it's a means of raising self-esteem or taking time to "put yourself first." But regarding the intentions of self-care, one that stood out when talking to young adults was it being yet another pressure to "fix" yourself. Rather than caring for the selves we have, some versions of self-care feel like sprints to create a better self instead. Like buffing up your ordinary self via extraordinary routines—ones that were often divorced from circumstances like not having time to practice self-care, not having money or health insurance to pay for your actual physical and mental healthcare, or having no space to figure out what it means to *truly* care for yourself in a way that's practical enough to be effective, but still feel good. The problem here is systemic: We cannot relax away overwork, fatigue, or plain old stress, and it places a bizarre amount of obligation and responsibility on us to repair ourselves, reorient ourselves, and squeeze in that meditation or journaling practice no matter what. It's another thing to do, another thing to be. In instances like this, "Take care of yourself!" can be half a motivational quip, half a tsk-tsk. And at times, that can come across as dumping the burden of structural crises that leave no time for actual rest or care onto individuals, another heap of self-reliance masquerading as self-compassion.

Having to think about my own self-care was a baffling exercise. I had things I did to relax—baking, watching movies, talking with friends on the phone—but frankly, I didn't want self-care activities; I wanted *no* activities, an actual break. The first time I saw someone reference "self-care," it was on Instagram (which isn't a shock, given that when you search #selfcare, you get upward of twenty-two million results). As for a lot of young women (especially white women, given the marketing and prices of a lot of this), elements within the broad genre of "self-help," including self-care, were something I constantly saw online, branded in rosy colors and girl-power fonts. And self-improvement seemed wired into how I thought about myself: If I wasn't trying to be better or calmer or more thoughtful, what on earth was I even doing? That advice is everywhere: Buying a jade roller will fix my skin, this certain meditation cushion will create a safe space to wipe away anxiety, and refocusing my mindset toward positivity will cure my chronic illness. Sometimes, a lot of this well-intentioned advice sounded like, well, if you *really* wanted to feel better, you would've figured this out, like the flaw was me not *wanting* it bad enough. That's the talking point that's everywhere else, anyway: Changing your life, becoming a better you, is solely a matter of *wanting* it. Of course self-care isn't immune to that particular strand of "best life" pressure.

Despite being someone who, personally, felt overwhelmed by all self-care was supposed to be, when I wound up at the doctor's office, after weeks of back-and-forth over insurance, I realized that the mentality around it all had caught me. While I logically knew that I couldn't bath-bomb my way to a functioning immune system, or gratitude-journal my way out of chronic illness, the pressure still bubbled. When the nurse asked if I'd been experiencing any stress and had any "stress-reducing practices," I remember thinking, *Oh no, I should've taken self-care more seriously. I should've done more.*

It might sound ironic that self-care itself can be a source of stress—and it is. It's not that self-care doesn't matter in young adulthood,[2] which is why there's value in what makes you feel good, comforted, or calmer. But between pressures of keeping up with the commodified version of self-care and the idea of fixing ourselves, it's easy to see how it'd be anything but relaxing.

"The idea of self-care has really been stressing me out," Brie, twenty-four, told me. When people ask her how she's taking care of herself right now, she says she doesn't even stop to think about it on a given day because so many other things are happening, and she's still trying to figure out a way for self-care to not "just be a shopping list." Brie wakes up at two thirty a.m. to get to work every day, so it's a matter of determining where self-care goes in the course of the day: go to work, get off work, self-care, check email; that makes it seem like yet another task she has to do.

Echoing that, Sanah, twenty-two, told me, "I felt the pressure to practice self-care 'perfectly' for a long time." She'd read hundreds of articles and lists highlighting various daily self-care routines but "sometimes, keeping up with my self-care routine felt more like work and less like self-care." It's obvious how self-care looks vastly different depending on your context: For Brie, it was a matter of not turning self-care into a chore, something she has to come home from work and do like she has to do laundry; for Sanah, she described self-care as a means of survival. She grew up in a household that struggled with domestic violence, and added, "If I had enough courage and persistence to get through the week, that was a radical act of self-care considering everything I had going on." Taking care of yourself, she said, should be unique and individualized, including tangible self-care strategies that are trauma-informed for some, not just the self-care lite we see available for purchase scrolling down our timelines.

"Self-care is definitely not always glamorous or easy," Sanah said. "Listening to yourself and assessing what you truly need is hard and uncomfortable." And that's what I'd been pondering while scrolling my way through ads for pillow scents designed to help me sleep better and desktop plug-ins created to make my computer screen "cozy": It feels like learning to care for ourselves is a pretty ordinary skill, one that demands more self-reflection than online shopping and more attention to what actually makes us feel good as opposed to what looks good, and is fundamentally about building a habit more than it is treating yourself. So how can we actually learn what it means to take care of our ordinary selves without obsessing over the calmer, more organized, most present, most tuned-in people we could be? So much of caring, it seems, means realizing we do not exist to be fixed.

I wanted to see what it looked like to organize your life around self-care, mostly because I was puzzled by the assumption that not only should we all have the time, resources, and energy to do it, but there were certain means of self-care, something that feels pretty personal, that were more popular than others. Following the advice of some "starter guides," I downloaded a self-care plan that was organized around different areas, like work, physical fitness, and relationships. If nothing else, I figured, it'd unpack what was self-improvement and what might honestly dip into the self-care category. The plan's intentions were noble, but as soon as I made it to step two, where I was asked to explain barriers standing in the way of my accomplishing activities that boost well-being, I felt a hot surge of unnecessary, entirely superficial stress. *Okay*, I thought, strategizing, *what gets bumped in pursuit of things that make me feel good? Well, I can't miss these meetings for work but that isn't self-care. It'd make me feel better to run the errands I've been putting off, but that isn't contributing to my well-being, either. It's just a chore.*

Brie brought up something similar in our conversation, but for her, it was more a matter of reflecting on how she was feeling on a given day, and what that means in terms of how she takes care of herself. It's what self-care looks like in the most practical sense of it all, she said. For Brie, that looks like taking a little bit of a self-inventory: "You just came home from work and you're tired, so then your self-care today is take a nap. Or oh, you haven't read a book in a couple of days or you really want to finish reading this book, so your self-care is read the book," she added. Same thing with emails and texts: When emails are piling up and making her nervous, she responds to get that number down; if she doesn't have the energy to respond to a text or message in the moment, her self-care is to not, and to be as transparent as possible when she is ready to respond. What Brie listed were simple, day-to-day things: They didn't come couched in the kind of language that almost sounds like motivation, encouraging you to do more. "The only thing standing in the way of your care is you," read one Instagram quote picture. Nor did they require any special products or timeline. The reflection made self-care something that was adaptive, little things that seemed to improve the everyday instead of glamorous turning points and life makeovers.

Changing your self-care to fit what's happening in your life on a given day might seem obvious, but the more common talking point seemed to be scheduling in dedicated self-care time—not that that is a bad thing; if we don't plan it, when are we supposed to find time to do it? There's something to be said for staying open to the idea that our needs might change and shift as we do. After all, it's easy to feel *guilty* for taking time to take care of ourselves, or, honestly, do anything just for fun. How often have you looked forward to doing something luxurious or relaxing or fun and then experienced an anxiety pang that you weren't using that time to study or reply to emails or clean the house? It's one reason the simple, personal things have to be the ones that count the most.

Sanah described self-care as being mindful and understanding what you need in the moment, then working to make it happen. "Sometimes, what you need could look like taking a bath, going on a run, or making yourself a cup of hot tea," she said. "However, sometimes self-care can simply look like lying in bed and watching your favorite TV show. Self-care can even be doing nothing." She also mentioned that society sells a formula for self-care and self-love, and while parts of that might be helpful to some, "the most important way that you can practice self-care is listening to yourself and assessing your own needs."

The simple stuff may not pop up in sexy marketing campaigns around how having a tub desk to put your wine on after a stressful weekday will change your life, or how the only thing standing between a revitalized self and your current self is a self-care kit ordered from Etsy, but it feels like the most profound, and most practical. Even when speaking to Dr. Alfiee M. Breland-Noble—a pioneering psychologist and founder of the AAKOMA Project, which has received recognition for its approach to engaging marginalized youth and empowering them to care for their mental health—about how self-care relates to optimal mental health, she pointed to something seemingly simple. Optimal mental health is knowing your baseline, cultivating your environment in healthy ways, and giving attention to your mind, body, and spirit. Knowing your baseline, or, as Breland-Noble described it, knowing on a cellular level what you feel like when life is just okay, feels like a big factor here. "Not when it's super, awesome, amazing, wonderful," she clarified. "Not when it's, 'This is the worst day of my life.'" But on a day when everything is just okay. "'I'm not really too worried about anything. I'm not really too upset. I'm not really too happy,'" she continued. "Most of us have no idea what that feels like. We don't know what that feels like because we don't stop."

Imagine the relief of just stopping. Of pausing. Not to attain, or strategize, or patch a hole, but to re-center. Breland-Noble said self-care is what it sounds like: "Your opportunity to take the best care of yourself so that you can be the best person that you can be," she told me. "So you can utilize your gifts and talents so that you can grow, so that you can mature." She is an avid meditator, and every week on her nonprofit's Instagram page they host a meditation on Instagram Live. "That's your spirit, right?" she said of just pausing to breathe. "That's portable. Breathing. It goes where you go. You don't need any special tools for that."

One of the reasons it felt so important to ask about optimal mental health as it related to self-care is how often the two get conflated. In marketing materials that tell us to find our centers, usually through a product, and reminders popping up, like activewear email subject lines, that only *we* have the power to change our lives, mental health still gets treated as something we can self-care solutions to. The distinction—between general self-care that might make us feel good and actual mental health treatment—matters, especially given the issues young people are facing with health insurance, which prices many out of getting the help they want or need.

Over one-third of American adults will develop an anxiety disorder in their lifetime, with 32 percent of thirteen- to seventeen-year-olds already meeting criteria for diagnosis, according to a policy brief from the Berkeley Institute for the Future of Young Americans, "The Anxious Generation: Causes and Consequences of Anxiety Disorder Among Young Americans."[3] According to some research, anxiety is considered a growing problem for young adults (no kidding, you might be saying).[4] And research points out that—unsurprisingly—poor mental health is associated with material disadvantage and unemployment, income, and debt, and mentions some factors potentially contributing to this anxiety spike in young people, including economic stressors, technology and social media, and sociopolitical factors.[5] During the pandemic, findings from the CDC, as reported by the *New York Times*, showed that young adults, in addition to Black and Latino people of all ages, were describing increases in levels of anxiety, depression, and suicidal thoughts, with almost 11 percent saying they had suicidal thoughts in the month before the survey. The greatest cluster within that number being Black and Latino people, unpaid caregivers for adults, and essential workers.[6] Another poll, conducted by NORC at the University of Chicago and cited by ABC News, found that adults under thirty-five were especially likely to report negative feelings, or experience physical or emotional symptoms associated with stress and anxiety.[7] Why bring up mental health when talking about self-care, if they're separate things? Well, because not only has self-care been commodified into a product that's not just fun and fancy, but life-changing, it's also used as a version of the bootstraps mentality, just wrapped prettier. Especially for young adults, who get dinged for being too sensitive and too focused on themselves, sometimes it feels easier to quietly hunt for solutions rather than admit that we're struggling, or need help we can't give ourselves. Self-care, as the pandemic showcased again and again, is not a solution for actually needing help. If you can't afford to see your therapist, an eye mask that's scented with cucumber likely isn't going to feel revelatory. If you can't afford to take off work, taking a "personal day" is akin to asking someone to commute on a unicorn. And, for that matter, telling people to "take care of themselves" or "seek help" can feel shallow if they don't have the tools or resources or time to do those things.

While Breland-Noble doesn't know about the whole "mindset" idea—"Because mindset, I think, does not account for structural racism and discrimination that people of color and marginalized people encounter," she said—she does mention what we're doing with our minds. "What are you actively, consciously thinking about on a day-to-day basis that feeds optimal mental health?" Sometimes, that's doing the best you can with what you have, and acknowledging that. In emerging adulthood, specifically, the trademark feeling of "in between" that carries so much possibility and freedom can also hold uncertainty, fear, and stress. And knowing how to ground yourself during upheaval, whether that's moving or changing jobs or shifting relationships with friends, is necessary. When you factor in that another defining characteristic of emerging adulthood is self-focus, things get slippery. Focusing on ourselves could slip from conscious, practical consideration of what actually calms us down or makes us feel good into the panicked effort to fix ourselves to live up to whatever ideal we have beyond work and friendship and hobbies, being the sort of person who never is on their phone after nine p.m., wakes up at six a.m. to journal their thoughts, or has mindful coloring art that's good enough to hang on the wall of the bathroom. It's not that these things are bad self-care; it's that it seems while we're doing what we can with what we have, it might be worth listening to what we just actually want to do.

To that end, it was a relief to hear that self-care can actually be doing nothing. The things we do to rejuvenate ourselves, to give ourselves more energy, fall into the same realm as "sleep and rest and, you know, frankly just staring into space," Christine Carter, PhD, author of *The New Adolescence: Raising Happy and Successful Teens in an Age of Anxiety and Distraction* and *The Sweet Spot: How to Accomplish More by Doing Less*, told me. "So when I talk about self-care, I'm really thinking about recovery time," Carter explained. It's why we enter young adulthood and immediately wish to regain every nap we refused to take as a kid, or why you read that sentence and considered putting this book down just to close your eyes for a second. Not to log your sleep cycle or track the hours of sleep you get or figure out which essential oils go in your bathtub without leaving a ring around it or debating whether you'll go to yoga or a bootcamp class in the morning. Nothing. We want *nothing*. The "I'll sleep when I'm dead" mentality is a holdover from the first industrial revolution, this idea that "busyness is a sign of our significance or our value." When that factory model shifted to online, people's "sense of worth and their productivity became acquainted with time spent on the job," Carter told me. It's what makes us anxious about recovery time, or any time spent not working, she said, "so instead of recovering, we engage in self-development." The slippery slope between self-improvement and self-care seems like yet another extension of how busyness and productivity are signals of our value. "A lot of personal growth is very taxing," Carter said. "And while a very good thing to do, it is not the same thing as self-care." It isn't that self-improvement is always a negative thing. It is, however, that self-improvement can "really be about not being good enough," Carter clarified.

If anything, caring about yourself is the opposite of earning it.

The very idea of self-care as something to be earned marked a turning point that felt more like an off-road swerve in my own health. First, I should have been able to fix anything wrong with me through sheer force of will, and second, if I was going to take a sick day, or a personal day, I better have first earned it. It's why I didn't notice when I started getting exhausted walking up the street to the bodega that was on my corner when I lived in New York, or when I felt dizzy carrying a normal-size basket of laundry. *I need to work out harder*, I thought, *I'm out of shape*. I didn't pay attention when I consistently slept through the night and woke up feeling as though I'd stayed out all night, ten nights in a row. *I need to try to get more sleep; I'll keep my phone away from my bed and take melatonin*, I planned. My inability to focus I chalked up to needing to slow down and finally getting around to starting a meditation practice. It was months of signs I should've caught, springs of water bursting out of a ship containing holes I never saw, because I patched them with good-intentioned efforts to improve my overall life, attempts to solve what was going wrong by adding good things in. The bonus rounds of more to do—even objectively good things, like working out and meditating—seemed to have made it worse.

And I am not the only one who has attempted to steer self-care toward self-improvement—mostly because the line between the two has never felt particularly well-defined. Ellie, twenty-one, sent me a Twitter message saying she'd spent all of college feeling that self-care was overwhelming—and that after a solid four years of hearing the term, she still isn't positive of exactly what it means. Sometimes, it's linked to health needs, other times, it's about life needs, and sometimes, it's just temporary fixes to get through. She explained that she conflates self-care with life management: Because one of her goals for self-care is peace of mind, self-management takes center stage as she has her whole life written out in a planner and Google notes, tracking goals, schoolwork, exercise, and whatever else comes to mind. When she had a semester where her anxiety was "off the charts," she felt she was supposed to fix it by adding *more* rigidity into her life—even healthier food, even more exercise. Even her "realistic," as she described it, version of self-care didn't help. She just needed real medical attention, noting that her doctor helped her find a solution, but she shouldn't have had to suffer with anxiety for so long.

Ellie believes young adults need opportunities to form healthy self-esteem that aren't tied to accomplishments and trajectories, with resources that support it. She mentioned mental health organizations launching national health initiatives to educate young adults on taking better care of themselves, which could also theoretically take the form of college campuses and workplaces providing opportunities for that education—and giving students and workers the capacity to actually enact it, too. It's a good question: Where *do* we learn how to take care of ourselves? It's fine to say it's a personal practice, but without resources, some young adults are going to start from zero on establishing care practices that feel conducive to their everyday lives. Sometimes, sitting through another webinar or getting a chipper email reminder to log off and take time for care does nothing when the structures of your life offer no space for that.

"I constantly felt and sometimes still feel like I wasn't good enough at self-care," Ellie said. "Honestly, I've been evaluating a lot of elements of my life for who knows how long, and I recently realized that I shouldn't constantly be measuring myself. No wonder I never feel good enough—I'm constantly comparing myself to myself or another ideal." It's hard to take care of yourself if you don't think you're worth it. These ideas of "earning it," or self-care shape-shifting into self-improvement, felt like they were pointing toward another facet of having an extraordinary, best self: If we're going to do it, we're going to do it all on our own.


Perhaps it seems like a rebuttal of the "self" part—and the fact that self-care at its best seems to rely on inherently personal things—but part of the glamorized marketing of self-care is self-reliance. It's presented luxuriously: Even when you look up "self-care" in stickers to put on your Instagram Story, the first one says "All about me," followed by "Self-love is the best love," and "Growth mindset." Presented this way, self-care is a means of hitting pause and rejecting the relentless urge of your to-do lists and over-obligations. Sounds pretty good, right? But a close look at how self-care is marketed begs some questions—mostly, does caring for ourselves mean conforming to the version of care that commodification amplifies? What about care in terms of our communities? It's not a secret that self-care has been commodified and exploited by companies who stand to make a profit off us wanting to feel better, but sometimes it feels worth acknowledging that our societal structures both encourage a self that we're always bettering and wear us down to the extent that *anything* feels better than this.

"There's a particular reason that sort of hollowed-out version of radical wellness and self-care becomes very popular," Petrzela, the New School professor, told me. That's because, despite the radicalism and genuine countercultural origins of a lot of it, at its heart, it's about individualism in many ways. The ideas of empowering yourself originated by Black activists and radical feminists can sound like "some traditional forms of American individualism, which are all about bootstrapping and are all about *the only person you can trust is yourself*," Petrzela explained. She thinks one of the reasons self-care and wellness have been so seamlessly commodified and commercialized is because they have an "easy alliance" with this conservative way of thinking in the United States. It's also what makes elements of self-care insidious. That it's all on you. Especially during a moment where so much of our society's safety net is being shredded before our eyes, she said, that's jarring, the idea of "Is it my fault if I'm sick? Did I not do enough yoga?"

There's also a connection to that trendiness and the hyper-self-reliance that treats self-care like it should be the balm for *everything*, a solution and an agent of change instead of just practical living as a human being. That fine line—between self-care, the fix, and self-care, the practice—gets trampled over when it is presented as something we should purchase, without addressing who profits when we do, who has access, and why "care" in this manner ultimately seems to involve picking products yourself, paying with your dollars, and solving whatever it is solo. The idea of "fixing" something, even if it's a mostly good thing, feels like another bloom off the giant plant of capitalism that tells us not only is there a product we need to care about ourselves, but that, when using whatever the product is, self-care can be productive, too.

"I love a good face mask as much as the next girl, but despite what Instagram ads want me to think, spending an exorbitant amount of money on glam products at Sephora or buying the latest bougie subscription product—literally just saw an ad for an overnight oats subscription called Mush—doesn't actually do much for the emotional, mental, spiritual, and physical needs of mine that self-care is supposed to tend to," Lexi, twenty-one, said. She hadn't heard the term "self-care" until college, and explained that she thinks it has a lot to do with the "immigrant experience": Her mother immigrated to the United States when she was young, and Lexi had what she described as a "very bicultural upbringing." As Lexi explained it, when you're assimilating to a new country, getting basic needs met, keeping your community tight-knit without many emotional or physical boundaries, stigma surrounding mental healthcare, and rigid gender roles—women tending to everyone's needs but their own—were all factors. The gendering of self-care is something Lexi thinks about often, describing it as one more way the patriarchy profits off women's insecurities, not unlike diet or beauty industries. "I just don't see any of my male friends being subject to the same self-care culture," she said. "They're surely, for the most part, taking care of themselves and living as functional adults, but don't make a point to talk about it or post about it on social media because it's not trendy for them."

This isn't to say that buying things isn't a form of self-care. If a new nail polish or bath salts boost your mood and bring some comfort to your routine, it's wonderful; other products that appear on self-care lists are therapeutic, including weighted blankets that help some with insomnia or anxiety, diffusers, and heating pads that loosen up muscles or quell aches. It's just that that conversation should likely be followed by the fact that learning to take care of ourselves isn't just trendy—it's necessary, and it doesn't have to be fancy in order to make a difference. Lexi pointed out that, some days, her self-care is cooking a nutritious meal, doing yoga, and writing in her journal, while others, it's eating Oreos and watching *When Harry Met Sally* for the eight hundredth time, because both are restorative in different ways. "No amount of self-care routines and charcoal face masks are going to help us when we live in a society that constantly denies us our basic needs, when we're drowning in student debt, when most of us are struggling with mental health issues or have a loved one who is, when we don't have equitable access to healthcare and are generally just watching the fabric of American society come undone," Lexi added. She pointed out that we can't show up for ourselves and each other if we don't take care of ourselves, including creating a society that better tends to our needs, and those needs being met becoming normalized, especially for marginalized communities.

Other young adults echoed Lexi's point that material circumstances really do impact this hazy idea of self-care. It shouldn't be a means of propping ourselves upright, and remaining productive and functional even as our world, workplaces, and schools crumble around us: We have to hold it together, but society certainly doesn't. Brisa, twenty-six, said that the biggest thing that's shifted how she can take care of herself is her financial situation becoming more stable, so she doesn't have to weigh when she can go to therapy again based on her next paycheck. "What your financial situation is or your physical situation is affects what your self-care looks like and what kind of self-care you need," she added. Brisa deals with chronic pain and described a situation too many people know too intimately: Her last job was hourly, and she took her time increasing her hours because she wasn't sure she'd physically have the energy, but she needed money to go to the doctor and to therapy. It's an endless circle, and it isn't challenging to see how, when your basic needs aren't met, it creates a domino effect of feeling bad, being unable to sustain yourself, and thus being unable to afford the basic help you need, through no fault of your own.

This isn't just in products. It's employers offering perks like free meditation app subscriptions instead of putting in place structures that would allow people to actually take care of themselves, like equitable wages; adequate family, medical, and personal leave; remote work flexibility; and health insurance. It's students on campuses needing universities to fund understaffed wellness and counseling centers, and to be treated as human beings with complex lives instead of high-performing robots who only think about school, and instead, schools offering opportunities to pet dogs and have hot chocolate during finals weeks. It's in stories—that unnervingly echo each other—of young people going to school counselors or employees going to bosses and asking for specific help, or time off, to receive treatment for physical or mental health issues, being met with condescending remarks about how they might feel better if they just took an hour to themselves. It's employers or schools sending out "surveys" on burnout in order to address needs, then never doing more than collecting thoughts in order to say they did. When functioning this way, self-care feels underhanded, a sly gimmick to remind us that, really, whatever we're feeling is all our fault anyway, and we should be able to fix whatever it is without assistance or support. It subtly implies that if we're burnt out, anxious, sick, overworked, stressed, or otherwise overwhelmed, it's our own doing, which is how the solution—"Practice self-care!"—feels like a box-check buzzword created to remind us that, hey, if you didn't squeeze in that hour of yoga to your workday, are you really prioritizing yourself? Never mind that your world, workplace, school, or society may not. What are *you* doing to alleviate the stress you likely didn't create on your own in the first place?

Needing help came up as self-care multiple times. "Self-care looks like letting someone else help," said Ashby, who just turned thirty and has a two-year-old. "I have this irrational idea that I-am-woman, hear-me-roar, and I must do everything in all corners of my life or it won't be right, so I try to remind myself it's okay to let someone else do something for me so I can have a physical or mental break." Juggling a busy career, alongside her husband who is doing the same, along with parenting, makes it tough to find time for self-care. And when she does get the time, Ashby explained, she puts pressure on herself to get things done that she typically can't while her two-year-old is with her, like cleaning or running errands. She said, "Self-care looks like peace for me. Peace of mind knowing there isn't really anything I need to do, so I can sit back and turn my brain off for a little while." She said she thinks self-care also doesn't have to be a big, extravagant plan. "Honestly, going to lunch by yourself is so awesome," Ashby said, explaining it's quiet, you're nourishing your body, and you get to do so while not stopping your child from choking on chicken nuggets or spilling water in her lap because she's insisting on using a "big girl" cup. You have to fill your own cup up first before you can give everyone your best self, she added. It's a reminder of how much can happen during this phase of life that might impact how we take care of ourselves, especially for emerging adults who are caretakers or parents and might face additional barriers to self-care. It also seems worth acknowledging that what it means to care for ourselves, to create space to take care of ourselves, might shift over time: What worked at one age with one set of life circumstances may not feel the same in another.

Figuring out what self-care means for you is key, according to Petrzela. "I think if you're being sold something really hard, then really think hard about what you're getting out of it," she continued, because so much of self-care these days is products people are selling. "So before you buy those essential oils or that membership to some streaming yoga platform, think about what you get out of it, because we know what they get out of it—they get your subscription purchase, right?" Thinking of self-care in a range of ways, from canceling plans or commitments to self-discipline to thinking about long-term objectives for how you want life to feel and moving toward those, can be helpful.

As if on cue, an email with "self-care" in the subject line bounced into my inbox, outlining "self-care strategies to get you through the week," including links to purchase agendas to help organize my "best life"—that's a quote—and a list of nail polish colors that are supposedly calming. I scrolled through the lists and searched for references for things people had mentioned to me as being a real part of caring for yourself: Community, recovery, healing—or doing nothing—didn't appear. Those things aren't for sale, it seems. I still struggle with the belief that intentionally caring for myself means I must be broken, and that broken things need fixing.

Caring, including caring about yourself, is the most ordinary thing we could do in a day, and perhaps the one that has been most muddied by our modern pursuit of it. That includes, of course, the trappings of capitalism and lack of security that hoist up this version as the end-all, be-all to taking care of yourself. It is not a failure to reflect on how you feel. It is not a character flaw to realize some things feel too heavy to carry alone. It is not selfish to want to tend to yourself—nor is it selfish to follow your own instincts about what that might mean for you. We can bath-bomb and girls'-night-in to our hearts' content, but at the same time, reflect on nurturing different aspects of ourselves through a variety of means. It means not rejecting opportunities to slow down; it means, where we can, holding our societal structures accountable for acknowledging that extraordinary isn't a standard we've chosen. Mostly, it means allowing ourselves the capacity to feel ordinary, to notice how we're feeling. In other words, just feeling at all.

# 10

# WHO ANSWERS WHEN YOU CALL

*On being part of the "loneliest generation"
and building our communities*

A FEW YEARS AGO, I BEGAN A WEIRD PRACTICE THAT'S THE closest I've ever come to journaling: I started writing down the ways people describe loneliness, probably because I was lonely myself. And it felt distinct from any other feeling: nostalgia, but without the memories; longing, but without awareness of what I was reaching for. Writing it down made it feel specific, tangible, a thing most of us were experiencing. When I riffled through the notebooks and random pieces of paper and notes in my phone that had collected all of the snippets of conversations I'd had on loneliness, there were countless mentions of "failure," like being lonely carried a sense of having failed to make friends or be social, like it was a feeling you could outrun if you just packed your calendar full enough. Others described it as a lack of being seen—like being surrounded by people who don't actually know you or your life or what matters to you at all, or standing with your back against the wall in a crowded room, surrounded by the hum of people talking, and not being able to join in yourself. The "opposite of what you see on Instagram" is a description I think about every time I see a picture of friends, faces pressed together and beaming in the glow of an iPhone flash. People who had wide circles of friends in college described loneliness, and the absence of social circles that had quelled it with easy access to meeting new people, as a turning point in their transition to young adulthood, something confidence-shaking and disorienting. Even introverts, like myself, discussed the surreal difference between craving time to recharge and actually feeling alone in ways that were both fleeting—like a Saturday night without plans—or consequential, like not feeling they had people to cheer them on during major life events. The complexity of how people put words to this feeling was fascinating, but what struck me was the omnipresence of it—we aren't alone in feeling lonely. It hardly ever gets said, but growing up isn't just adventurous, transitional, and new. Emerging adulthood, it would seem, is lonely.

A 2019 poll reported that millennials are the "loneliest generation," with 30 percent stating they "always" or "often" feel lonely.[1] Another 49 percent said they have somewhere between one and four "close friends" (which, frankly, sounded like a lot).[2] A 2018 survey by health insurer Cigna that reported on twenty thousand adults across the country using the UCLA Loneliness Scale found that most Americans are actually considered lonely, or view themselves that way. It also reported that younger generations had higher loneliness scores than older ones, claiming that "Generation Z (adults ages 18 to 22) is the loneliest generation."[3] Finding where you fit in the world, working out who you want to be, is sometimes an inherently lonely proposition. It demands the big questions no amount of studying or plan-B planning could've prepped us for, until we live through them: *What matters to me? How do I feel when I'm alone? Who is going to be in my life? Who should be there, and how should it feel?*

And we know emerging adulthood is generally a time of transition: moving, for school or work or just out of your parent or guardian's house; losing communities, like school or college towns or first jobs; starting over, on repeat, reinventing your identity and discovering what you really want life to hold. That amount of potential for change—and trying to navigate the GPS of your own life—feels ripe for amplifying loneliness. What that can end up feeling like, at least for some, is accidentally surrounding yourself with whoever you can, attempting to tweak yourself and your expectations into groups you find yourself in, or putting your head down and charging forward into the hustle, alone. Alone even when you don't want to be. Alone when you feel you're losing yourself in it. Alone with the guilt that you should be independent enough to handle it, and the sinking crush that you just aren't. Yet, somehow, a state of being that exists in all age groups, that pops up whether you have twenty friends or two, that can find you even when you're surrounded by people, feels disorienting, like a betrayal of what young adulthood is supposed to be, according to some: toggling between circles of friends and blissful independence.

It's hard to paint the broad strokes of what sometimes gets interpreted as loneliness—isolation, sadness, or even a misunderstanding of introversion—onto a young person who is supposed to be at the peak of their social experience. It's easier to point to what the *opposite* of loneliness looks like for young adults: solo backpacking adventures; table settings for a dozen or so "best friends" at a dinner party; cozy evenings with wine and Netflix and movie boxes of candy from CVS with friends you've had since childhood; people hovering near you at a party, eager to catch up and see your glow of likability reflected onto them. If anything, loneliness seems uncomfortably indiscriminate, drop-kicking you into longing and nostalgia whether you consider yourself popular or unpopular, connected or disconnected, an introvert or an extrovert.

At times, it even feels like loneliness is a side effect of wanting other people in your life in the first place. Maybe that's what is so rattling: The realization that we want other people is a risky proposition. In certain moments, it felt as though loneliness was specifically being alone, like living away from family and friends and having no one to call if I got sick or I needed help. In others, I swear I could see the fog of loneliness waft over crowded rooms, where I stood smiling and small-talking and clutching a red Solo cup during social gatherings, trying to put myself out there and be the sort of person other people would want to be friends with, wondering if everyone was just naturally better at making friends than I was.

Tiptoeing the narrow line between being alone, often necessary for self-reflection and refilling your tank, and being lonely is another thing we're establishing for ourselves. Solitude, voluntarily, can feel healing, a pause to reflect, a nice breather from a world that's overstimulating and breathless in its hustle. Loneliness, on the other hand, is a "distressing feeling" that accompanies thinking one's social needs aren't being met by the quantity or quality of their relationships, according to some research.[4] That means, yes, you can spend a bunch of time alone and truly never feel lonely, and you can also be surrounded by people, have seemingly thriving relationships, and still feel lonely. And, it's important to note, loneliness isn't a blanket that spreads over everything equally. In research on loneliness in late adolescence, researchers made the distinction that "state levels of loneliness refer to momentary feelings of loneliness in daily life, whereas trait loneliness refers to a baseline measure of how lonely adolescents feel in general."[5] This obviously doesn't just apply to young people, but the clarification is important. And it isn't as simple as "Just make plans!" I recall multiple times when I came home from an evening out or dinner with a group and felt loneliness surge more strongly than it had before I left. Puzzlingly, sometimes reaching out—textbook advice that seems to get doled out—made me feel lonelier, like I was bothering people, self-conscious that they wouldn't see me as a friend.

By no means is loneliness unique to emerging adulthood, either, but it feels like all around us are versions of what it looks like to be fulfilled by relationships, encouraged by your own independence, and thanks to the virtue of our phones, never technically alone. Not for one second, when I came home to a dark apartment for what felt like the thousandth night in a row, home late from work with no friend to call and gossip with or grab an after-work dinner with, did I imagine anyone was lonely but me. There must've been something uniquely wrong with me, I thought, to feel this alone in it all. But the more emerging adults I spoke to, the more it seemed feeling lonely was quite ordinary—which would've been comforting to figure out sooner.

There is a particular stinging stigma that comes with the pervasive belief that young adults, just by virtue of age, aren't supposed to be lonely. We, the young people, are supposedly always on our phones, Snapchatting, TikToking, texting our friends—how could we even have time to feel lonely? And if we do, there must be something wrong with us; we're either too codependent or just not reaching out enough. The reality of friendship and connection and loneliness

is far more fluid. In the 2018 BBC Loneliness Experiment, sixteen-
to twenty-four-year-olds surveyed had the highest loneliness levels
and 40 percent said they "often or very often feel lonely."[6] Another
survey, this one from Australia, pointed out that adolescents still
have relatively stable structures, like family and school, in place (assuming they had those to start with; some teens can't rely on support from their families), while young adults might find significant
life events or big transitions more problematic. As a result, the survey said, "young adults reported higher levels of loneliness, social
isolation, social anxiety and depressive symptoms than adolescents
aged 12–17 years."[7] And that's backed up by the research regarding
loneliness in adolescence, which notes "adolescence is characterized by
important social transitions that may impact the experience of loneliness."[8] If moving out of the familial home as a teenager could impact loneliness, it's not hard to see how shifting relationships and life
transitions in young adulthood would, too. The trappings of modern
life might add to loneliness—it's hard to imagine a world where we
no longer have a real-time feed of things we've been left out of—but
there's also an argument to be made, that young people feeling lonely
could also have to do with some parts of young adulthood itself.

   "I just wish that people were more open about loneliness and
talking about this," Alicia, nineteen, shared. During her first year of
college, she was afraid to admit she was lonely, because it seemed as
though everyone else was having so much fun going out with friends.
She realized the more she talked about loneliness, more and more
people admitted they were going through it, too—everyone was just
too afraid to say it out loud. Echoing Alicia, multiple people in their
mid-to-late twenties addressed loneliness as taking them aback, describing some of the highlights of young adulthood as surprisingly
lonely, including some significant so-called milestones: moving to

college, launching a dream career, signing a lease on an apartment with people who drifted from "friends" to just "roommates" a few months in. Others pointed to seeing everyone they know having weekend plans or taking trips, panicking over who to ask to be in their weddings, not having a circle of people who understood their background or culture, or not knowing how to make new friends. In all the chaotic newness of these transitions, so full of possibilities, for a lot of emerging adults, it also marks the first time you feel truly in it alone. Here you are, responsible for your own life, for your choices, for your circle. Society collectively markets it as exhilarating, and sometimes, it is. We think of loneliness in the sad and solemn moments; it also happens in the objectively happy ones.

I could pinpoint how I felt like a failure, even if it felt somewhat shameful and superficial to admit out loud: no plans on a single Friday night *and* no longer feeling pleased with myself for being able to see every movie alone; watching the slow trickle of people surrounded by other people scroll across social media; getting sick and wishing I had someone to take care of me, even though I technically could myself. But I couldn't define what I wanted: A close-knit "girl gang"? A wide circle of friends? The ability not to feel lonely when I was alone? The longer I believed I'd failed by being lonely, the more anxious I became about reaching out; the more comfortable I got with that loneliness, the less I prioritized acknowledging the obvious rebuttal to a hyper-self-reliant culture: I was not invincible to needing other people, just like enjoying alone time did not make me invincible to loneliness.

The "invincibility" factor here is an interesting one; there seems to be such heft placed on the ability to go it alone in young adulthood—maybe because you're making the leap to a different phase and the new experiences, responsibilities, and choices that come with it. But the pressure to "do it yourself" sometimes gets used as a marker for how independent, capable, and together you are. "I do see where in American culture there is that hyper-independence," Alicia said, naming a desire to study abroad as an opportunity for people to learn what it's like to be alone. "But I think it's important to realize that not a lot of kids have the opportunity to say that, because we've been alone for so long, you know?" As a first-generation college student, Alicia pointed out that not every student has the privilege of *showing up* to college with a built-in network of support systems, and it's not hard to see how that could also apply to jobs and cities. That in and of itself can be isolating, to feel you're the only one who has showed up to the metaphorical party without any guidance on how to navigate it. Forging that path can be super lonely, Alicia said, observing that while some people crave independence, for her, it's the opposite: Her family is incredibly tight-knit, constantly WhatsApp-ing each other from all over the world, and she wishes she was closer to them.

As with everything, circumstances shift loneliness: A study from the UK, "Barriers to Belonging: An Exploration of Loneliness Among People from Black, Asian and Minority Ethnic Backgrounds," found that discrimination, racism, bullying, and xenophobia are all triggers to loneliness that go overlooked too often.[9] Meanwhile, other research, which looked at how certain population groups express and address loneliness, pointed out that marginalization's "very nature brings about a sense of disconnection, dissociation from society at large, and a sense of aloneness and loneliness."[10] It even appears in the workplace: A 2020 Cigna study that looked at loneliness at work found that Hispanic and Black workers surveyed were more likely to report feeling alienated from coworkers and emotionally distant at work. For young people who don't see themselves and their experiences represented, loneliness takes on additional layers, ones of potential social isolation. It feels part of addressing loneliness in young adulthood, as people navigate different parts of their identities, is underscoring the fact that not only does it not feel the same to everyone, there are painfully real stigmas, circumstances, and types of social exclusion that bring about loneliness as a side effect. Loneliness may be part of the human condition, but the manner in which it unfolds seems to be different for everyone.

"I think what's interesting about loneliness is that, in itself, it's not a bad thing," said Kasley Killam, who is the founder of Social Health Labs, a graduate of the Harvard T. H. Chan School of Public Health, and an expert on well-being that comes from community and connection. I was calling cross-legged from the floor of my bedroom, where I'd been sheltering in place in response to the coronavirus pandemic that shut down society as we know it. Talking to young adults about loneliness during a pandemic that demanded social distancing added an otherworldly layer of what it means to be lonely. Young people loaded their lives into boxes and vacated college dorms, sometimes with only a few days' notice; found themselves stuck inside for weeks on end with roommates they hardly knew; or retreated back to their hometowns because rent became unaffordable due to COVID-19 job loss, because they needed to be caretakers, because it was safer. It took a feeling young adults experience anyway and screamed it into a megaphone: Not only are we lonely, some of us are actually alone.

What brought me to Killam's work was an article she'd written for *Scientific American* in which she detailed opportunities to connect without contact during the pandemic. In the article, Killam pointed to data that said the proportion of individuals who belong to a community group, like a volunteer club or sports league, tanked from 75 percent to 57 percent over the past decade, and pointed out that even without the pandemic keeping us unto ourselves, most of us were already suffering from poor "social health."[11] "Social health" caught my attention, because, despite reading all the information on chronic loneliness as a health risk, my mind still categorized it as my own personal failing, something other young people articulated to me, too: *If I was likable, it wouldn't be hard to make friends. If I was really independent, I wouldn't feel so bad seeing photos of people I know squished together around a tiny bistro dinner table, glowing with the light of tea candles and good conversation. I wouldn't be so needy.*

"Loneliness is a signal that your body sends to tell you that you're not getting something that you need," Killam said. "It's just like hunger, thirst, or fatigue." *Need.* It's when loneliness becomes chronic, or when you spend more of your time feeling lonely than you do feeling connected, said Killam, that it starts becoming associated with poor health outcomes, including depression, high blood pressure, and heart disease.[12] Loneliness has tangible ramifications on our physical and mental health, too: Physically, research shows lack of social connection heightens health risks as much as smoking fifteen cigarettes a day,[13] while other studies link chronic loneliness to depression, anxiety, and self-harm, among other health issues.[14]

Those nuances are one of the reasons that attempting to define loneliness feels akin to catching lightning bugs, flickering off and on in the dark. Some lapses of loneliness we can see coming from a distance—when you move to a new city where you don't know anyone, for example—but how do we explain loneliness that happens when we're surrounded by people, or when we *have* friends? For individuals raised on an ideology—not just at home, but at school, at work, in our interactions and self-perception—that there's nothing we aren't capable of doing ourselves, it can be disorienting to realize things like community, friendship, and a sensation that you're seen, acknowledged, and valued aren't just individual choices, but actual needs. If loneliness is a signal that we need something, it's easy to see how we could warp it into some self-deficiency: *That means I'm not enough alone, that I alone can't fulfill myself. There's something missing from me.* "You're not meant to go it alone" is something I heard a lot but didn't comprehend until I realized feeling lonely did not mean something was broken within me.

When we think about mental health, we think of things like therapy, just like exercise and sleep are good for our physical health. So, what can we do to improve our social health in order to buffer the effects of loneliness? "It's helpful to think about social health as its own separate dimension because of how large an impact relationships have on our bodies and minds," Killam continued. "Plus, thinking of it this way can help people to prioritize connection and recognize that there are different ways of strengthening their social muscles, which, in turn, influence other dimensions of health." I assumed the solution was simple, and I was just incapable: Be likable, make friends, and enjoy this moment in adulthood, where one night besties pile around the Friendsgiving table, and other nights are spent alone, answering only to yourself on what you want for dinner. But turns out, when debating how to strengthen that social muscle—"Just get involved!" or "Just reach out!" often feel too broad to be helpful—there are questions you can ask yourself about what this actually looks like for you, since it isn't a one-size-fits-all fix. "What interactions are nourishing for me? What is draining for me? Who are the relationships that I really want to prioritize?" Killam said. We also have to think more widely, when it comes to social health, than just one-on-one relationships. It's also about broader communities and networks, including outlets like workplaces, schools, organizations you're involved in, or activities you do.

So many life transitions that upend our sense of community and stability occur in emerging adulthood. New schools, new jobs, new cities, and new beginnings are dazzling, until the lights dim and you realize you have to rebuild communities to sit with you when life is hard and heavy, laugh at a stupid joke your boss told in an all-staff meeting, or spend weekends cooking dinner and playing cornhole in a backyard with. Community, friendship, and feeling connected aren't extras we luck into. Acknowledging the need to connect, instead of the fear of neediness, creates opportunity to prioritize making choices about communities and relationships.

The shame surrounding loneliness was obvious as people described feeling bad for admitting it, for all kinds of reasons: shame because they were more social than peers they knew but still felt disconnected; guilt over alone time they felt was critical to their mental health, but seemed like a silly thing to choose when they were so lonely otherwise; embarrassment for not being good at making friends as an adult. Versions of it popped up in conversation after conversation: Young people who felt like their social lives were inadequate when compared with peers, disappointed in themselves for not "being out," "doing more," and "really living," even if they described being generally satisfied with their social lives. Young people who admitted to feeling betrayed, having gone from being hyper-social college students, never without a buddy, to a lonely adult, too tired from the workday and general life maintenance to make new friends. People feeling they needed something, and not knowing exactly how to ask for it—or who to ask. It made me think of how, especially when people are between communities—not a student anymore, trying to forge friendships beyond our families, pacing around the so-called real world—most don't just want to be included and invited, but valued and seen.

"I just have maybe six people who I'd probably take a bullet for, and then a bunch of people that I kind of know," Liz, thirty, said. She was good at having relationships with people, and had a lot of them, until she reached college and found herself in a traumatic relationship that was isolating. It was traumatic enough and lasted long enough, Liz told me, that the effects carried into her adult life, where, for a long time, she struggled to make connections deep enough to invest time in. Despite describing herself as a "social person," she told me that the issue is not having "medium-level friends." Having different kinds of friends feels like one of the most gloriously freeing—and vulnerable—things about this life stage, where you suddenly might have work friends, school friends, friends you grow up with, neighborly acquaintances you exchange pleasantries with in the hallway or whose mail you get when they're out of town, transient friends you only know because they're good friends with *your* friend. If it sounds like a lot of people, not every person will have friends in every category, and it's not necessarily a big number. But it feels important, because sometimes, we're so zeroed in on what friendship, companionship, and community are "supposed" to look like, we forget how they sometimes feel.

"I think people forget that most things in life take work when you want them to matter to you, and friends are included in that," Janice McCabe, PhD, associate professor of sociology at Dartmouth College and author of *Connecting in College: How Friendship*

*Networks Matter for Academic and Social Success*, said. We underestimate that friendships take work, McCabe explained, because they're somewhat of a chosen relationship; they aren't built in like some family circumstances are, but there are reasons we should do that work. First is the emotional support they offer, including support for the other stressors in our lives, like work, family, or even romantic relationships; friends can be really valuable for talking through the day-to-day struggles or joys, McCabe added. Because we think these chosen relationships should be fun, we might be hesitant to bust out the calendar and schedule friend time, but it's easy for time to flit by, and suddenly, you're exchanging "We should really catch up!" comments with someone for the tenth time.

"I think that in the rush to build up your career and the pressure of having to sustain yourself, like, you can put work first as opposed to friendships just for fun," Alicia told me. Something she's been working hard to do is making the conscious effort to call friends and chat with them about more than work—even if she met them at work, she steers the conversation beyond it. Most of the conversations I'd had with young people from their late teens into their late twenties revolved around fear of lacking "deep connections," "best friends," or "friends who felt like family." Many expressed grief that relationships they'd had since childhood didn't fully carry into young adulthood, or, at least, didn't feel the same. Mourning the loss of best friends certainly isn't a singularly young adult experience, but the time does feel ripe for shifting ideas of what a friend should be: Moving to a college campus forces a togetherness that we think should equate to closeness, best friends, and full social calendars. But in the "real world" that follows, friends scatter, for jobs or graduate school or moving home for family responsibilities or romantic partnerships. Between competing responsibilities of work, romantic relationships, family, school, and other aspects of our day-to-day lives, too often, friends become second tier. It's an enduring misconception: "People like spending time with friends, it's fine, but it's kind of a waste of time," McCabe said, noting that it isn't at all a waste of time. In McCabe's own research, some college students she interviewed said that their friends were actually what kept them in school and on their campus. "So that kind of emotional support, just that sense that you belong, you're important, you're valued," Mc-Cabe told me, "I think is something that is so important to us as human beings and [is] something that friends can certainly provide."

Suddenly, without the safety net of always having people around, there's a startling realization that the skill set required to "make friends" gets a whole lot more complicated when life isn't organized around structures supporting friendship and community, like school or your soccer team or neighborhood. Distance means reimagining how you deepen relationships, since it can't always be spending every Saturday night together or bumping into each other. It feels like modern friendship for emerging adults demands prioritization: In a world where everything is begging for your attention, where so much is in transition, how do you decide what friendships or relationships to prioritize? How do you find the communities to have those relationships to begin with? When I asked how we can maintain strong bonds, McCabe said one way is to take stock of important relationships in your life, then ensure you're giving those relationships attention. While a lot of the focus goes to *making* friends, maintaining friends is also important. The banality of building long-term bonds with other people and with your community doesn't look or feel like the extraordinary versions of friendship and togetherness: orbiting around a dozen best friends at a time, arm in arm at festivals, biking around on trips, cozied up around brunch tables with shared plates of French toast, sprawled out with guitars and snacks on a blanket in a park. There's an ordinariness to loneliness, it seems, but also ordinariness in its opposite—community is a commitment, and friendships and connections take work. Everyone will require different degrees of socializing and solitude to feel happy, included, and safe. The universality feels like no one wants to feel lonely but almost certainly at some point in life will, and we all need friends in our own ways.

And friendships and communities don't have to look like a single thing: Your BFF can be as significant as the work buddy you pass in the hallway, just in different ways. You might have ten close friends or float between groups. You might cherish small talk and socializing in line at the grocery store, or deep conversations with just two close friends. The important thing, it seems, is feeling seen, heard, and held up by people around you—which, maybe, comes with knowing you can "belong" in different circumstances and with different people in different ways. To belong as a young adult means not just opening yourself up to the idea of new groups, new ways of forging connection, and new communities, but reflecting on what it means for you to feel fulfilled beyond just, well, you. It's terrifying, intimidating, vulnerable; it means answering the call for other people who want to belong, too.

Of course, we do have amplified perceptions of what connection *should*—or is going to—look like, which might be why so many of us nervously recount not knowing how to make friends in a new city, break into a new group at school, or sustain a friendship that spans different time zones. There are a lot of projections of young adult togetherness. Colleges are brilliant at marketing the type of friendship you'll find there: you, among a group of like-minded friends sprawled across the university lawn, then wearing school-spirit sweatshirts a decade after walking the graduation line. The idealized version of togetherness pops up in other contexts, too, like moving to a city where you don't know a soul and are adopted immediately into a group, or having a meet-cute in the office, where you and a coworker are bonded for life. All around us are the narratives of wedding parties of a dozen friends, adventures that bond you because of where you went or food poisoning you got along the way, and roommates who are family as well as friends. It isn't that these things *don't* happen. It's that they don't always unfold the way we assume they will, setting us up to be jerked around by loneliness and unnerved by our apparent inability to make friends.

What people don't understand about their twenties, Dr. Meg Jay said, is that, second only to old age, "it's the loneliest time of life." Some of it is structural, she said, because people are "settling down," finding partners, and having kids, if they choose to, on average later than they were in decades previous. Jay said this can be good for a lot of reasons, but it does create a five-to-ten-year period where people are "between families." After our first conversation, when I called Jay again to ask about this idea of "between families," she pointed out that while many (though not all) twentysomethings grew up in some kind of familial structure, their twenties might be the first time they "feel like [they] don't really necessarily have a nest of any kind or a guaranteed go-to support system." It's worth noting that not every young adult grew up in a traditional, "happy" home; Jay explained that a "childhood home" may not feel fit to return to, or returning may not developmentally be the best thing to do when you feel displaced. This time of life does feel "like this place where I could go anywhere, I could live with anyone," Jay told me. "Which sounds like wonderful freedom, but actually doesn't feel all that great in a lot of ways, because it just feels like all of this could change and none of this matters." It's another example of the layers of loneliness, and I was intrigued by what Jay called our "emotional immune system"—our connections or relationships. The "emotional immune system" reminded me a lot of social health, and combining the two makes it evident that, despite my own personal best efforts and a society hell-bent on self-reliance having a moral value assigned to it, we just aren't wired to go it alone.

And it's really stressful when we begin to see that lack of support as an inherent personal failure, a typically Western train of thought. "In general, Western cultures are more individualistic," Jay said. "'Me, me, me, I need to find myself, be by myself, you know, do me,'" Jay continued, pointing out that other cultures give more thought to how communities help you, and how you help your community. Being self-reliant, and having those skills, is great, and important, including in young adulthood. But, Jay mentioned, "we also know that the happiest, healthiest people also lean on others and connect with others, and don't feel personally or professionally isolated." In the depths of my own loneliness, that's how it felt: that I was failing as a human being. I tried to join groups that already felt solidified, because people knew each other from college and had the sort of friendship that seemed to extend lifetimes; I struggled to turn one-off coffee dates into something that wasn't a special occasion. Then, in turn, I felt I should be empowered to do things like go to events for work solo, always the one to volunteer to take a picture for a couple or a group of friends.

The line between individuality and isolation, or togetherness and loneliness, can feel blurry, especially now. To realize that maybe our connections and communities are the greatest needs and strongest foundations on which to build ourselves can feel heavy, because it demands that we rewire a lot of what we've spent our young adulthood doing: focusing inward, examining what we want, and using every stride toward improvement and betterment to chase it down. How many times have you had the best intentions of seeing friends on a weekend, only to collapse, exhausted, onto the couch on a Friday night, and then use the remainder of your weekend, if you're not working, to handle the day-to-day life logistics like laundry and grocery shopping? Ordinary things, like routine phone calls, making your way through awkward first times at meetings, in clubs, or on teams, and reaching out don't fit the extraordinary versions of friendship and togetherness, where you're constantly doing things with other people. It takes time and energy and work, and it baffles me how long I spent thinking the opposite: *If I was likable, and meant to not be lonely, this would be effortless!*

The stress of making new friends, and having a preconceived idea of what that entails, can spark the notion that these seemingly mundane things—little routines, casual interactions, reaching out—come *later* after you "have it together." After reading dozens of messages from lonely young adults that began with a version of "I know I'm responsible for my own happiness, but . . ." it dawned on me that self-sufficiency has been so amplified, we've forgotten it's okay to want others to contribute to our happiness, too. Personal responsibility has been taken so seriously, out of necessity, that the idea of answering to other people feels too stressful. And when you're at the start of so much—careers and résumé-building and finding cities and making sure you're doing enough, enough, enough—something as ordinary as reaching out becomes a chore, buried underneath more extraordinary pursuits.

The illusion of always being connected via phones and tweets and Instagram Stories feels like another addition here. Just because we're online doesn't mean we're connected, but physically being alone, thanks to social media, means we don't totally have to sit solo with ourselves, either. In my own life, I've often wondered whether the constant scrolling and *seeing*, technically, friends' lives play out via social media blunted the need to actually reach out to them, rather than spurring it. That's a miss on my part—watching someone's life isn't the same as being part of it, and at best, social media feels like it could be a tool to facilitate joining in, not watching from afar.

This was exacerbated by COVID-19, only, suddenly, we were hyper-reliant on devices, because that's where coffee dates and standing dinner dates and birthday parties and wedding showers and graduations were unfolding. So much of the dialogue surrounding this time was about reaching out to people, checking in, leaning on your friends, even from a safe social distance or digitally. Suddenly, that's all we had, and all that really mattered. And it made me wonder why it took a pandemic for that to be sorted into a collective priority, a reminder that so much of our well-being is, in fact, tied to other people, that we need each other, more than we get many opportunities to admit.

The antidote to loneliness, especially in young adulthood, isn't to thrust yourself into every social scenario possible. Instead, it seems, it's about acknowledging having community and feeling connected as a *need*, and prioritizing scenarios where that feels meaningful. It seems these efforts can be small, even. Kasley Killam told me we're likely not going to remember who liked our posts. "What matters is the long conversation that you had with a friend over the phone where you talk about challenges you were going through, or the really genuine compliment that someone gave you out of the blue," she said. Those were the things that felt most precious: When someone at an organization I was new to reached out via Instagram, and gave me an entry point. When I could look forward to a scheduled Sunday phone call with a friend across the country. When a friend and I, who had grown apart, began sending handwritten notes back and forth—something to anticipate. There's social media for this, too, it's worth noting, especially for those of us who find online connection more accessible: There are all kinds of communities young adults mentioned finding, from support groups to activism groups who spend their time coordinating and organizing to clusters of Twitter friends to networks of pen pals. In other words: lots of ordinary reaching out.

In Liz's efforts to create opportunities to meet those "medium friends," she started a dinner club with two of her best friends. It's a standing invitation, and they reach out to others to join— particularly people they'd like to develop deeper relationships with. "[We] just open the house and people who are available can come." She also used Meetup.com to start a book club, an echo of the flood of virtual book or podcast clubs run through Instagram or Zoom that I've seen pop up on my own social media recently. Small starting points, like a shared activity, can give everyone a rallying point when you're trying to break the ice and meet people, which can feel like casting lines out to a still lake. Liz framed it to herself as: "If someone just kind of puts themselves out there and tries to create a space for these people, maybe people will show up." She said it's scary, but possible, and especially in a place that's transient, with people who are busy, the opportunity to have something sustained is important.

Brie, twenty-four, mentioned "transitional friendships," thinking of her three best friends who have known each other since high school. A lot of friendship hinges on seeing each other every day, Brie said, and the fact that they still care about each other and hang out, even as they've grown up and incorporated more people into their lives, is a big deal. "We're all transitioning in our lives in these different ways and it affects our friendship in that we don't all get to just hang out in the basement of one of our parents' houses watching movies and playing video games all day," Brie said. She's trying to remind herself that that's okay, and part of growing up—even though their schedules rarely sync up, they make the effort to keep connecting anyway.

Kendall, twenty-six, shared that she found a sense of belonging through volunteering, a means of connecting with like-minded people. "There is this automatic sense of vulnerability in volunteering for a cause that is special to you because you're showing some part of your heart to those around you right from the beginning, and they are showing that to you as well," she said. "The more we can say as a society, 'It's okay to feel lonely when you're surrounded by people' or 'It's okay to not have the most likes on a picture online' or 'Having three best friends that you can go to for everything is enough,' the better people will feel about making these decisions," Kendall told me. When push comes to shove, she said, you need people to show up and support you through the good, the bad, and the even worse, and sometimes, online followers don't cut it. "As I've entered my adult life, I've learned the value of true friends that you can call on no matter what," Kendall added, "and [who] will answer those calls."

As a kid who never quite fit in, who then grew into an adult who wondered how to find belonging, for a long time, I only had a mental image of what not being lonely looked like: I thought if I was worthy of people, I'd have them, and that bonds were something I'd earn on an as-needed basis once I got comfortable with truly being alone. Instead, when I talked to emerging adults about how they were filling their own needs for connection, a theme materialized: steadiness, dependability, sustainability. Making a concrete plan instead of exchanging the dozen "We should hang out sometime" messages. Sitting in nature, going on walks or hikes. Blocking time specifically for phone calls, text catch-ups, and FaceTimes, or taking one hour, even if it was once a month, to meet for coffee and dessert. Writing letters. Finding local causes to volunteer for, or help with. Potluck clubs for people all learning to cook, bonding over slightly burnt dishes. Ping-Pong leagues set up in a garage. Reconnecting with old friends through something they posted on social media. Knowing that staying in because you need to sleep and wanting to socialize don't have to be opposing forces; a ten-minute call with a friend and a nap might serve you better. Acknowledging that loneliness isn't a signal of brokenness, but a cue that you're still here—that you're in need of people because, as you grow into your life, you want others to grow with. We're just answering each other's calls, after all.

# 11

# "THE BEST FOUR YEARS OF YOUR LIFE"

*On how college sets us up for young adulthood*

"THESE WILL BE THE BEST FOUR YEARS OF YOUR LIFE!" IT'S what people told me the first time I dropped out of college as an almost-nineteen-year-old buckling under the pressure of needing time and space to find herself and help her mental health, while simultaneously needing to pick a major, a city, and a career plan before she could even legally drink alcohol. "You know this is your future?" I remember the woman in the registrar's office informing me with the tone reserved for parents catching their kid sneaking back into the house after a night out. *Of course I know*, I wanted to counter. It seemed like the only things I "knew" had to do with my future: what it should look like, the gravity of it, the numerous ways I was ruining it by just standing there. My future, the vague, all-consuming ideal we're taught to live for, felt like a more dominant force in my life than my present. That was all changing in the drafty hallway at the small university forty-five minutes from my hometown. I was dropping out.

Of course, there was a little more to it than that: The privilege to move home until I figured out what I was doing. The job I'd been commuting to throughout my freshman year, which I could increase my hours at to full-time. And when I returned to school, nearly two years after the fact, I found a program that gave me academic credit for those work experiences, which saved me money and time. But in that moment, when I decided to drop out of college, I felt I had ruined my life before it had even begun, a thread that ties together the stories of dozens of young people I've spoken to who all felt changing their major too late, losing a scholarship, going to a "lesser" school, or not going to school at all was going to determine the outcome of their life. In retrospect, the pressure to have my life figured out, sealed and signed on the dotted line for student loans by eighteen, still feels unrealistic and insurmountable, but familiar enough to remember the ache of thinking it was all downhill from here—I'd ruined the most formative social, work, and academic experience of my *life*, professors warned me, friends told me. Now I was a *nontraditional* student, finishing assignments on the floor, using a box from work as a mini-desk, and replying to professors' emails on breaks at work. I might have shattered my own myth of the perfect college experience, but what I didn't realize at the time is I was building a life that felt more like me—something every young person should have the opportunity to do, especially in college.

We call it a rite of passage, because college is spun as the start of who you are as a young person. For many young adults, it's the first time they have the opportunity to leave their hometowns, or not. We have college rankings and "best of" lists, where you can see exactly where your education and formative experiences fall on the scale of what is perceived as impressive. You start making critical decisions about your future—taking on debt, deciding where to live, entering courses of study that supposedly outline the career path you're going to take—which, by the way, you're supposed to have determined before you sign for those loans. Too many of the common talking points still go: If you don't go to college, you're a slacker who didn't make the most of their potential; if you do go, you're also irresponsible, because whatever you decided, there's someone waiting to tell you that you could've done it cheaper, or chosen a better major. It gets dismissed as "Kids these days are too sensitive; they can't handle stress!" when downplaying this time of life as formative. Then, it gets amplified as "the best four years of your life," when highlighting it as the *most* formative. Pegging anything as the "best of your life" is a gutting amount of pressure whether you're eighteen or sixty, because, deep underneath the wild freedom that's supposed to illustrate, you're left wondering whether the self-doubt and uncertainty and terror will linger forever.

That's why the "traditional" experience—and being a "traditional" student, for that matter—feels so frustrating: What does it mean to be a traditional college student anymore? According to the Georgetown University Center on Education and the Workforce, as of 2015, 70 percent of full-time college students were working while in school, something that stood to negatively affect them academically if they worked too many hours, and negatively affect them personally if they couldn't work enough to live.[1] A 2018 report[2] thoroughly debunked the myth of every college student being a recent high school graduate who is simply weighing which major to pursue: Around 41 percent of college students in 2018 were twenty-five or older, despite many universities being slow to accommodate needs that make education more accessible to them, including childcare, flexible class schedules, and more expansive financial aid and payment plans.[3] According to a survey of eighty-six thousand students by the Hope Center for College, Community, and Justice at Temple University, "45 percent of college students said they experienced food insecurity in the prior 30 days, 56 percent of respondents reported experiencing housing insecurity in the previous year, and 17 percent had been homeless in the previous year."[4] Based on their report "#RealCollege During the Pandemic," 58 percent of students, who were responding to the survey in the midst of the pandemic, were experiencing basic needs insecurity.[5] Students weren't just going to school during the pandemic, a feat hard enough: They were working or attempting to find work after experiencing job loss or job insecurity, navigating getting their basic needs met as multiple resources shut down around them, parenting, taking care of relatives or loved ones, among other responsibilities, *also* during a pandemic.

There's also a persistent idea that students pursuing post–high school education only attend residential four-year universities, leaving out the thousands of people who lay a foundation for their lives at community colleges, vocational schools, or pursuing a trade. And a subset of this myth also pretends that all students have to focus on is what happens in the lecture hall for that hour and a half, as if life beyond school pauses simply because you're a student. It doesn't, because college students—whatever kind of school they attend, whether they're full-time or part-time, whatever their age—aren't just students. They're people, with complex lives and stressors and expectations even beyond what they do in classes or on campuses.

For lots of young people, college represents access and opportunity and chances for freedom, reinvention, and discovering a "true self." For others, it feels midway between an identity crisis and existing in a pressure cooker. When I asked Pearl, twenty-one, whether she felt collegiate pressures had informed her identity as a young adult, she was swift to correct me, explaining that the word "inform" was too passive in regard to what college does to your identity. "College more so chokes or conforms your identity rather than informs," she told me. She sees it split into two categories: It "smacks you on the head and tells you that your identity isn't good enough," leaving you to mold yourself to fit into affluent or popular communities on campus, or "strips you down to your vulnerable state," where the actual self-discovery begins. "Either way, you morph your identity through the growing pains of college," she said. I wondered why today's students believed the myth of college being the best four years of life persists, and Pearl explained it seems to be said about "white, privileged people who don't have to deal with discrimination that marginalized people deal with on campus, specifically on PWIs" [predominantly white institutions]. "People think the height of your life is your college years, which, the more I think about postgrad life, the more I think that is not true," she said. "There are so many opportunities out there that people fail to see or look for." It never appears on glossy brochures or school-spirit tees or acceptance emails: The idea that any rite of passage will contain the best of your years isn't just inaccurate; it's depressing. It's not a matter of whether or not any person loved college or didn't. But it is about how an entire society has hyped up one four-year chunk of time as the best you're ever going to be, while ignoring the identity pressures and life pressures that compose it.

When I talked to adults in their mid-to-late twenties about whether college was their best four years, most seemed skeptical to attribute who they were now solely to the experience they'd had then. Nearly everyone regretted the money they spent on college, and there was a lot of repetition that, at the time, they didn't realize how much that would factor into what they experienced later. Some people loved their social lives at school, whereas others pointed to incidents of harassment and assault, discrimination, or ostracization that they felt were embedded in their campus's culture. Stuffing college into a one-size-fits-all, glorified cornerstone of young adulthood leaves out that for a lot of people, their higher education experience wasn't just okay—it was awful.

Rarely now does college get to be the blank slate students are told it will be. The expectations, from internship offers to studying abroad to meeting your lifelong friends, pile up before students today have emerged from high school. But for Rebecca, twenty-nine, it really *was* that fresh start. Now that she's returned to graduate school, she's already seen a significant shift between the experience she had and ones students today have. In fact, she'd likened college to a popular conception of marriage, in which your partner is supposed to be everything—the love of your life, your best friend, your therapist, your financial support, your whole world. "I think college has become the same thing," she told me. "You're supposed to find yourself, learn everything, get job skills, become financially independent. And it's like, how in the world can one institution be all those things?"

Rebecca went to community college at fifteen, after growing up in a religious family who kept her out of public education for fear of government brainwashing. At age eighteen, without any support from advisors at her community college or adult mentors, Rebecca applied to a four-year university and was accepted as a junior. She went from only having been alone in her parents' house once or twice to being an adult, taking classes that changed her worldview and gave her "the language to describe my upbringing in a way that I'd been searching for almost my entire life." It's a reminder that education can feel an awful lot like freedom when we don't measure it by grades and rankings and categories all designed to make us the "best" of something. Rebecca was there to learn for the sake of learning, without the hyper-awareness of competing in every class, the pressure to always be doing more, and looking over her shoulder to see who was doing it better.

In her transition from a twenty-year-old graduate who considered her undergrad experience the foundation of her identity to returning to graduate school at twenty-five, academia, she thinks, is the place where this "self-optimizing bullshit came into being." Within a year or two of being in graduate school, she said, she no longer thought of herself in isolation, in terms of her work or performance. "I only thought of myself in terms of, 'What's everyone else doing, and am I doing as good as everyone else, and am I spending every waking second working? And if I'm not, am I a bad person?'" What had once been enough suddenly wasn't, and she doesn't know how long after graduating it will take to break that cycle of thinking, if it ever happens. "It's been traumatizing, and I don't know how I would have made it through community college, undergrad, or my first job if I'd had this paralyzing problem of comparison and self-doubt that I have now," she told me. Now, as a PhD candidate who frequently works with undergraduates, she feels for students who end up distraught over an A minus. "All that matters is that they get the best grade possible so they can go to law school or business or medical school or join a start-up, and there's almost nothing I can say to them that makes them feel any better," she explained.

It's a thing we love to dismiss in young adults, this obsession with grades and gold stars. It's where you hear comments on young people being incapable of managing failure, or quips about how if you can't handle a bad grade, you'll never be able to handle a real job. Which, of course, ignores how many students are, in fact, managing both at once. But the reality is a generation has been nudged into the conviction that we're all one bad grade, one mistake at work, one flaw away from losing our future, our present livelihood, and any substantial employment that might provide us with health insurance. It's not about the grade itself. It's what the grade indicates about you. Plus, young adults today know that taking out loans doesn't mean you'll get a job that can pay them back; that following your passion or your talent doesn't necessarily mean you end up fulfilled; that even doing your best work, at school or at work or in your personal life, might not suffice, according to expectations, bosses, or professors. Sometimes, college feels like a fast and expensive way to realize even your best isn't enough.

It's like watching the ivy of capitalism coil around our feet, tethering us to educations that are increasingly expensive—much like the rest of our lives. "People are desperate to find the magic bullet to feel safe in a society where there is no longer a clear-cut pathway to a good life," Rebecca said. The best path we can come up with, in her words, is to be "the best student ever. Go to school and then get some soul-crushing job where I work eighty hours a week and at least I have a paycheck and health insurance, and at least I can sleep at night over that, even though my personal life and my overall well-being may be falling apart." I thought of all the students and recent graduates I'd spoken to who had pulled all-nighters recently, eager to prove themselves to their professors or bosses or just keep up with everything churning down the conveyor belt toward them faster than they could possibly assemble the pieces of a "good life." How shameful it is that this feels like a best shot at security. "And this thought of just having a simple existence . . ." Rebecca continued. "Nobody can just be simple. If you're not constantly trying to be the best thing ever, life is no longer worth living, because who are you outside of self-optimization?" It's a question that, when we talk about emerging adulthood and college, we better start coming up with better answers for.


There's a tremendous amount of pressure regarding young people getting into college—America even had its very own higher education scandal, where celebrities scammed to get their kids into elite universities, dubbed Operation Varsity Blues, underscoring the classism, "elite" school fixation, and parental collegiate obsession that still exists. Maybe it's because costs have skyrocketed or the college prep process feels like it starts around first grade, but by the time they actually make it to college, no wonder students are stressed out, overwhelmed, and as one student who recently endured the admissions process phrased it to me, "soulless," having poured so much of their energy and self-worth and time into building a future that begins at collegiate gates. All this breathless hype "makes it feel like you have to follow a specific plan and everything has to go a certain way and it has to be done on a specific timeline, and if you can't get it done in that timeline, something's wrong with you," said Dr. Jessi Gold, assistant professor in the Department of Psychiatry at Washington University School of Medicine in St. Louis, and a specialist in college mental health, medical education, and physical wellness.

Having to decide a life plan so early, she said, doesn't leave a lot of flexibility in your choices, given many haven't had time to determine their own "identity and values. But you're supposed to be choosing what you're going to be doing forever." Looking back on the decisions I made involving higher education and achievement—and more so, the desperation with which I made them—I feel shame. But I also see a young person doing her best to square her evolving life values, goals, and reality against what felt like a stopwatch. Plus, it's finding that balance: You're supposed to be having fun and enjoying all this, but every second spent having fun feels like sacrificing time finding your purpose, Gold said. It becomes a culture of work hard, play hard, but sleep ends up not being included, because of this constant pressure to be doing something productive.

It's also worthy of consideration that perception of college might be shifting for students today, maybe because of cost, maybe because of the pandemic—which, in a lot of ways, shattered the "traditional college experience" myth as we know it—maybe because they've chosen a different path. If time is so precious, if these years are so coveted, some young people are reconsidering how they do college and if they do it at all: It's presented as both an aspiration and a life practicality, an opportunity you both have to earn and pay for. Students described opting to take gap years, working full-time instead, or pursuing a couple classes at a time as they continued working as opportunities to craft a college experience that fit with their lives, rather than them working to fit it. Not every option will be available to every young person—and there's still a need to have a conversation about what accessible, affordable (and tuition-free) college looks like, and how that would change opportunities and expectations surrounding it. But what it means to be a college student should be reconsidered, anyway, to keep up with the lived experiences of people—and maybe imagine a system in which higher education works to fit the life of a student, rather than them working to fit it.

The idea that every college student is eighteen to twenty-two and attends a four-year university is "a part of this American Dream ideal that we have about owning a house and having a specific number of kids and being married," said Xorah, sixteen. It feels like part of that same path. Xorah is a community college student pursuing her associate's degree in early childhood education. She thinks part of the reason community colleges aren't centered in conversation around young people and school is that they have a "negative connotation" as being somehow lesser—the exact opposite of Xorah's experience. She explained that her school is incredibly responsive to adapting to the needs of students and, because it's smaller, is open to change, is affordable, and offers academic and personal support as well as a diverse student body. While that "American Dream" ideal may not reflect the experience of the majority of Americans, she explained, "it's like a dream that we have in our collective mind . . . In my parents' generation, it was super important that you go to college," and that if you wanted a good job, if you wanted to be stable, you got a college degree. "I think that that is kind of being questioned, because there are so many different mediums to be able to be successful. And success looks so different today, and even the idea of success is super diverse today."

The college experience grabbed the first-job experience and bound itself to it tightly. For a lot of students, what happens at college isn't totally about what happens at college—it's also about what comes after. According to some data, 41 percent of recent college graduates (and 33.8 percent of college graduates, in general) are currently working a job that doesn't require a college degree, with the average student debt, depending on what source you read, estimated as somewhere between $29,800 and $37,200. For some, it's even worse if you go and don't graduate, which is the case for a lot of young people who end up disenchanted with collegiate life, have circumstances that keep them from staying enrolled, or simply can't afford to stay.[6] According to data from the National Student Clearinghouse Research Center, six out of ten college students who began school in fall 2012 hadn't earned a degree six years later.[7]

Megan, twenty, said she thinks schools realize that we need them more than they need us. "I think the thing is, at the end of the day, colleges are institutions," she said. So, she explained, she can be grateful for her experience and that you could "theoretically" say that these four years are the most important time of your life, but that emphasis will never be reciprocated by the school. "Regardless of how my experience is, I'm just a number to them; I'm just a student ID number; I'm just a FAFSA ID number." That shows up in how schools treat students, too. For example, Megan's university talks frequently about the importance of taking care of your mental health, but if you need to take a semester off for physical or mental health, you're penalized, losing things like your guaranteed housing or standing for class registration. "I had this realization my freshman year of college that it came down to, like, do you have money? Or do you have time?"

Alexis was fired from her resident assistant job because of how outspoken she was regarding the lack of support they gave RAs; she was supposed to be a worker first, student second, she said. Currently, she's taking a mental health–related leave, which she said was "literally the hardest decision I've had to make." She's a first-generation student who is independent from her parents, and said when it came down to it, if she didn't take the leave of absence, she'd likely cause harm to herself. "And there's no reason in me putting myself through this if I know I just need to pause," she said. When she was trying to explain she literally can't afford to fail, her friends suggested taking out additional loans, scholarships, or asking her parents. Even during the summer, when she was supposed to be taking a break and caring for her mental health, she was working eight-hour shift jobs, including overnight at Wawa, and trying to get a second job at Starbucks or the Cheesecake Factory. "My loan, and the debt that I have, I just see it as a means to an end. It's that hope that I'll be able to get out of this cycle of poverty," she said. "When we say we can't afford to fail, we really do mean it."

It's not just a financial thing, though that's bad enough. In honor of May's Mental Health Awareness Month, Student Loan Planner surveyed the relationship between mental health and student debt and found that one in fifteen student loan borrowers has considered suicide because of their loans.[8] It's echoed by other data, like a study published in the journal *Social Science & Medicine* that found that student loan debt took a toll on early adult mental health, and found evidence that student loans are associated with poor health outcomes and psychological functioning in early adulthood.[9] It seems like an obvious answer to the "Why are all today's young people so stressed?" question. Well, the cost of education, deemed necessary to getting a job, has risen. Meanwhile, job precarity feels as though it is everywhere. Degrees still double as status symbols, though we know that's a farce. So desperate are young people to maximize anything that might look like an opportunity, "Should I just go back to graduate school?" is seen as a viable solution to problems of being underemployed, being unemployed, or wrestling with debilitatingly low self-esteem. And a swath of the population still tells people who took other paths—who decided they couldn't afford college, didn't feel it was in their best interest to attend, or otherwise opted out—that they missed out on an experience considered critical to living your "best life" as a young adult.

The crushing pressure is what happens when you stick an institutional price tag on something, connect it to the job market, *and* make it a social experience. Despite data that shows Americans believe in higher education as a public good, it remains an individual financial pressure, and the myth that all it takes is working hard and getting good grades to set you up for a good life has been debunked.[10] Higher education might be considered a necessity, but it's not a guarantee.[11] "We're one of the few societies [where] people have to spend so much money to go to college," Dr. Anthony Rostain, emeritus professor of psychiatry and pediatrics at the University of Pennsylvania and coauthor of *The Stressed Years of Their Lives: Helping Your Kid Survive and Thrive During Their College Years*, told me. In the past, Rostain says, college was always seen as a step toward upward mobility but not perceived as a necessity the way it is now. About seventy years ago, he explained, the biggest infusion of funding toward college came in the form of the GI Bill, which provided educational assistance to veterans and servicemembers, making it possible for them to attend college or other postsecondary training programs. In the 1960s, student scholarships and loans were provided via the US Departments of Defense and Education.

But then, social programs like that were "systematically whittled down," Rostain said, in the aftermath of the Vietnam War, "so that more of the burden of the cost, not only of college but of healthcare and the like, is growing. It's being leveraged onto people rather than society." This happened alongside the defunding of alternative pathways to successful careers and occupations like trades, or vocational or certificate programs, he said, and suddenly high schools began to see themselves as college prep schools. And so young adults' futures were planned around whether they went to college, and for some, where they went. Why does this history matter? Well, if we're out to grapple with our extraordinary selves, it's important to tackle the systems that have pushed people to be extraordinary in the first place.

In 2020, the COVID-19 pandemic took everything we know about the college experience and dragged an eraser across it: Students were forced off campus, leaving behind classes, communities, and in some cases, the only home, food, or Wi-Fi they had. Classes pivoted to Zoom, leading to fierce debates about the validity of online learning—as if learning online, last-minute, during a global pandemic, is at all similar to learning online in a program created for it, with professors knowledgeable in that space. Gone were packed dorms filled with friends and pizza, in-person extracurriculars where you had a chance to do stuff you aren't graded on, and the residential "college experience" as it had been marketed.

"I'm absolutely grieving several aspects of my college experience," said Moira, a twenty-year-old junior. They were supposed to go on a study-abroad trip, complete a summer undergraduate research experience, and visit graduate schools, among other things. Now, they find themself missing the "smallest, silliest things," like coming back to their dorm room to find their roommate's fashion project sprawled across the floor, going to the dining hall at midnight for bad chicken fingers, saying hello to acquaintances. The grief has come with another interesting element, though: "I also don't feel pressure anymore to be a stereotypical college student," they told me. "I never went to a party and I don't drink, and while the majority of my friends don't, either, there was always this feeling that I was the odd one out and the suspicion that when I looked back on my four years here, I would regret how I had spent my time. That's gone away."

While there are definite downsides to not having in-person learning, Moira said, more time in their life has opened up opportunities for keeping in touch with friends, working on independent academic projects, and hobbies. The impact of COVID-19 on campuses is tangible, including the spread of the virus and how many students were thoroughly displaced by it: Not every student has a safe place to be "sent home" to, jobs—and the subsequent ability to pay tuition—were lost, and as it exacerbated other dimensions of privilege, COVID-19 beamed a bright light on massive equity gaps on campuses that had always existed. It also seemed like more and more people were having conversations about what it means to be a college student. For some students who had worked their entire lives to get to college, losing one of the precious four years felt like something had been stolen from them—something they'd dreamed of, and sacrificed for, that they didn't feel could be recaptured. Others described feeling like "the bubble finally popped," and giving themselves leeway for the first time—gone were the pressures to join every club, go to every tutoring session, and make an appearance at every party. Instead, students were trying to keep each other safe on campus, and off it, create ways to make the experience meaningful anyway.

The idea of creating your own meaning—and doing it your own way—in college doesn't get enough airtime. This seems to be, in part, because there's so much emphasis on staying on the clear-cut trajectory of a major or timeline of a four-year college degree. But because of the cost, experimenting with classes or taking additional time to graduate, even if you need it, doesn't really seem feasible. It often doesn't feel like it leaves a whole lot of wiggle room for students to make mistakes, let alone find themselves in life circumstances beyond their control. Kayla, a twenty-six-year-old graduate student who is enjoying her grad experience far more than undergrad, said she'd experienced a "profound disillusionment" in light of her school's response to COVID-19. "I watched paid, professional adults—all of whom supposedly champion critical thinking, searching for truth, and empirical data—absolutely fumble their way through this virus response," she said. While she knows there's a massive amount of privilege in the fact that her own logistical shifts, including accessing remote learning, were feasible and comfortable, "I do think it's important to know that the ivory towers collapsed in a big way."

She had intentionally gone across the country for graduate school to experience "a new way of living, of being, of eating, of relating to the space around me," and grappled with a sense of being robbed of that time when she went back home to quarantine. But she's in the final year of a school counseling program, and her greatest anxiety is career-related since she has no idea what she'll be inheriting in terms of job market, public schools, and public health. Still, Kayla said during undergrad, "I remember feeling plagued by a sense of guilt that I was doing college 'wrong.'" Now, she explained, there are no crushing social pressures in addition to academic challenges—most of the people she's in class with are kind and friendly, but are in school for careers, not to "meet their future bridesmaids," something someone said to Kayla during undergrad.

When I dropped out of college, I was sure I had decimated my future with my own uncertainty. Goodbye to the chances to try new opportunities if I could afford to take them, or courses of study, or

meeting new people. But the failure around my collegiate expectations felt freeing: So much of my own unhappiness and anxiety and
uncertainty around my college experience came from following a
path I didn't feel I'd picked in the first place. It didn't match that
I didn't feel ready to move away from home. Or that I needed to
work while in school and had an off-campus job I didn't want to give
up. Mostly, it didn't feel as though it matched me being *so* unsure—
instead of slowing down and looking at how different pieces could
make a puzzle that fit my life, I panicked, worried that I was behind, and that if I didn't go to college *right then*, in the "traditional
way," it meant I'd squander my opportunity to define my life. Expectations feel insurmountable. "It's almost like, again, where's the
place to grow and make mistakes and hate what you're doing for a
little bit and not give up?" Rostain asked. I floundered for a while, a
thing we're never supposed to admit lest we betray we don't know
everything yet (never mind that we aren't supposed to). But eventually, I found my footing, and with it, a degree: A full-time job and
full-time online school felt nearly impossible, as I stayed up late into
the night always doing one or the other, and wondered if I was missing out on what college was "supposed" to be. But it set me up for
the kind of adulthood I embraced, not just one I thought I should
aspire to: Deciding to finish college a different way gave me the opportunity to have dreams beyond just getting through.

Those transitions and pressures are something we need to talk
about more with young adults, and it shouldn't take a pandemic to
get us reevaluating the pressure of a one-size-fits-all college experience. Ashae, twenty-two, is the first person in her family to graduate from college, which has radically changed her relationship with
them. In addition to walking what she called uncharted territory,
since her family hasn't had the same experience she's had, she ex-

plained there was "a lot of pressure placed on me in terms of what career I choose, because ultimately, it is the expectation that I will be the one to take care of my family." As a kid, she told me, she dreamed of buying her mother a house in a nice neighborhood, affording access to the best doctors for her grandmother, and taking her younger sister on vacations. We don't talk about these dreams as if they are real for young people. "In college, especially my senior and junior years, I felt a lot of pressure to feel like I had everything together," she continued. She was involved in several organizations on campus in which she held leadership positions, in addition to being a resident assistant and writing tutor. "I wanted to be able to be a good role model, even though I often didn't feel like one at all," she said. "It's imposter syndrome. I didn't feel worthy of anything, especially the love of my peers." That's carried into her career and young adulthood beyond college, too. Ashae thinks of being laid off at least once a day. "I think, if I were to be fired tomorrow, how would my life look, what would I do? Who would take care of my grandmother? I think of how my mom would probably have to loan me some money, and the thought of this destroys me." At every "high" she's reached, she thinks constantly about the lows that may follow, and finds herself overcompensating by trying to reach "perfection," showing up to work an hour early every day, making herself available to her manager, and staying at the office late. "And yes, I know these are great practices to have, but sometimes I feel as if I am overexerting myself just to drown out my thoughts." It's too easy to look over the shoulder of the person beside you and see them, thriving in class and raving at parties, and think that you aren't doing enough to create a life that looks like that, too.

Now, college is bookended with this "best life" pressure. College has changed the high school experience entirely and, in some cases, feels like it's moved up the timeline of young adulthood. College isn't like spontaneously blowing your dollars on a luxury vacation, something impulsive and impractical. It's tying your hopes to the idea that sacrifice—financial, personal, academic—will pay off later. Today's young people are grappling with the knowledge that putting the heft of your worth and money into a future may not pay off in ways it once had. Of course that has personal repercussions on how college shapes our sense of self. It's why we rarely talk about that part of the college experience—the uncertainty.

What was once a time for exploration is now carefully organized into what those experiences get you—and it feels they have to be helping you achieve something or earn something, because if not, how did you have the luxury of free time, anyway? Doesn't that mean you aren't working hard, or taking this seriously? More specifically, how are you paying for that? "It's okay to have an identity crisis now and then when you're growing up," Dr. Rostain said. "It's almost like we've scheduled people out of the chance to experience their own uncertainty as anything other than a sign of weakness." And this isn't a phase in college, either. Because so much of identity formation takes place during the teens and twenties, not all habits we form in college remain in college.[12] You don't spend four years pulling all-nighters and have a sleep schedule that snaps back to normal the day after graduation, so you certainly don't spend four years building an identity that consists of hustle then suddenly know how to find work-life balance after you exit the hallowed halls of higher education. The "scheduling people out" of experiencing uncertainty is a young adult firewall: If you're working every minute, you'll never be able to say you didn't do enough if things don't work out. Responsibility is supposed to protect us. I recounted to Rostain what I kept hearing from young adults, that so many young people feel a crushing amount of pressure to never fail at anything, from transferring schools to taking a leave of absence to allowing any part of their life plan to be derailed. It feels like a commentary on who you are as a person. "I see this in my office, my consultation room, again and again," he said. "The internalization of that message: *I can't afford to fail*. It's such an impossible set of demands that people place on themselves."

College has changed what it means to fail, because so much is at stake, all the time. I spoke to multiple people who have failed a class, something experts like to say is a normal and healthy part of life—except it's been a barrier that's kept them from graduating college, being one class away from finishing and unable to pay to re-take it. Not getting a good job out of college means falling behind on student loan payments, which could mean hurting your credit score, which could eventually affect your ability to successfully rent an apartment or own a home. The margins for error feel significantly slimmer, and so many of these critical decisions—education, loans, first jobs—are intertwined with the timeline we've laid out for the college experience. The stakes of failure feel higher, but what really makes them feel different is that it seems as though those stakes are starting to fall into place earlier.

"I think that someone could look at my college experience and they'd think that it was the ideal college experience," said Andrew, twenty-three. He'd attended school on a full merit scholarship and held elite internships throughout his college career. He was always doing work outside the classroom, he explained, and was even in a fraternity. But there was another side people weren't seeing: Andrew had been working, in general, from a young age, applying a level of stress and pressure that extended even beyond the typical strains of college. Despite all the impressive work Andrew was doing outside the classroom, he was ultimately kicked out of his scholarship program due to a low GPA. One of the high-powered internships had been a negative experience, with both the company and Andrew himself mutually knowing he wouldn't continue with them following that summer. "I was on and off antidepressants and antianxiety medications my entire college career," he explained. More than half that time, he said, he spent trying to self-medicate with drugs and alcohol. Looking back, Andrew said, his high school experience seems "truly unreal"—he took ten Advanced Placement classes, captained the debate team, played JV soccer, played in the orchestra, and led an education advocacy campaign. "I was doing way more than I needed to be doing at that age and putting myself under way too much pressure," he explained, and in spite of outward achievement, because he was surrounded by teenagers doing equally impressive things, he often felt he wasn't doing enough. "That I was not good enough. I ignored the effect this had on my mental health and ultimately self-medicated with drugs and alcohol. In the middle of all of this, I came out of the closet."

Getting kicked out of the scholarship program, once in college, was a wake-up call, he said, as he was embarrassed, ashamed, and spent the bulk of his senior year hoping no one noticed. "In my head, I was a failure, an imposter that should never have been given the scholarship in the first place," he said, adding that maybe he should never have even been admitted to his school to begin with. It's a raw example of what "achievement"—considered to exist outside circumstances impacting a student personally, to be earned at all costs—looks like from the inside, and how early the stress of never being enough, doing enough, starts by the time one gets to college.

He realized he was letting his mental health have far too much control over his life, Andrew explained. "That I was distorting reality and undermining my own self-worth. And that my education environment was officially toxic."

Nearly every young person I spoke to about their college experience—some currently in school, some who graduated several years ago—referenced it as a turning point in their mental health. For some, it was the first time they had access to mental healthcare or counselors; others described the bulk of the experience as being detrimental. "I wish that we were more specific about the type of mental healthcare that the young Black and brown people, specifically, should seek out in spaces that kind of enforce racial inequity," said Cherisse, a twenty-one-year-old who works while in school, adding that being unable to talk to your peers or professors about things is the especially isolating part. She's glad to have had professors who understood when she advocated for herself, but also realizes she's a "bold" person, and not everyone may be able to advocate for their mental health or know how. "I know that people fall under the radar, people fall off with their grades or get overwhelmed because they don't really have anybody to guide them," said Cherisse. She only recently got a therapist, and there's so many reasons young adults may or may not pursue that kind of treatment, she added, noting that one year of college when her mother lost her job, Cherisse didn't even have insurance. She thinks while, in school, students are taught to "ask for help" in the general sense, they don't always know who to call, and sometimes the help they need isn't offered. She said, "Intentionally teaching young Black and brown kids getting out of high school, navigating into their adult life and college, teaching them how to truly advocate for themselves," and giving them access to people who can help them mentally, is critical.

During my own college career, I was hustling, I was achieving, but little of it was driven by curiosity or exploration, two things I thought college would provide in spades. And I was a white, privileged student with a job. First-gen students, low-income students, students of color, students who are queer, and students who are marginalized all face challenges that often go undiscussed, because our society still believes that as long as we get them to college, the rest figures itself out. It doesn't matter if they don't have counselors who understand the communities they come from and how the college transition isn't one-size-fits-all. It doesn't matter that no one had conversations about the ramifications of loans; they'll figure it out later. It doesn't matter that social pressures, like getting to make friends, finding a support system, and having community, get dismissed as a "bonus" of college rather than some of the most foundational things that happen to us as people (that's true of having support and community even outside the collegiate context). More and more, though, young people see they don't have the luxury of "figuring it out later," which is why conversations about the selves we create in college, and how we treat those selves, have to begin now.

In all the years of hearing how college shapes our careers, our friendships, and ourselves, when it comes to higher education, emerging adults are faced with more questions than answers, ones that cannot be answered by scribbling in an A, B, or C bubble with a number two pencil: *What if I've done everything right and it still doesn't work out? What if I don't know what I'm doing; I just know I'm working so hard at it? What am I even doing?* There are a lot of moments I remember from college. I remember the first time we were required to read aloud in class, and how my cheeks flamed red when I stumbled over words I'd never heard spoken aloud as classmates coasted through them. I remember a professor telling me I didn't take getting a degree "seriously" because I was working while in school. I remember how I felt I was failing more often than I was doing much else, and I wish I'd known that was normal, but I also wish I'd known that failing wasn't the end of the road. The college experience has changed. But if I could tell my college self anything, I'd tell her to ease up on the pressure that college must be the best of you. I'd encourage her to be honest, about who she is and what she wanted and when she felt lost. And I'd tell her that so few of the things she learned that would eventually become who she is would be included in her GPA.

# 12

# A NOTE ON GROWING UP

"... like being special, I think."

"Making it on my own."

"Not being lonely."

"I imagine it feeling like being free."

"Space for the small things that mean the most."

"I know I'm supposed to answer something about money or independence but I really think my best life would be one where I felt good enough."

WHEN I STARTED WONDERING ALOUD WHAT "LIVING YOUR best life" meant, and unpacking the mounting expectations, stressors, and abject insecurity that took us from wanting a good life to yearning for an extraordinary one, I began by asking people what it meant for them. Some emerging adults I spoke to pointed to tangible goals: They wanted to buy homes, pay off debt, travel the world, start a new career, find partners, and make new friends. But people also voiced a feeling—feeling taken care of and cared for; feeling secure in who they are; feeling like their life choices belonged to them. In many cases, it felt like a life well lived took the stereotypical "best life" we've come to know as extraordinary and shattered it, letting the glittery expectations of all we're supposed to be crash to the floor, and reveal how we really feel.

One of the most fundamental things that's become clear is that other people's opinions of your life, choices, and preferences are not automatically more valid or insightful or exciting or wiser than your own. Nor should expectations that come from outside be the final say in who you should be—obviously, circumstances influence all of this, and we don't operate outside our circumstances. But there's worth in what we feel we know about ourselves and our lives. Sometimes, that feels like a trust fall: *How much do I trust that I know about myself? Do I know what matters to me—and do I find myself worthy enough of making those calls? What do I want? How do I want my life to feel? And all these extraordinary metrics—at what point do they shift from being aspirational ideals to being placeholders for self-worth?*

When I began writing, I was smack in the middle of a seemingly extraordinary life that felt like the opposite. I was living in New York City, supporting myself with a collection of part-time jobs to pay the bills and freelance writing. There was not one sparkly Instagram Story of how the sunset looks sinking below Manhattan's grid that told the truth about what was happening: I was homesick and detached; I was losing myself to someone else's version of ambition, my sense of levity and outlook on life rendered rigid by the idea that I wasn't good enough to deserve to feel good; the belief that I was flunking young adulthood because I was supposed to have more figured out by now, and couldn't muster the energy to. I was sick, and sad. There was always just the endless and empty pursuit of more, and I could keep a running list of ways I could prove myself, remake myself, and change my own life—over and over, until I became a perpetual work-in-progress instead of a human being who was learning and growing and faltering each day. It was a lot of searching—not in the cool, adventurous way, but in the frantic, longing way.

I built up fantasies of me—well, not so much *me* as a version so altered and amplified that it didn't look a whole lot like me at all; the sort it's easy to imagine yourself into when everything new seems to shine and it feels like only a matter of time until you grow into yourself in all the ways our dreams tell us we will. I'd be the kind of person who said an enthusiastic yes to everything and was known for being up for anything. My ambition would glow like heat off a bonfire, surrounded by well-meaning watchers holding their drinks and trading versions of their stories; it would be the glue that matched all the fractured misdirections and try-hard mistakes and false starts into a neat ladder rather than winding paths. I could give worldly advice and take care of my parents and grandparents.

And somehow, now, I find myself discovering, again and again, it's not just the overeager yeses but the thoughtful noes—what you say no to—that make a life; I've noticed that ambition for the sake of ambition is hollow, a mirage that evaporates and changes shape when you reach out to grab it. I find myself asking what it means to be proud of yourself, when you know there's always more you could be; I think about caretaking as a role that grows with me, including how I'll take care of me. I'd heard, over and over, about in-betweenness as part of this time of life. But I'd imagined it differently: it feels like juggling the many parts of myself, and my life, and deciding what holds up when it comes down to what matters, what's beyond my control, what I should be trying to change for myself or others. I imagine everyone has a different version of their own in-betweenness.

While that alone isn't a groundbreaking realization about emerging adulthood, what I realized I was searching for *was*: It wasn't to be told I was special, or extraordinary, or the best. It was to hear that I was enough. And then, I heard that echoed back to me, from so many people who gave their time and energy to sharing their stories and perspectives.

Right now, back in my hometown, listening to people talking about their twenties and finding themselves and what feels forma-tive versus what's supposed to be, I searched again for words to cap-ture what I am feeling: Nostalgia, like I am missing who I used to be? Fear of missing out, like there's probably more to this story, and maybe more to life, than I've seen? Then, I thought of the boxes that held the contents of my life; of birthdays that tally up our years on earth, and so-called rites of passage, like graduations and promo-tions and weddings, that mark that we've kept going—according to someone's standards, anyway. I thought of looking around and real-izing you're the adult in the room; of friends you talked to every day who you haven't heard from in a long while; of dreams you grew out of; of seeing the freedom and fearlessness of my childhood self give way to more uncertainty, more caution, more confusion as a young adult—and the chasm between growing up and feeling grown look-ing wider and wider.

It struck me that growing up feels like a weird form of grief: grieving what could've worked out, and what didn't; grief for who or what you tangibly lost; grief for what could've been. I wished I'd had a roadmap on how to grow into myself: how to take opportu-nities without chasing what I thought I was supposed to want; how to acknowledge the big questions, of what it all means and who I am, without feeling like I skipped the chapter the class was reading aloud; how to not worry quite so much about following the trajectory we're told is the best and only one; how to notice imperfections without feeling I needed to tattoo them on me, as stamps of my faults; how you don't have to know everything—including about yourself—to be worthy, to be valid.

Deciding your life, deciding who you're going to be, feels like freedom—but that doesn't mean we're immune to questioning whether we're figuring it out fast enough, if we're falling short, if it's not turning out like we planned. So many of the things that truly shape our lives are occurring every minute, even when we don't realize it: when we listen to what's important to us; reach out to someone; dismantle the scales of what is supposed to hold value; care for ourselves and for others; structure a belief system that aligns with how we want the world to feel; heal from what's harmed us. It's not meeting a standard of extraordinary, of growing up, of living your best life. It's just what makes *your* life.

There isn't a question: The structures around young adulthood have changed. This book isn't intended to be a Band-Aid slapped on the open wound of a society that took the phrase "Move fast and break things" literally and applied it to people. This remains a time of life profoundly shaped by marginalization and injustice, and this book isn't going to fix that. More broadly, a lot of the advice that gets hurtled toward young adults feels like empty platitudes: Telling someone to make peace with their flaws, give up their stressors, or live more simply isn't going to cover it. But I hope amplifying ordinariness can contribute to a shift in the way we think about our lives. Over the past more-than-a-year, speaking to young adults from different locations, backgrounds, and circumstances about the pressures they'd internalized, the messages they'd taken to heart, and strain of living a "best life" has distilled some of the growing pains and stressors and changing definitions of success into a simple lesson: Some of the most extraordinary things about our lives are, in fact, the ordinary ones. The person we met by chance that changed everything. The thing we said yes—or no!—to that rerouted the path. Knowing loneliness isn't a character flaw, but a sign we aren't in it alone. That craving acknowledgment, acceptance, belonging, and even wanting to be liked are *normal*, not betrayals to the great solo adventure of finding yourself. That failure is rarely final and is mostly someone else's definition of failure anyway. That we become more of ourselves when we let the right people in. That we're becoming more ourselves all the time. That, where we can, we could embrace the glorious mundanities and follow timelines that feel truest to us; try to give ourselves permission, where it's in our power, to live as we are—not solely for who we could be. Where it's possible, we can make it better for those who come after us, since emerging adulthood doesn't stop with a single generation. It'll keep changing, with new challenges and stressors and, yes, even adventures. And in spite of it all, our best lives will be the ones that feel truest to us—not to the ideal of what we should be, but to this, right now, right here: our ordinary selves, savored.

# ACKNOWLEDGMENTS

To Sarah Haugen, my brilliant editor and partner in all things ordinary: From our first phone call, working with you has been like having a multiyear conversation with a friend. You made this sharper, more detailed, and braver; your patience and thoughtfulness are invaluable in an editor, and amazing in a friend. Partnering with you on this book has been a tremendous honor and an experience I'll cherish for the rest of my life.

To Jamie Carr, my incredible agent, friend, and partner in this book, for the leap of faith you took with me that's changed my life in every possible way, the countless hours you spent helping shape draft after draft of what would turn into this book, and for your fearlessness, compassion, and endless words of wisdom. I'm inspired by you, grateful for you, and glad to learn from you—and count working with you as one of life's precious gifts.

To The Book Group, for their support and remarkable work.

To the spectacular team at Harper Perennial, who went above and beyond, especially Courtney Vincento, Amanda Hong, Nick Davies, and Megan Looney.

To my mom, as if words will ever capture it all: From telling stories with my toys on the floor of your studio, to trying to forgo math to do more "stories" at school; from growing up hearing lines like "That caviar is a garnish!" to conversations about anything and everything bubbling over at our kitchen table. I'll spend the rest of my days trying to live up to the example you set, repay all you do for us, and capture the zest, humor, and empathy with which you live. You've been there through every wrong turn, humiliation, and rough draft read aloud over coffee, armed with Nancy Meyers movies and reminders of what matters at the end of the day; the one who never wavers, who I'll always aspire to be like, who taught me the power of ordinary things.

To my dad, who, from building me a ballet barre to letting me consistently blow through office printer ink growing up, has always been an exemplar of what it means to build dreams—through sacrifice, struggle, and second-guessing, with humor, humility, and hope.

To the family pets: Tom Hanks the Cat, Rory the Sheepdog, Butters the Kitten, Matt's Margo, and and Meowmeow the Little Black Cat, who we all miss—because spending so many hours tethered to a computer screen is nothing without good company, and pets love you regardless.

To Matt, for always showing up—wherever, whatever time, and bringing the lightness of adventure into everything, always.

To Luke, for his sense of humor, capacity for dreaming and work ethic that's worthy of awe, and our shared tendency to worry out of love and care.

To Annie, the Bean, the person I aspire so much to be like. The ultimate consultant on everything in this book, the person I go to with everything, and keeper of cherished coffee dates. Your affinity for poetry and art, your sense of wit and wonder, and your advice have saved me a hundred times, and restored my soul a dozen more.

To Graham, for pulling over when I see pink skies that must be documented for the collection of good-sign sunrises and sunsets, elaborate takeout traditions, space heaters to write in front of, and sending email love letters.

To Madysen, who grabbed me by the hand when I didn't know I was sinking and has been a dear friend ever since. I'm grateful for your book recommendations, our shared enthusiasm for pizza, breads, and candy, and our long-distance phone catch-ups.

To the Kentucky Student Voice Team, an incredible group who have been so generous with their time, insight, and work over the years, for always making time to speak with me, and doing powerful work across Kentucky.

To the Student Voice Team, endless providers of education and insight, and leaders in creating a world that is truly student-centered.

To Grace Williams, whose brilliance and insight brought so much perspective to these pages. Thank you for your generosity of time, thoughtful and candid observations, and for lending your talent to this project.

To Megan Wahn, fact-checker extraordinaire, whose care, incredible attention to detail, and amazing eye brought so much to this book. I'm so fortunate to have you as such a big part of this process and grateful you brought your extraordinary skill to this book about ordinariness.

To the incredible people who spoke to me for this book, who made time to share their expertise, journeys, insight, and perspective between their own day jobs, highs and lows, and lives unfolding. The fact that I was trusted to tell small parts of so many people's amazing stories is the honor of a lifetime, and I am grateful beyond words to all who took time out of their days to be part of this book. Their stories are the heart of it all, and my thanks will never be enough.

# NOTES

## 1: ON BEING ORDINARY

1. Settersten, Richard A., Timothy M. Ottusch, and Barbara Schneider. "Becoming Adult: Meanings of Markers to Adulthood." In Scott, Robert, and Stephan Kosslyn (eds.), *Emerging Trends in the Social and Behavioral Sciences.* Hoboken, NJ: John Wiley and Sons, 2015. https://health .oregonstate.edu/sites/health.oregonstate.edu/files/faculty-staff/profile pubs/settersten_et_al-becoming_adult-emerging_trends.pdf.
2. Ibid.
3. Vespa, Jonathan. "The Changing Economics and Demographics of Young Adulthood: 1975–2016." United States Census Bureau, April 2017. https:// www.census.gov/content/dam/Census/library/publications/2017/demo /p20-579.pdf.
4. Ibid.
5. Arnett, J. J. "Emerging Adulthood: A Theory of Development from the Late Teens Through the Twenties." *American Psychologist* 55, no. 5 (2000): 469–80.
6. Arnett, Jeffrey J., Rita Žukauskienė, and Kazumi Sugimura. "The New Life Stage of Emerging Adulthood at Ages 18–29 Years: Implications for Mental Health." *Lancet Psychiatry* 1, no. 7 (2014): 569–76.
7. Munsey, Christopher. "Emerging Adults: The In-Between Age." *Monitor on Psychology* 37, no. 7 (June 2006). http://www.apa.org/monitor/jun06 /emerging.

## 2: "FOR THE EXPERIENCE": ON WORK IDENTITIES, DREAM JOBS, AND DOING IT "FOR THE EXPERIENCE."

1. DeFilippis, Evan, Stephen Michael Impink, Madison Singell, Jeffrey Polzer, and Raffaella Sadun. "Collaborating During Coronavirus: The Impact of COVID-19 on the Nature of Work." National Bureau of Economic Research, 2020. https://www.nber.org/papers/w27612.
2. Ibid.

3. Golodryga, Bianna, and Sarah Boxer. "Graduates Face Worst Job Market on Record." CNN, May 20, 2020. https://www.cnn.com/videos/business /2020/05/20/job-market-2020-graduates-coronavirus.cnn-business.
4. "Deeper in Debt: Women & Student Loans." AAUW, February 25, 2020. https://www.aauw.org/resources/research/deeper-in-debt/.
5. Ibid.
6. Weller, Christian E. "African Americans Face Systematic Obstacles to Getting Good Jobs." Center for American Progress, December 5, 2019. Accessed October 2, 2020. https://www.americanprogress.org/issues /economy/reports/2019/12/05/478150/african-americans-face-systematic -obstacles-getting-good-jobs/.
7. Spievack, Natalie. "For People of Color, Employment Disparities Start Early." Urban Institute, July 25, 2019. https://www.urban.org/urban-wire /people-color-employment-disparities-start-early.
8. Schwandt, Hannes. "Recession Graduates: The Long-Lasting Effects of an Unlucky Draw." Stanford Institute for Economic Policy Research, April 2019. Accessed October 2, 2020. https://siepr.stanford.edu/research /publications/recession-graduates-effects-unlucky.
9. Cech, Erin A. "The Passion Principle: Self-Expression, Career Choice, and Inequality Among Career Aspirants." https://drive.google.com/file /d/1ieixmat2WGwPVu0UYNTu2J0eOXOfSIS2/view.

**3: A WAITING ROOM: ON HOME, AND HOW WE BUILD IT**

1. Leopold, Josh, Mary Cunningham, Lily Posey, and Tiffany Manuel. "Improving Measures of Housing Insecurity: A Path Forward." Urban Institute. Accessed October 5, 2020. https://www.urban.org/sites/default /files/publication/101608/improving_measures_of_housing_insecurity .pdf.
2. Karabanow, Jeff, Sean A. Kidd, Tyler Frederick, and Jean Hughes. "Toward Housing Stability: Exiting Homelessness as an Emerging Adult." Western Michigan University, Journal of Sociology & Social Welfare 43, no. 1 (March 2016). Accessed October 5, 2020. https://scholarworks .wmich.edu/cgi/viewcontent.cgi?article=4000&context=jssw.
3. "Youth and Young Adults." National Alliance to End Homelessness, October 21, 2016. https://endhomelessness.org/homelessness-in-america/who -experiences-homelessness/youth/.
4. Katsiaficas, Dalal, Carola Suárez-Orozco, and Sandra Isabel Dias. "'When Do I Feel Like an Adult?': Latino and Afro-Caribbean Immigrant-Origin Community College Students' Conceptualizations and Experiences of (Emerging) Adulthood." Emerging Adulthood 3, no. 2 (2014): 98–112.
5. Scannell, Leila, and Robert Gifford. "The Experienced Psychological Benefits of Place Attachment." Journal of Environmental Psychology 51 (2017).

https://www.researchgate.net/publication/315986136_The_experienced
_psychological_benefits_of_place_attachment.

6. Dallago, Lorenzo, Michela Lenzi, Douglas Demaree Perkins, and Massimo Santinello. "Place Attachment in Adolescence." In Levesque, Roger J. R. (ed.), *Encyclopedia of Adolescence*. New York: Springer, 2011. https://doi.org/10.1007/978-1-4419-1695-2_403.

7. Ibid.

8. Love, Shayla. "There's a Chemical in Your Brain That Makes You Want More." Vice, August 14, 2018. Accessed October 5, 2020. https://www.vice.com/en/article/d3e53w/theres-a-chemical-in-your-brain-that-makes-you-want-more.

9. Fry, Richard, Jeffrey S. Passel, and D'Vera Cohn. "A Majority of Young Adults in the U.S. Live with Their Parents for the First Time Since the Great Depression." Pew Research Center, September 4, 2020. https://www.pewresearch.org/fact-tank/2020/09/04/a-majority-of-young-adults-in-the-u-s-live-with-their-parents-for-the-first-time-since-the-great-depression/.

10. Winsor, Morgan. "Why Adults in Different Parts of the Globe Live at Home with Their Parents." ABC News, May 27, 2018. https://abcnews.go.com/International/adults-parts-globe-live-home-parents/story?id=55457188.

11. Nova, Annie. "The Pandemic May Cause 40 Million Americans to Lose Their Homes." CNBC, July 30, 2020. https://www.cnbc.com/2020/07/30/what-its-like-to-be-evicted-during-the-coivd-19-pandemic.html.

12. Bailey, Peggy, and Douglas Rice. "Pandemic Relief Must Include Comprehensive Housing Assistance for People Experiencing the Most Severe Hardship." Center on Budget and Policy Priorities, July 27, 2020. https://www.cbpp.org/research/housing/pandemic-relief-must-include-comprehensive-housing-assistance-for-people.

13. Dey, Judith, and Charles Pierret. "Independence for Young Millennials: Moving Out and Boomeranging Back." *Monthly Labor Review* (December 2014). https://doi.org/10.21916/mlr.2014.40.

14. Rentfrow, Peter Jason. "Statewide Differences in Personality: Toward a Psychological Geography of the United States." *American Psychologist* 65, no. 6 (2010): 548–58.

15. Chopik, William J., and Matt Motyl. "Is Virginia for Lovers? Geographic Variation in Adult Attachment Orientation." *Journal of Research in Personality* 66 (February 2017): 38–45.

## 4: FINDING YOURSELF, COMMODIFIED: ON HOBBIES, EXPERIENCES, AND WHAT CREATES IDENTITY

1. Sokol, Justin T. "Identity Development Throughout the Lifetime: An Examination of Eriksonian Theory." *Graduate Journal of Counseling*

*Psychology* 1, no. 2 (2009). https://epublications.marquette.edu/cgi/view content.cgi?article=1030&context=gjcp.

2. Ibid.

3. Layland, Eric K., Brian J. Hill, and Larry J. Nelson. "Freedom to Explore the Self: How Emerging Adults Use Leisure to Develop Identity." *Journal of Positive Psychology* 13, no. 1 (2018): 78–91.

4. Ibid.

5. Pine, B. Joseph, II, and James H. Gilmore. "Welcome to the Experience Economy." *Harvard Business Review*, July–August 1998. https://hbr.org /1998/07/welcome-to-the-experience-economy.

6. Eventbrite. "Millennials: Fueling the Experience Economy." AWS, October 4, 2020. https://eventbrite-s3.s3.amazonaws.com/marketing/Millennials _Research/Gen_PR_Final.pdf.

## 5: CRACKS: ON PERFECTIONISM AND BEING ENOUGH

1. Hill, Andrew P., and Thomas Curran. "How Perfectionism Became a Hidden Epidemic Among Young People." The Conversation, January 3, 2018. http://theconversation.com/how-perfectionism-became-a-hidden -epidemic-among-young-people-89405.

2. Ibid.

3. Shulman, Michael. "Perfectionism Among Young People Significantly Increased Since 1980s, Study Finds." American Psychological Association, January 2, 2018. Accessed October 3, 2020. https://www.apa.org /news/press/releases/2018/01/perfectionism-young-people.

4. Curran, Thomas, and Andrew Hill. "Perfectionism Is Increasing over Time: A Meta-Analysis of Birth Cohort Differences from 1989 to 2016." *Psychological Bulletin* 145, no. 4 (2019): 410–29. https://doi.org/10.1037 /bul0000138.

5. Ibid.

6. Smith, Martin M., Simon B. Sherry, Vanja Vidovic, Donald H. Saklofske, Joachim Stoeber, and Aryn Benoit. "Perfectionism and the Five-Factor Model of Personality: A Meta-Analytic Review." *Personality and Social Psychology Review* 23, no. 4 (November 2019): 367–90. https://doi .org/10.1177/1088868318814973.

7. Sherry, Simon, and Martin M. Smith. "Young People Drowning in a Rising Tide of Perfectionism." The Conversation, February 5, 2019. http://theconversation.com/young-people-drowning-in-a-rising-tide-of -perfectionism-110343.

8. Herman, Keith C., Kenneth Wang, Reid Trotter, Wendy M. Reinke, and Nicholas Ialongo. "Developmental Trajectories of Maladaptive Perfectionism Among African American Adolescents." *Child Development* 84, no. 5 (2013): 1633–50.

9. Ortega, Norma E., Kenneth T. Wang, Robert B. Slaney, Jeffrey A. Hayes, and Alejandro Morales. "Personal and Familial Aspects of Perfectionism in Latino/a Students." *Counseling Psychologist* 42 (2013): 406–427. https://doi.org/10.1177/0011000012473166.

## 6: GOOD LITTLE CATHOLIC GIRL: ON ASKING BIG QUESTIONS: DO I HAVE MEANING?

1. Barry, Carolyn McNamara, and Mona M. Abo-Zena. *Emerging Adults' Religiousness and Spirituality: Meaning-Making in an Age of Transition.* London, England: Oxford University Press, 2014.

2. Krok, Dariusz. "When Is Meaning in Life Most Beneficial to Young People? Styles of Meaning in Life and Well-Being Among Late Adolescents." *Journal of Adult Development* 25, no. 2 (2018): 96–106. https://doi.org/10.1007/s10804-017-9280-y.

3. Masci, David. "Many Americans See Religious Discrimination in U.S.—Especially Against Muslims." Pew Research Center, May 17, 2019. https://www.pewresearch.org/fact-tank/2019/05/17/many-americans-see-religious-discrimination-in-u-s-especially-against-muslims/.

4. Gayman, Deann. "Study Tracks Divide in Religious Affiliation, Prayer Among LGB Emerging Adults." University of Nebraska–Lincoln, June 26, 2020. Accessed October 5, 2020. https://news.unl.edu/newsrooms/today/article/study-tracks-divide-in-religious-affiliation-prayer-among-lgb-emerging/.

5. Kramer, Stephanie, and Dalia Fahmy. "Younger People Are Less Religious Than Older Ones in Many Countries, Especially in the U.S. and Europe." Pew Research Center, June 13, 2018. https://www.pewresearch.org/fact-tank/2018/06/13/younger-people-are-less-religious-than-older-ones-in-many-countries-especially-in-the-u-s-and-europe/.

6. "1. Religious Affiliation Among American Adolescents." Pew Research Center, September 10, 2020. https://www.pewforum.org/2020/09/10/religious-affiliation-among-american-adolescents/.

7. Ter Kuile, Casper, and Angie Thurston. "How We Gather." Sacred Design Lab. https://sacred.design/wp-content/uploads/2019/10/How_We_Gather_Digital_4.11.17.pdf.

8. "Younger Millennials Who Are Unaffiliated (Religious 'Nones')." Pew Research Center, May 12, 2015. https://www.pewforum.org/religious-landscape-study/religious-tradition/unaffiliated-religious-nones/generational-cohort/younger-millennial/.

9. "Why America's 'Nones' Don't Identify with a Religion." Pew Research Center, August 8, 2018. https://www.pewresearch.org/fact-tank/2018/08/08/why-americas-nones-dont-identify-with-a-religion/.

10. Ibid.

11. Badshah, Nadeem. "UK Muslims Prepare to Take Ramadan Online." *The Guardian*, April 23, 2020. http://www.theguardian.com/world/2020/apr/23/uk-muslims-embrace-technology-for-ramadan.

12. Schwartz, Charlie. "Planning a Coronavirus Passover: Tips for a Virtual Seder in a Year Unlike Any Other." *USA Today*, April 3, 2020. https://www.usatoday.com/story/opinion/2020/04/03/coronavirus-passover-virtual-seders-zoom-column/5106887002/.

13. Haque, Fahima. "Celebrating Eid al-Adha Amid a Pandemic." *New York Times*, August 1, 2020. https://www.nytimes.com/2020/08/01/us/eid-al-adha-coronavirus.html.

14. JTA Staff, Shira Hanau, Philissa Cramer, Ben Harris, Cnaan Liphshiz, Gabe Friedman, Marcus M. Gilban, and Curt Schleier. "Want to Attend an Online Yom Kippur Service? Here Are Some Options, Based on Your Interests." Jewish Telegraphic Agency, September 17, 2020. https://www.jta.org/2020/09/17/culture/want-to-attend-an-online-rosh-hashanah-service-here-are-some-options-if-you-register-now.

### 7: ONLINE IN REAL LIFE: ON BEING—AND BROADCASTING—YOURSELF ONLINE

1. Bjornsen, Chris. "Social Media Use and Emerging Adulthood." In Zupančič, M., and M. Puklek Levpušček (eds.), *Prehod v odraslost: sodobni trendi in raziskave* (Emerging Adulthood: Current Trends and Research). Ljubljana, Slovenia: Znanstvena založba Filozofske fakultete Univerze v Ljubljani, 2018. 223–61. https://www.researchgate.net/publication/324542908_Social_Media_Use_and_Emerging_Adulthood.

2. Awad, Germine H., Carolette Norwood, Desire S. Taylor, Mercedes Martinez, Shannon McClain, Bianca Jones, Andrea Holman, and Collette Chapman-Hilliard. "Beauty and Body Image Concerns Among African American College Women." *Journal of Black Psychology* 41, no. 6 (2015): 540–64.

3. "Sociologist: Women Judged More by Their Looks in Various Spheres of Life." Science in Poland, February 21, 2018. Accessed October 5, 2020. https://scienceinpoland.pap.pl/en/news/news%2C28321%2Csociologist-women-judged-more-their-looks-various-spheres-life.html.

4. Anderson, Joel R., Elise Holland, Courtney Heldreth, and Scott P. Johnson. "Revisiting the Jezebel Stereotype: The Impact of Target Race on Sexual Objectification." *Psychology of Women Quarterly* 42, no. 4 (August 22, 2018): 461–76.

### 8: HEARTSICK: ON DATING, CHOOSING, AND LOVE

1. Schalet, Amy T. *Not Under My Roof: Parents, Teens, and the Culture of Sex.* Chicago, IL: University of Chicago Press, 2011.

2. Rauer, Amy J., Gregory S. Pettit, Jennifer E. Lansford, John E. Bates, and

Kenneth A. Dodge. "Romantic Relationship Patterns in Young Adulthood and Their Developmental Antecedents." *Developmental Psychology* 49, no. 11 (2013): 2159–71. https://doi.org/10.1037/a0031845.

3. Xia, Mengya, Gregory M. Fosco, Melissa A. Lippold, and Mark E. Feinberg. "A Developmental Perspective on Young Adult Romantic Relationships: Examining Family and Individual Factors in Adolescence." *Journal of Youth and Adolescence* 47, no. 7 (2018): 1499–1516. https://doi.org/10.1007/s10964-018-0815-8.

4. Blair, Sampson Lee, and Timothy J. Madigan. "Dating Attitudes and Expectations Among Young Chinese Adults: An Examination of Gender Differences." *Journal of Chinese Sociology* 3, no. 1 (2016). https://doi.org/10.1186/s40711-016-0034-1.

5. "Why More Religious Singles Are Searching for Love Online." PBS, April 11, 2013. https://www.pbs.org/newshour/nation/why-singles-are-going-to-religious-online-dating-in-a-fractured-dating-market.

6. Zhang, Xing, and Sharon Sassler. "The Age of Independence, Revisited: Parents and Interracial Union Formation Across the Life Course." *Sociological Forum* 34, no. 2 (June 2019): 361–85.

7. Lamont, Ellen. "If You Want a Marriage of Equals, Then Date as Equals." *The Atlantic*, February 14, 2020. https://www.theatlantic.com/ideas/archive/2020/02/if-you-want-marriage-equals-then-date-equals/606568/.

8. Ibid.

9. Heino, Rebecca D., Nicole B. Ellison, and Jennifer L. Gibbs. "Relationshopping: Investigating the Market Metaphor in Online Dating." *Journal of Social and Personal Relationships* 27, no. 4 (June 2010): 427–47. https://doi.org/10.1177/0265407510361614.

## 9: WHEN SELF-CARE DOESN'T CARE ABOUT US: ON SELF-CARE AS SELF-RELIANCE, AND WHAT IT MEANS TO TAKE CARE OF YOURSELF

1. Harris, Aisha. "A History of Self-Care: From Its Radical Roots to Its Yuppie-Driven Middle Age to Its Election-Inspired Resurgence." Slate, April 5, 2017. http://www.slate.com/articles/arts/culturebox/2017/04/the_history_of_self_care.html.

2. Arnett, Jeffrey Jensen. "Emerging Adulthood." Noba. Accessed November 13, 2020. https://nobaproject.com/modules/emerging-adulthood.

3. Scheffler, Richard, Daniel Arnold, Hinnaneh Qazi, Jessie Harney, Lauren Linde, Grayson Dimick, and Niki Vora. "The Anxious Generation: Causes and Consequences of Anxiety Disorder Among Young Americans: Preliminary Findings." Berkeley Institute for the Future of Young Americans, Goldman School of Public Policy, July 2018. https://gspp.berkeley.edu/assets/uploads/page/Policy_Brief_Final_071618.pdf?source=post_page.

4. Scheffler, Richard M. "Anxiety Disorder on College Campuses: The New Epidemic." Berkeley Institute for the Future of Young Americans, Goldman School of Public Policy, April 2019. Accessed October 5, 2020. http://youngamericans.berkeley.edu/wp-content/uploads/2019/12/Anxiety_Disorder_on_College_Campuses_UCB_Study_FINAL.pdf.

5. Hoffman, Jan. "Young Adults Report Rising Levels of Anxiety and Depression in Pandemic." *New York Times*, August 13, 2020. https://www.nytimes.com/2020/08/13/health/Covid-mental-health-anxiety.html.

6. Ibid.

7. Mumphrey, Cheyanne, and Jennifer Sinco Kelleher. "Poll: Pandemic Takes Toll on Mental Health of Young Adults." ABC News, September 11, 2020. https://abcnews.go.com/US/wireStory/poll-pandemic-takes-toll-mental-health-young-adults-72946698.

## 10: WHO ANSWERS WHEN YOU CALL: ON BEING PART OF THE "LONELIEST GENERATION" AND BUILDING OUR COMMUNITIES

1. N.d. Yougov.Com. Accessed December 18, 2020. https://today.yougov.com/topics/lifestyle/articles-reports/2019/07/30/loneliness-friendship-new-friends-poll-survey.

2. Ballard, Jamie. "Millennials Are the Loneliest Generation." YouGov, July 30, 2019. Accessed October 5, 2020. https://today.yougov.com/topics/lifestyle/articles-reports/2019/07/30/loneliness-friendship-new-friends-poll-survey.

3. "Are You Feeling Lonely?" Cigna. Accessed October 5, 2020. https://www.cigna.com/about-us/newsroom/studies-and-reports/loneliness-questionnaire.

4. Hawkley, Louise C., and John T. Cacioppo. "Loneliness Matters: A Theoretical and Empirical Review of Consequences and Mechanisms." *Annals of Behavioral Medicine: A Publication of the Society of Behavioral Medicine* 40, no. 2 (2010): 218–27. https://doi.org/10.1007/s12160-010-9210-8.

5. Van Roekel, Eeske, Maaike Verhagen, Rutger C. M. E. Engels, Ron H. J. Scholte, Stephanie Cacioppo, and John T. Cacioppo. "Trait and State Levels of Loneliness in Early and Late Adolescents: Examining the Differential Reactivity Hypothesis." *Journal of Clinical Child and Adolescent Psychology: The Official Journal for the Society of Clinical Child and Adolescent Psychology* 47, no. 6 (2018): 888–99.

6. Hammond, Claudia. "The Surprising Truth About Loneliness." BBC, September 28, 2018. https://www.bbc.com/future/article/20180928-the-surprising-truth-about-loneliness.

7. "The Young Australian Loneliness Survey." VicHealth. Accessed October 5, 2020. https://www.vichealth.vic.gov.au/media-and-resources/publications/young-australian-loneliness-survey.

8. Van Roekel, Eeske, Maaike Verhagen, Rutger C. M. E. Engels, Ron H. J. Scholte, Stephanie Cacioppo, and John T. Cacioppo. "Trait and State Levels of Loneliness in Early and Late Adolescents: Examining the Differential Reactivity Hypothesis." *Journal of Clinical Child and Adolescent Psychology: The Official Journal for the Society of Clinical Child and Adolescent Psychology* 47, no. 6 (2018): 888–99.

9. Amadi, Paul, and Ruwaida Adam Mohammed. "Barriers to Belonging: An Exploration of Loneliness Among People from Black, Asian and Minority Ethnic Backgrounds." The British Red Cross and Co-op. https://www.redcross.org.uk/about-us/what-we-do/we-speak-up-for-change/barriers-to-belonging.

10. Rokach, Ami. "Loneliness of the Marginalized." *Open Journal of Depression* 3, no. 4 (January 2014): 147–53.

11. Killam, Kasley. "How to Prevent Loneliness in a Time of Social Distancing." *Scientific American*, March 12, 2020. https://www.scientificamerican.com/article/how-to-prevent-loneliness-in-a-time-of-social-distancing/.

12. "Signs and Symptoms of Chronic Loneliness." Cigna, March 2019. Accessed October 5, 2020. https://www.cigna.com/individuals-families/health-wellness/chronic-loneliness.

13. Novotney, Amy. "The Risks of Social Isolation." American Psychological Association, May 2019. https://www.apa.org/monitor/2019/05/ce-corner-isolation.

14. Ducharme, Jamie. "COVID-19 Is Making America's Loneliness Epidemic Even Worse." *Time*, May 8, 2020. https://time.com/5833681/loneliness-covid-19/.

## 11: "THE BEST FOUR YEARS OF YOUR LIFE": ON HOW COLLEGE SETS US UP FOR YOUNG ADULTHOOD

1. "Seventy Percent of College Students Work While Enrolled, New Georgetown University Research Finds." Georgetown University Center on Education and the Workforce, October 28, 2018. https://cew.georgetown.edu/wp-content/uploads/Press-release-WorkingLearners__FINAL.pdf.

2. "College Today: More Students Are Older, Working, Supporting Others." Lumina Foundation, June 3, 2019. https://www.luminafoundation.org/news-and-views/college-today-more-students-are-older-working-supporting-others/.

3. Dedman, Ben. "Misconceptions About Today's College Students." Association of American Colleges and Universities, November 2018. https://www.aacu.org/aacu-news/newsletter/2018/november/facts-figures.

4. Goldrick-Rab, Sara, Christine Baker-Smith, Vanessa Coca, Elizabeth Looker, and Tiffani Williams. "College and University Basic Needs Insecurity: A National #RealCollege Survey Report." The Hope Center for College, Community, and Justice, April 2019. Accessed October 5, 2020.

https://hope4college.com/wp-content/uploads/2019/04/HOPE_real college_National_report_digital.pdf.

5. Goldrick-Rab, Sara, Vanessa Coca, Gregory Kienzl, Carrie R. Welton, Sonja Dahl, and Sarah Magnelia. "#RealCollege During the Pandemic." The Hope Center for College, Community, and Justice. https://hope4 college.com/wp-content/uploads/2020/10/Hopecenter_RealCollege DuringthePandemic_Reupload.pdf.

6. Redden, Elizabeth. "41% of Recent Grads Work in Jobs Not Requiring a Degree." Inside Higher Ed, February 18, 2020. Accessed October 5, 2020. https://www.insidehighered.com/quicktakes/2020/02/18/41-recent-grads -work-jobs-not-requiring-degree.

7. "Completing College—National—2018." National Student Clearing-house Research Center, December 18, 2018. https://nscresearchcenter .org/signaturereport16/.

8. Lockert, Melanie. "Mental Health Survey: 1 in 15 High Student Debt Bor-rowers Considered Suicide." Student Loan Planner, updated September 4, 2019. https://www.studentloanplanner.com/mental-health-awareness -survey/.

9. Walsemann, Katrina M., Gilbert C. Gee, and Danielle Gentile. "Sick of Our Loans: Student Borrowing and the Mental Health of Young Adults in the United States." *Social Science & Medicine* 124 (January 2015): 85–93.

10. Public, A. S. A., and PRIVATE GOOD. n.d. "Americans' Views of Higher Education." Columbia.edu. Accessed November 23, 2020. https://www .tc.columbia.edu/thepublicmatters/reports/Research-Brief-2-v10102018 .pdf.

11. Teachers College Newsroom. "An Investment That Pays Off for Society." Teachers College, Columbia University, July 14, 2018. https://www.tc .columbia.edu/articles/2018/july/americans-believe-in-higher-education -as-a-public-good-a-new-survey-finds/.

12. Arnett, J. J. "Emerging Adulthood: A Theory of Development from the Late Teens Through the Twenties." *American Psychologist* 55, no. 5 (2000): 469–80.

# ABOUT THE AUTHOR

RAINESFORD STAUFFER HAS WRITTEN AND REPORTED FOR the *New York Times*, *New York* magazine's "The Cut," *WSJ Magazine*, *Teen Vogue*, *Vox*, and *The Atlantic*, and has appeared on CNN *Newsroom* and NPR's *On Point* and *Weekend Edition*. She is a journalist, speaker, and Kentuckian.